The Garretts of Columbia

– THE –
GARRETTS
of COLUMBIA

A Black South Carolina Family from
Slavery to the Dawn of Integration

DAVID NICHOLSON

THE UNIVERSITY OF
SOUTH CAROLINA PRESS

© 2024 David Nicholson

Published by the University of South Carolina Press
Columbia, South Carolina 29208

uscpress.com

Manufactured in the United States of America

33 32 31 30 29 28 27 26 25 24
10 9 8 7 6 5 4 3 2 1

Library of Congress Cataloging-in-Publication Data
can be found at http://catalog.loc.gov/.

ISBN: 978-1-64336-454-4 (hardcover)
ISBN: 978-1-64336-455-1 (ebook)

Portions of "The African" first appeared, in slightly different form,
in the Spring 2017 issue of *Carologue*, a publication of the
South Carolina Historical Society.

For my son, Andrew,
and his cousins, Nia, Corinne, and Elena,
and their children after them.

". . . but as servants of God we have commended ourselves in every way. . . . We are treated as impostors, and yet are true; as unknown, and yet are well known . . . as having nothing, and yet possessing everything."

—*2 Corinthians 6:4–10*

CONTENTS

CONFESSIONS OF A
WEARY INTEGRATIONIST

This book's taken me nearly sixty years to write. I began it Thanksgiving Day in 1965, my first year at Sidwell Friends, the prestigious upper Northwest private school that's long served Washington's elite. Richard Nixon's daughters went there but didn't graduate. So did Chelsea Clinton and Barack Obama's daughters, though, of course, Sasha and Malia came long after I'd graduated. I count just twenty-one of us in the 1966 yearbook—thirteen in the ninth, tenth, and eleventh grades, and eight in the school's equivalent of elementary and junior high. We were less than one percent of the entire enrollment.

I was fourteen years old and a sophomore that Thanksgiving. Dinner was hours off, so I lay on the couch in the living room, a book facedown on my chest, my head turned to the television and one of the parades. The doorbell rang. My sister, Phyllis, went to open it.

"Mom!" she called.

The surprise—almost alarm—in her voice made me get up.

It was one of my classmates, a boy I'll call Tom Roberts. His mother was there, too, flanked by his father, his brother, and a younger sister, their arms laden with dressing-stuffed turkey, a substantial baked ham, green beans, a salad, sweet potatoes, macaroni and cheese, pumpkin pie. (I may be confusing the candied yams and macaroni and cheese with my mother's. Perhaps the Robertses' was a more WASP-like bounty—mashed potatoes and diced mixed vegetables from a can.)

"Good morning!" they cried cheerfully. "We've brought you Thanksgiving dinner!"

I was too stunned to speak, too stunned even to be embarrassed.

Wondering who it might be, my mother, Ruth, came out of the kitchen where our own turkey was slowly roasting. Years before, in happier times, she and her seven brothers and sisters would gather for holiday dinners in this same house on S Street in Washington, the house she'd grown up in, the house she came back to after she fell ill and fled her marriage. But Mattie, their mother, had been dead six years. All of Mattie's children except Mac, the youngest, were married with families of their own. Two had been gone from Washington since the 1950s: Phyllis[1] (Mattie's third daughter) was in England with her Air Force officer husband, and Kemble (the next-to-youngest) in Cincinnati. It might have been ne'er-do-well Mac, genial and half drunk though it was still early, his three-year-old marriage already fraying, and with nowhere else to go. None of the others would have paid a surprise visit; all were at home, anticipating dinner with their own families.

I should note that Ruth was a natural aristocrat who seldom offended anyone by accident. My sister, Jo, remembers her side by side with a white woman in a downtown department store, the two of them considering the same black blouse. Holding it against her chest to gauge the size, the white woman gushed, "You know, black is just so distinguished." To which my mother replied, without missing a beat, "That's what we've been trying to get you people to understand for years."

On this particular Thursday in 1965, however, Ruth simply said, softly, so our visitors could not hear, "Close the dining room doors, Phyllis." Ceiling-high oaken sliding doors shut, table with Mattie's white linen tablecloth hidden, sparkling, special-occasion china out of sight, Ruth graciously accepted the dinner we did not need.

Tom and his family left in a few minutes, suffused with the warm feeling that accompanies bestowing charity—and all of us collapsed laughing: my mother and I, my sisters Phyllis and Jo, our younger brother, William. How foolish, how arrogant, to assume that, Black, I must be poor and my family unable to afford Thanksgiving dinner.

Once we'd exhausted our laughter, my mother sighed. "All this food! What are we going to do? We can't eat two turkeys." She thought for a moment, then went to the kitchen to telephone Miss Gloria. Miss Gloria lived around the corner with her two children, a nephew, and a series of semirespectable boarders who sojourned in her basement. She was a heavy woman with thick, wobbly arms, a sweet dimpled face, and lemon-cake-colored skin. Once, years before when she'd been younger, she'd favored

Etta James and stepped out with a fighter who'd held several championship belts. Now, she worked nights behind the counter of a doughnut shop.

In a few minutes, Miss Gloria was at the door, flanked by her son and the nephew who stayed with her. "Oh Ruth, thank you," she cried. "Thank you so much. I don't know what we'd have done about Thanksgiving this year." The boys took charge of the boxes, bags, and aluminum pans. Miss Gloria said "Thank you," once more. My mother closed the door. And we all laughed ruefully again, marveling at the ways of white folks.

◆　◆　◆

Ruth is gone, as is my brother. Phyllis and Jo say they don't remember that Thanksgiving. Neither did Tom Roberts when I e-mailed him some years ago. But I remember my laughter curdling when I realized I might arrive at school and find he'd told everyone. I needn't have. Perhaps he was as embarrassed as I was. Perhaps he was more sensitive than I give him credit for. At any rate, no one seemed to look at me sidelong. The next day, I worried a little less; even less the day after. Soon, I'd completely forgotten. For years, I didn't think about that Thanksgiving at all. When I began to brood about it again, it wasn't coincidence that I was approaching sixty and beginning to understand that if, at sixteen, I'd believed in the full and complete integration of American society, I must now face the possibility that King's would always be an impossible dream. An enduring case of willful mistaken identity made it impossible for Tom's family, and mine, to transcend our shared, difficult history. Blinded and blinkered, both families saw what they wanted of the other, not who each really, truly was.

When that Thanksgiving scene returns to me now, it's as unwelcome as a two-in-the-morning phone call from a drunk college classmate babbling apologies for slights I'd long forgotten. I've rewritten it time and time again in my imagination so that Ruth thanks the Robertses and tells them haughtily they could have saved themselves a trip, and the cost of the turkey, if they'd called first. Or invites them in so they can see past the sliding doors into the dining room and the table awaiting the bounty she's preparing. *How wonderful that you've come to share Thanksgiving with us,* she says. *Dinner won't be ready for two or three hours, but there are parades and football on TV, and how thoughtful of you to make sure there'll be enough food!*

She didn't say either, of course, choosing to indulge the Robertses. After all, they *were* trying to do the right thing and perhaps—though it's hard enough cooking for one family!—Mrs. Roberts even prepared the dinner Miss Gloria and her brood wound up enjoying. All the same, we laughed (not in their faces; we were too polite) at the clumsiness of their good intentions. Goodness of intent aside, it's still impossible for me to see the Robertses' awkward charitable act as anything except a kind of racial charade in which all of us played the parts assigned by history. It wasn't the first time my family took part in that kind of role playing. It wouldn't be the last.

It took seventy-three years for Sidwell Friends to integrate, but even then, the school admitted just one black student. (Was he sometimes lonely? I wonder about that.) That was in 1956. Things hadn't improved much seven years later. The number had increased to . . . seven, which makes the twenty-one of us in 1965 a significant increase.[2]

As I said, these numbers come from the 1966 yearbook some senior talked me into buying when I was just a sophomore. Was it Amy, the cheerleader I still daydream about, leaping mid-yell, bare-legged in pleated gray skirt and black-and-white saddle shoes? I craved the ease with which she and her football-hero brother sauntered through their golden lives. Another of the seniors who, once school was done, drove away in convertible Beetles, Mustangs, or Camaros? No—more likely, it was one of the ink-stained wretches on the yearbook staff.

If you'd asked me then what Friends was like, I'd have shrugged and muttered that it was fine. And it was, most of the time. I was grateful to be rid, finally, of the taunts and bullying I'd endured at Jefferson Junior High because I didn't wear the right clothes or like the right music. (Ruth couldn't afford to buy me the gabardine slacks, Ban-Lon shirts, or Chuck Taylors other boys wore, and when it snowed enough to earn money shoveling neighbors' steps and sidewalks or running errands, I bought 45s by The Beatles, Rolling Stones, and Kinks at Record City downtown, not the Supremes, Temptations, or Sam and Dave.) Something of a chameleon, I managed to fit in well enough to find friends almost as soon as Sidwell started that first September. I was a good enough mimic to fool myself, too—it took years and years to acknowledge the discomfort and estrangement that came with being part of the integration generation. Someone's written that those of us who were the first at schools like Friends weren't there for our own good but for the benefit of the white students. I can't say it wasn't true.

At about the same time, I joined the Sea Explorers, a boating-oriented Boy Scouts program. En route to an otherwise all-white gathering of Ships (as our units were called), I remember our Skipper admonishing us, "Now fellows, don't segregate yourselves." Someone from the Black Student Fund, which provided the money for me to go to Friends—when I wrote the organization's twentieth-anniversary history, one founder told me it was started by John F. Kennedy supporters who feared that JFK and his brother would be politically embarrassed by revelations their children attended all-white private schools—might have said the same thing if there'd been an orientation to prepare us. There wasn't, despite it being scarcely a decade after 1954. Though we weren't the first to have thrust on us the burden of representing the race, we were the first to interact with whites on terms of putative equality.

Inevitably, mistakes (as they say) were made.

There was the junior varsity coach who called me and another boy Heckle and Jeckle after watching us flail during tryouts for the team. (He'd begged us to come to the first practice because he assumed all Black kids played basketball.) There was the white boy whose first greeting was, "Hey, man, you dig soul music? I dig soul music." (I preferred The Beatles because Janis, the girl I had a crush on in junior high school did.) There were the heads that turned my way when topics in class touched on race and questions—"Why didn't Africa have any great powers? Or any history for that matter?"—for which I had no answers. There were the girls who made clear their interest and, equally clear, their lack of interest in my meeting their parents. Just as well. The Black women who served us when I *did* eat at someone's home were always introduced by their first names. "Why, she's just like part of the family," one mother crowed proudly.

When I brood about these things that happened, years and years before trigger warnings and social justice coordinators, I find myself wishing I'd known some of the stories I'm going to tell here, as well as others I'm saving for another book. Stories about the ancestor who bought his freedom and land to call his own; stories about the great-great-great-great grandfather who quit the United States for Liberia; stories about Papa, the great-grandfather who read while walking between the handles of a plow; stories about the great-uncle who died a missionary in Nigeria; stories about the uncle who landed on Utah Beach not long after D-Day. The worst of the fighting was over, but things, he remembered, "were still plenty hot."

They believed in America, all the men and women from the tribes of Simonses, Garretts, Millses, and Hunters whose stories I'll tell. It's an old-fashioned sentiment, like faith in kumbaya and integration. But why else would they have sacrificed to educate themselves, their sons, and their daughters; sent sons to fight in two world wars; preached the gospel of education, thrift, good manners, and moderation, all in the face of a world that denied their abilities and their essential humanity? It may be more accurate to say they believed in the *possibility* of America. Still, it's the only reason that makes sense to me.

"You are as good as any," my grandmother, Mattie P. Simons, used to tell her children after they moved from a narrow street hard by Union Station to a new home within walking distance of Howard University. There were still maids, laborers, and waitresses among their new neighbors; now there were teachers, a doctor, and a dentist as well. "You are as good as any," Mattie reminded her children, "and better than most."

She was right, of course. But, before I get too far ahead of myself, a confession: It isn't true that I began to write this book that Thanksgiving Day back in 1965. I was fourteen, remember?, and only a high school sophomore. The Robertses weren't the Robertses, and Tom wasn't my classmate's name. As for the rest, as I lurch between discovery and imagining—everything else I'm going to tell you is as true as I can make it.

- 1 -

The African

Of all the stories Ruth might have told back then, I wish she'd told the story of The African. (I was in my thirties when she finally did, had slunk home after finishing the Writers Workshop at the University of Iowa—shaken in my belief of myself as a writer and owing thousands in student loans.) She called him that as we talked while folding copies of *Black Film Review*, the magazine I'd started. The African, as if he were an archetype, a mythic figure to be remembered with awe. His real name had been taken from him, of course, once the slave ship in which he was chained landed in Charleston and he was led to the auction block. But he was called other names in other stories passed down over six generations, his surname always Dublin, his first name sometimes Bob, sometimes Samuel, sometimes Prince. Whether chosen or forced on him, whether Bob or Samuel or Prince, The African's acceptance of the new name (and his later actions) showed him a practical man. He put down where he was, made the best of where he'd found himself, reinvented himself as an American.

How else to explain his purchasing his freedom and then land, delivering his wife and two of his children from slavery? He didn't free them because he couldn't, and so the story doesn't end happily. All the same, I'm glad I know it.

If he'd been able to read or write, The African might have left traces to help me understand his life. Likely he could do neither—South Carolina had forbidden "mental instruction" of slaves since at least 1740. What little I do know about him, then, comes from scant mentions in manumission papers, deeds, a lawsuit, auction sale bills, census records, and a scattering of newspaper stories. There's an advantage in that: Not knowing who he was, I can make him who I need him to be.

Slaveholders sometimes mocked their captives by giving them heroic names like Titus, Pompey, or Caesar, but the appellation "Prince" may have come from The African's great-grandson, Casper George Garrett. Called C. G. Garrett in contemporary newspaper stories (and sometimes granted the honorific "Professor"), he was Papa to his children and grand-children. His wife Anna Maria (Mah-RYE-uh) Threewitts Garrett, was Mama. I'd have called them that if I'd known them—they were my great-grandparents. I'll call them that here.

Born near the small town of Laurens in western South Carolina just after the Civil War, Papa was nurtured by his mother, educated by North-ern missionary schoolteachers, and encouraged by a cohort of farm folk who recognized his talents. When he was just out of his teens, he jour-neyed to Columbia to attend Allen University, the pride of the S.C. Afri-can Methodist Episcopal (AME) Church. With the exception of five years as principal of a Winnsboro Colored Graded School, he'd remain in his adopted hometown the rest of his life, teaching at Allen, editing and pub-lishing three newspapers, serving as an active AME layman, and dabbling in Republican politics. He and his wife would rear ten children.

Devoted to his students—many remembered him fondly as the inspi-ration for their own careers as teachers and clergymen—and to his alma mater, Papa served Allen for several decades. He was passionate about the causes he espoused, vehement in his likes and dislikes, always ready to speak out against injustice inside and outside the Church, real or per-ceived. He and The African labored in different fields, but in his own way, Papa was just as determined. Surely this great-grandfather with the tenacity and the courage to remake his life must have been held up as an example.

And yet, though Papa was closer to The African than we are, he passed on fewer than one hundred words about his ancestor. "My grandmother's father," he said, "was a young prince of the blood royal who, after being brought to Charleston, refused to be enslaved. He went upstate, bought land in the early eighties, married a slave woman, built a home and bought his wife and all his girl children. Through the treachery of his guardian, the old man lost his plantation, and the children unbought. He was a highbred, grand old man who took no insult and suffered no master. Death had no terror for him when his or his children's rights were invaded."[1]

Papa's account comes from the South Carolina edition of A. B. Caldwell's *History of the American Negro*, a collection of mini-biographies of "representative men and women of the race." It was published a century after The African purchased his freedom, long enough for fact to have become myth. So there's probably more than a little exaggeration in Papa's story—any captive who "refused to be enslaved" would have quickly found himself crippled or dead—and the wishful thinking of a generation seeking to distance itself from the painful past. Many had been born in slavery. Those, like Papa, who did not have to endure it must have glimpsed welts scarring older folk. At night, in front of the fire, they heard whispered tales as horrifying as ghost stories. Little surprise, then, that another of Papa's stiff-necked, mustached contemporaries in Caldwell's *History* also maintained royal ancestry, claiming a grandmother who'd been "a princess of the Crow tribe in Africa." A second asserted "a strain of white blood from grandparents on both sides." A third's mother was "Cherokee Indian." And *her* father, he said, was "half white."[2]

Some of these claims may be true—one man has straightish hair and resembles a mournful Henry Winkler, with the actor's long nose and thin lips. Even if they aren't, though, they're interesting as examples of a complicated (and ongoing), response toward slavery. Papa and others Caldwell included in "the best element of the Negro race"[3] were closer to the experience than we are, but the conundrum of how to hold slavery endures. Even Ralph Ellison's Invisible Man's grudging acceptance—"I am not shamed of my grandparents for having been slaves. I am only ashamed of myself for having at one time been ashamed."—seems easier said than won. For most of our history, we *have* been ashamed, almost as if we believed our ancestors would have done more to protect their families and themselves if they'd truly been men. But it's wrong to blame them, as wrong as it would be, say, to blame a woman for having been raped or a man for surrendering his wallet at gunpoint. The African and his cohort were chained and forced into coffles by ruthless, greedy men with more powerful weapons and better technology, men who may even have been haunted by nightmares from their own distant pasts. The root of the word *slave* is Slav, which hints at something Ruth said once that I've never forgotten: "If you go back far enough, everybody was a slave."

Exaggeration aside, I'm inclined to trust Papa on the essentials. He was a lawyer and a newspaperman, committed to the truth, though telling it as he saw it didn't always serve him well. He didn't name the "young prince," but he knew that his grandmother, The African's daughter, was named Nancy and that she'd married a man named Samuel. His father was also named Samuel. His mother had been named Martha Hyde.

There were other stories, too. In one, The African's called Bob Dublin and is a "chieftain" brought to South Carolina "from the Congo" shortly before the end of the Civil War. He had two daughters, Harriet and Sally. Another version calls Dublin's wife Nancy and his daughters Sally and Mary. The names are important. With the exception of Harriet, all can be documented in connection with the man who may have been The African.

◆ ◆ ◆

It was Ruth who found the manumission papers. I wish I could write that they were among the thousands of letters, diaries, photographs, and other documents she uncovered in the mid-1970s in the attic of the house on S Street. It would make a better story. Her father had bought the house in 1928 when she was only six years old, and Ruth had grown up there hearing of the maternal ancestor called Bob (or Samuel or Prince) Dublin. Now, among everything she found in the attic were copies of programs for two reunions of "the Dublin Clan" in the 1930s. Noting the common surname Dublin—she was, after all, a manuscript librarian at the Library of Congress—Ruth took the train to South Carolina.

She found what she was looking for in the Laurens County Public Library, microfilm of a deed of manumission dated January 4, 1819, for "a certain Negro man" named Dublin. In it, one James Hunter acknowledged that Dublin had paid him twelve hundred dollars and was now "emancipated and set free." Relinquishing all claims, James signed in the presence of two witnesses, Sophia and S. B. Lewers. Five Laurens District freeholders signed a supporting affidavit.

It's a telling document once one manages to decipher the spidery antique handwriting. Dublin (only the first name is used) is described as "about twenty two years of age, black complexion, and about five feet two inches high." If the age is correct, he would have been born about 1797.[4] The freeholders' affidavit—required under an 1800 South Carolina law designed to restrict manumission and keep free Negroes "in due subordination"—certified Dublin as "not of bad character and . . . capable of gaining a livelihood by honest means." Thirty-one years later, the 1850 census would identify Dublin as a "mechanic," a term used for any skilled craftsmen. At the beginning of the twentieth century, however, he was remembered as "a good carpenter and industrious."[5]

He had to have been to come up with the twelve hundred dollars—equivalent to nearly twenty-five thousand dollars today—that he paid to ransom himself. But even if Dublin were a carpenter (and not a cooper, bricklayer, or blacksmith), it's nigh impossible to know how much he earned and how long he saved to buy his freedom. And if he were a carpenter, did he fashion trusses, joists, and walls on site, or was he a joiner who made doors and windows in his own shop? Was he a cabinetmaker, making beds, chairs, dressers, and other furniture, able enough to charge by the piece? Whatever his trade, wages were generally lower in the South,[6] so he would have been lucky to earn two dollars a day. I'm only guessing, but it might have taken him as long as eight years (which means, if the estimate of his age in the manumission papers is correct, he'd have been fourteen when he started) to save what he needed, depending on how much he returned to his master for the privilege of hiring himself out.

However he managed it, Dublin's timing was good. About two years after he freed himself, the state did away with private manumission and made emancipation possible only through legislative act. The change would have profound implications for him and his family.[7]

Other than the fact that Dublin managed somehow to pay him twelve hundred dollars, I don't know why James Hunter agreed to free his slave. One possibility is that he subscribed to what University of South Carolina historian Lacy Ford calls the "paternalistic ideal" some slaveholders began to embrace in the early 1800s as justification for the peculiar institution. (A term, I ought note, coined by John C. Calhoun, U.S. vice president, senator, and staunch defender of slavery, though he meant "peculiar" in the sense of "special," because he believed American slavery different from, and better than, slavery elsewhere.) Inherently contradictory, it attempted to put a kinder face on slavery by recognizing slaves as human, although lesser, uncivilized beings with limited possibilities for bettering themselves.[8] As Frederick Douglass put it, they wanted to "hold [their] slaves, and go to heaven too."[9]

There's also another, less hypocritically sanctimonious possibility. Seven years after Dublin purchased his freedom, James asked the Laurens District Court to prevent another man "from foreclosing on a slave mortgage 'on the ground of usury.'" After falling into debt "'while afflicted with something like a paralytic affection [*sic*] which produced in him a most deplorable state of bodily & mental imbecility,'" James mortgaged three of his slaves to one Charles Fowler. Charles had increased the interest. Unable to pay, James asked the court to compel Charles to reveal how he'd computed the interest on the mortgage and to return the slaves.[10]

If this were the same man who freed Dublin, had a pattern of becoming "embarrassed in his pecuniary affairs"[11] earlier led him to sell Dublin Hunter to himself?

◆ ◆ ◆

Perhaps it was only that they were aware of James's carelessness in financial matter, but powerful whites took an interest in Dublin. The signatures of Samuel Brown Lewers and his wife, Sophia, show that. Lewers, 1792–1852, graduated from South Carolina College (now the University of South Carolina) in 1811. He served in the War of 1812, became an attorney, and was admitted to the bar in 1815. Also a minister, he was one of the founders of the First Presbyterian Church of Laurens, serving as pastor from 1832 to 1850.[12]

His wife, Sophia (1795–1888), was the second daughter and third child of Charles Allen (1764–1856), a Virginian who fought in the Revolutionary War and who helped select the site on which the town of Laurens was built. Allen's name, followed by what may be the initials Q. M., also appears in the document. Appointed a judge by Governor Charles Pinckney, he must have been the magistrate who convened James, Samuel, Sophia, and the freeholders to approve Dublin's manumission.[13]

The record contains far more about the Lewerses than it does Dublin, but there's almost nothing about their relationship. Did they advise Dublin on how to proceed with the process of manumission? Might they even have helped him buy his freedom? It's possible, but not because they were particular friends of Black people. According to the 1840 census, the Lewerses owned nearly two dozen slaves. Likely, then, they helped Dublin out of guilt, seeking to assuage their consciences by embracing the "paternalistic ideal" that allowed them to help free one while keeping more than twenty in bondage.

On November 5, 1821, two years after gaining his freedom, Dublin purchased twenty-one acres of land from his former master. He paid $82.50. James did not sign—the document notes "his mark" above and below an X. (If he wasn't illiterate, perhaps he'd begun to suffer from the "paralytic affection"[14] that had sent him into debt.)

Dublin was not quite done. On March 25, 1823, he exercised his rights as a free man a second time, purchasing a woman named Sall and her two daughters, "Sophia or Mary" and Suzette.[15] It was an act of faith by a man of singular determination, another step toward the possibility he might make a life he could call his own.

The next part of the story's a long one. Bear with me. And understand that, even though Dublin's the hero of my tale, the official narrative scarcely mentions him.

A month before Dublin Hunter purchased Sall and her daughters, the Laurens Court deemed them part of the estate of a man named Charles Simmons. Charles had been dead for more than thirty years, so it was one more twist in a story of avarice and sibling rivalry that began about a decade after the end of the Revolutionary War. Sall and her children suffered, but without the greed of Charles's children, I might never have discovered their names.

Charles died in 1791 or 1792, leaving a will dated July 7, 1791. His wife, Elizabeth, distributed his property in accordance with his wishes. Three sons, John, Charles, and William, were to divide his three-hundred-fifty-acre plantation. Three daughters, Sarah, Elizabeth, and Jane, were bequeathed livestock (horses and cows), beds, and furniture. A fourth daughter, Mary, received only "five shillings sterling."

Not surprisingly, Mary felt slighted. So did Charles's namesake son—his father owned two more tracts of land that weren't mentioned in the will. Mary and Charles's resentment would simmer for decades. To complicate matters, John felt owed for work he'd done, so he took several hogsheads of tobacco from his father's plantation, sold them, and used the money to buy three slave children from one Major William Dunlap. The major went to Maryland or Virginia (accounts differ) and brought back "two Negro girls," Rose and Sall (who's also called Sarah in some documents), and a boy named Mose.

Rose's age is lost, but if a later bill of sale can be believed, Mose was two or three years old, and Sall was one or two. Nothing in the surviving court documents explains why John, a man who'd worked as his father's "croper [*sic*] or overseer," wanted children who couldn't have been much use in house or field.

They suffered a long journey, two hundred sixty miles as the crow flies if William went to Lynchburg, three hundred thirty if he went to Richmond, and even farther if the children came from Maryland. After the Middle Passage, it's the second family hegira. One account implies John bought the three after William came back, so perhaps William had gone north on his own accord and returned with several slaves, among them, a mother and her children. (This would mean he separated and sold Rose, Sall, and Mose with no more hesitation than if they were part of a sow's litter.) But if William was fulfilling John's commission, as another account implies, John wanted children, so William may have bought only the three. Did he take a wet nurse? Or was Rose old enough to care for Mose and Sall? Could she have carried the younger children, walking while William ambled ahorse? Did he bring a cart or wagon so that the children huddled in back, jolted, and jostled as the horse stumbled on the rocky path? I imagine Rose holding a rag soaked in milk or sugar water to Sall's mouth as Dunlap snarls over his shoulder for her to hush the squawling infant. And the blinkered horse plods on, as weary as the travelers.

Too young to know the full horrors of the future that awaited, the children endured simple survival as heroic as Dublin's purchase of himself. But their trials were not over.

John took possession of them, but only for a little while. His brothers and sisters were a contentious bunch—they complained about his seizing and selling the tobacco. To placate them—the documents suggest the slaves would become part of his mother's estate to be distributed at her death—he sold Mose and Sall to his mother for £50 on December 20 or December 24, 1793—Christmas Eve. Again, accounts differ. He kept Rose.

The elder Charles Simmons had been in debt when he died, so Elizabeth sold Mose to satisfy her creditors. Sall remained with her. Over the next twenty-nine years, Sall gave birth to five children—Amy, Nancy, Bob, Suzette, and Sophia.[16]

Dublin Hunter may have been the father of some or all, but I can't know for sure. The white men who took affidavits and recorded inventories and bills of sale didn't care. For them, the children were only property, and so, depending on the document, Amy is sometimes "Amie"; Bob, "Bobb"; and Suzette, "Lizette." Nancy is always Nancy. Sophia, who was also called Mary, had her names misspelled twice, once as "Sopha" and then, inexplicably, "Carly," though that last may be due to my inability to decipher the faded, ornate handwriting. The youngest child, she must have been named for Dublin's benefactress, Sophia Lewers.

It would not be the last time one of Dublin's descendants was named to commemorate someone who aided the family.

Elizabeth Simmons died in 1822, leaving Sall and her children to five of her sons and daughters. Sall and Sophia went to John Garlington (the "Register" who'd signed Hunter's deed of manumission), in trust for Elizabeth's daughter, Jane Simmons Franks. Sally Simmons Madden received Bob. Amy went to Elizabeth Simmons Smith. Two sons, William and John, received Nancy and Suzette, respectively.

Mary Simmons McCaa, the daughter to whom the elder Charles Simmons had left only five shillings, received nothing. But she'd already gotten hers—and set in motion the events that would reveal the names of Dublin's wife and children: Six years before Elizabeth's death, David McCaa sold David Anderson "all interest and claim" in Charles Simmons' estate due McCaa "in right of his wife Mary." David Anderson paid him six hundred dollars. A day later, Mary signed a document attesting that she'd voluntarily assigned her claims to her husband—Anderson wanted to nail down his claim.

A few months after Elizabeth's death, Anderson and the younger Charles Simmons sued John and the other heirs, claiming the distribution of Sall and her five children in Elizabeth's will had been unlawful because John had bought Sall "with monies properly belonging" to the elder Charles Simmons's estate. The court decided in Charles and David's favor, and on March 25, 1823, Sall and her children were sold. Dublin purchased Sall, Sophia, and Suzette for six hundred sixty dollars. An inventory taken the day before the sale estimated that Suzette was five or six years old and that Sophia was one. Amy—sold to Charles Smith—was about ten. Nancy—sold to John L. James—was about eight. And Bob, who was sold to Edward Garlington, was seven.

All the bill of sale says about Dublin is that he was a free man of color—otherwise, he could not have the purchased the three. It gives no clue about his relationship to the two girls, but my guess is that they were his children. Charles's suit calls all five children Sall's, but the ages make me think not all were Dublin's: He would have been about sixteen when Amy was born, and Sall 22. Sixteen's old enough to father a child, of course, but Elizabeth's will describes Sall and four of the children—Nancy, Bob, Suzette, and Sophia—as "Negroes." Amy, the oldest, is called mulatto. Dublin's own freedom papers describe him as of "black complexion."

Dublin celebrated two milestones about the time Sophia and Suzette were born—the purchase of his freedom and land to call his own. Coincidence? Perhaps. But he was in his twenties then, and it just may be that he was spurred to independence by the birth of his children. Also, if the girls weren't his, why would he have spent such a large sum—as much as sixteen thousand five hundred dollars today—to purchase them and their mother?[17] There's another, less appealing possibility, one suggested by Johnson and Roark in *Black Masters: A Free Family of Color in the Old South*: Perhaps Dublin understood owning slaves would assure his white neighbors that, although free, he "was no more antislavery than they were—namely not at all."[18] But if this were true, why take two young girls, one of them years from being able to work his land? Better to have purchased seven-year-old Bob and ten-year-old Amy. Sophia and Suzette must have been his If they weren't, then surely Dublin must have loved Sall enough to rescue two of her children from slavery.

There's another question that haunts me. If some, or all, of the other children were his, why didn't Dublin purchase them too? The most likely explanation is that he couldn't afford to. Amy was sold for three hundred twenty-six dollars; Nancy, for three hundred sixty-one dollars; and Bob, for two hundred thirty-six dollars. He would have needed nearly sixteen hundred dollars—about four hundred dollars more than he'd paid for himself, and nearly forty thousand dollars today—to take Sall and all five children.

If all were his, then Dublin lived the rest of his life with the terrible choice he'd been forced to make.

◆ ◆ ◆

A few weeks after Sall and her children were auctioned, Samuel Lewers "accept[ed] the trust and appointment as Guardian for Dublin Hunter a free man of color above the age of 15 years." As he had when signing the manumission papers, Samuel attested that Hunter was "of good character and correct habits."[19]

Dublin needed a white protector because of a law passed on December 21, 1822, in response to white fears of slave rebellion. Earlier that year, a free Black carpenter named Denmark Vesey had exhorted slaves in and around Charleston to rise up and slaughter their masters. Betrayed before the insurrection began, Vesey was hanged. As many as forty others were also executed. In the wake of the thwarted uprising, South Carolina lawmakers adopted several provisions restricting the rights of free Blacks. One required free Black males over age fifteen to find guardians. Another made it illegal for slaves to hire themselves out. Passed four years earlier, that last provision would have made it impossible for Dublin to buy his freedom.[20]

If he'd taken liberty for granted (living "head in the lion's mouth,"[21] he probably didn't), Dublin knew he could no longer. His guardian (as Johnson and Roark explain) had to be "a respectable freeholder of [his] district," and it made sense to seek one "as high up the social ladder as possible."[22] Clergyman, lawyer, and magistrate, Samuel met both criteria. But Dublin waited until May of 1823—about five months after the law was passed— risking the chance he'd be sold back into slavery. Any white man could have turned him in, and there was incentive to do so. The "informer" (the statutes use that word) would have been entitled to "one moiety [half] of the proceeds of the sale."[23]

Perhaps Dublin didn't know he needed a guardian. I think it more likely he didn't feel compelled to find one right away. If he was as skilled as he was remembered a half-century after his death, respect for the quality of his work gave him status and a measure of security. Once he'd rescued his family, however, Dublin moved quickly, obtaining his certificate of guardianship just five weeks later. No longer alone, he had a wife and daughters to protect.

◆ ◆ ◆

Except for the 1830, 1840, and 1850 censuses, and a scattering of newspaper articles, Dublin fades from the record after Samuel signed on to be his guardian.

In the first of the censuses, the one in which Carter G. Woodson found 7,921 "free colored persons" in South Carolina, Dublin is listed as head of a family that included a man between twenty-four and thirty-six years old, a woman aged thirty-six to fifty-five, and two boys and two girls under age ten. (If the David Anderson who appears on the same page is the same ordinary—an officer of the Court of Ordinary, forerunner to today's probate court—whose lawsuit resulted in Dublin being able to purchase his wife and children, his extracurricular efforts as huckster weren't all that successful: He's listed as owning just five slaves. By contrast, John Garlington, also listed there, held twenty-three.) Sall must have been the older woman—the difference in their ages is compatible with that given in other documents. The ages of the two girls also accord with what we know of Suzette and Sophia. Names aren't given; it's possible, though, that one of the boys was called Richard. All are erroneously listed as free—an 1820 law had made manumission possible only through an act of the South Carolina Legislature. As far as the state was concerned, Sall and their children were Dublin's property. That fact would have unfortunate consequences after his death.

It's harder, though, to account for the family members who appear in the census ten years later. Dublin's household consisted of nine persons— two boys under age ten, three males and one female aged ten to twenty-four, one man and one woman aged thirty-six to fifty-five, and one man aged fifty-five to one hundred.

If Dublin and Sall were the couple aged thirty-six to fifty-five, then who was the older man? And who were the others, and what were their relationships to Dublin? Two of the males aged ten to twenty-four could have been Richard and the other boy listed in the 1830 census. Was the third the husband of the woman aged ten to twenty-four? Or could it have been Bob, the unredeemed captive, who would have been about twenty-five by then? The female aged ten to twenty-four could have been either Suzette or Sophia, but what happened to the other girl? Were the two boys under age ten her children? Sall would have been almost fifty; still it's possible that one or both were hers.

Only three people appear in 1850, the last time Dublin's in the census. He's head of a three-person household consisting of himself, aged sixty-five; Sally, aged sixty; and Allen, aged fourteen, who could have been one of the younger boys counted the decade before.

If the age given in 1850 is correct, Sally would have been born about 1790, which jibes with what we know of the one-year-old Sall brought to South Carolina about 1792. Dublin's age is given as sixty-five, meaning that he would have been born about 1785. There's a twelve-year discrepancy between the birth year—1797—that can be inferred from the deed of manumission. Puzzling, unless the census taker simply guessed on the basis of Dublin's appearance.

He must have had a hard life if he appeared to be so much older than his chronological age. And yet I want to believe Dublin didn't live like a prisoner or slave, fixed on the immediate—the row hoed, the cow milked, the board planed, the shingle riven and drawn—to thwart despair. He suffered the unhealed wound of his failure to rescue all of Sall's children. He endured the losses that come to all men—the bittersweet departures of his sons and daughters to embark on their own lives, the diminution of aging. But I want to believe he enjoyed simple, ordinary pleasures—cool water to slake his thirst, the satisfaction of a full belly, Sall's warmth on winter nights, the pleasure of whispered endearments. And perhaps sometimes, bent over his workbench, stopped to contemplate a crisp curl twisting fragrant from the plane, the sweetness of right-fitting mortise and tenon, the gleam of a sharp-whetted chisel.

In the end, Dublin was betrayed by the encroachment of age and the diminishment of his abilities. That final census lists him as a mechanic owning fifty dollars in real estate. Either the value of the land he purchased in 1821 had declined severely, or he'd been forced sell all or part of it. Perhaps he'd used himself up making sure his family escaped slavery's horrors. Still, it was his triumph that, despite hard times and poverty, he and Sal enjoyed more than twenty-five years together outside of bondage before his death.

It was almost enough for a happy ending.

◆　◆　◆

Much of Dublin's story accords, in broad detail at least, with Papa's tale of his African ancestor. Like Papa's "young prince of the blood royal," Dublin refused to be enslaved, though he purchased his freedom instead of rebelling outright. Like Papa's prince, he "married a slave woman" and then purchased his wife and daughters. Papa had his African ancestor purchasing "all his *girl* children" (emphasis added), implying he was unable to free at least one son. Hunter left in slavery a boy (and two girls) who may, or may not, have been his children. Finally, Papa testified that "the old man lost . . . his children unbought" because of "the treachery of his guardian."[24]

The lost children may have been Amy, Nancy, and Bob, but there's nothing to suggest Samuel Lewers betrayed the trust he'd sworn to uphold. Instead, he did Dublin a kindness at least once. The year before Dublin purchased his wife and children, Samuel bought a "speckled cow & calf" for $10.50 at auction. According to the itemized "Sale Bill," the two animals were "taken by Dublin Hunter."[25]

Still, like the African prince, Dublin did lose his wife and children, so perhaps Papa's story captured the essentials. When Dublin died in the 1850s (one source says 1850; another, 1855), Sall and their children were caught in the contradictions of the system that permitted their husband and father to be free but not quite a man. Though they lived as if free and were listed as free persons of color in the 1840 census, all were his property, his slaves. After his death, they were sold to satisfy his creditors.[26]

And with that, Sall, her children, and their children's children disappear into history—Suzette, Sophia, Amy, Nancy, and Bob, and all the others whose names have been lost. All except one. Sold after his father's death, he was "determined to be free" and so would succeed in buying himself, not once, but twice. His name was Richard Hunter, though he's sometimes called Dick Nugent, after the man who first bought him.[27]

Accounts published after his death claim Richard "cheerfully accepted his changed condition." Perhaps. But he was a lot like his father, and his was the cheerfulness of a man determined not to wallow in self-pity. A "clever workman," he was "imbued with the idea of freedom," and so he negotiated an agreement with his new owner, a bachelor named Samuel

Nugent. He would pay fifteen hundred dollars—one hundred dollars a year for fifteen years—for his freedom. Samuel died a year or two after the start of the Civil War, still owed four hundred dollars. Richard was sold again, this time for eight hundred dollars. The purchaser was his wife, Eliza, a free woman of color. The couple had trouble raising the money, but, as "an act of faith and pure kindness," a "Laurens planter" named Clark Templeton "endorsed the note." (He could afford to—the 1870 census says he owned property worth nearly four thousand dollars.)

At war's end, Richard and Eliza still owed about five hundred dollars. They didn't have to finish paying Clark. Shrewd enough to understand it was in their best interest, they did anyway. Even if they couldn't foresee the ascension of white supremacy that would follow Reconstruction's abrupt end, Richard and Eliza must have known they were dependent on the goodwill of their white neighbors.

The money was well spent. Richard lived the rest of his life in Laurens County, operating a small farm on fifty acres purchased from Clark. He sold produce, fowl, eggs, and butter. After his death in 1902, newspapers throughout the country published stories praising his "industry, thrift and frugality." His decision to repay the debt was cited as "an example of inflexible business good faith," and Richard celebrated as "sober, honest, frugal and polite" and (an odious characterization) an "old-time Negro." For whites too young to remember the Civil War, he was a historical curiosity, relic of another age. But for those who'd lived through the war's privations and its unsettled aftermath, Richard's seeming fidelity served to alleviate lingering unease about the men and women who remained among them, no longer slave but not quite free.

Honesty and my time as a newspaper reporter and editor compel me to admit that some of what can be documented about Dublin Hunter accords with Papa's story, but much does not. One story published after Richard's death called Dublin "a full-blooded African, free born, [who] came to this country on his own volition. He was a mechanic and withal a thrifty Negro." His last name was supposed to have come from his guardian, a "storekeeper" named Thomas (not James) Hunter. According to this account, Dublin "married a wife whose freedom he purchased." Another newspaper had it that Dublin came to South Carolina from Africa in the 1830s and "probably received his training in some British colony."

Unfortunately, the newspapers don't tell us what peculiar sense of adventure would lead a free African to come to America and settle voluntarily in a slave state. And they don't deal with the difficulties he would have faced. Leery of increases in the number of free Negroes, legislators passed numerous laws restricting their entering South Carolina. Those who refused to leave were to be beaten until they complied. Black seamen were treated differently. If Dublin had been, say, a ship's carpenter, the law stipulated that he was to be seized and confined until his ship was to sail.

Discrepancies aside, this that gives me hope I might not be wrong in claiming Dublin as ancestor: Papa said his grandfather, Samuel, married a woman named Nancy. Both a Samuel Garrett and a Nancy Garrett appear in the 1870 census. Samuel is listed as a farm laborer, with Nancy as keeping house. He is fifty-three (or fifty-eight; the handwriting isn't clear), so he would have been born about 1812 or 1817. She's fifty-six, which means she would have been born about 1814. Both would have been old enough to be Papa's grandparents. (Because Samuel wasn't descended from Dublin Hunter, he probably wasn't named after Samuel Lewers.)

Eight-year-old Nancy was among the three children sold at the same time Dublin Hunter bought Suzette and Sophia. Assuming the estimate of her age was accurate, she would have been born about 1815. Were they the same woman? And was she Dublin's daughter? Perhaps: Samuel and Nancy's household included eight children, among them a one-year-old boy named Dublin.

Which brings us back to the family stories that identify The African as Bob Dublin. In those, he's married to a woman named Nancy and has daughters named Mary and Sally. All three names can be documented in connection with Dublin Hunter, though Sall(y) was his wife and Mary (or Sophia) and, possibly, Nancy his daughters.

There are other connections between Papa and the Hunters. The surname Hunter appears in those 1933 and 1934 Dublin clan reunion programs Ruth found, programs that also included Millses, Garretts, and Hunters. Papa named his fifth child, and fourth son, Colon (the Spanish for Columbus) Hunter Garrett. Given family naming traditions—children

were often named for older relatives and given surnames as first names—
Papa certainly knew of a connection with a relative surnamed Hunter.

In the end, though, perhaps it doesn't matter that I can say only that I'm
pretty sure Dublin Hunter was Papa's African, and thus my ancestor as
well. What really matters is that The African existed and that we remembered him for generations after he died. What matters is that Papa was
inspired hearing the stories about him. And what matters now, two cen-
turies after Dublin Hunter reinvented himself as a free man, is how I hold
him. "Some people are your relatives but others are your ancestors," Ralph
Ellison observed, "and you choose the ones you want to have as ancestors.
You create yourself out of those values."[28] No matter that Ellison was talking about literary, not literal, ancestors—I claim Dublin Hunter.

Of course, my need to be descended from some other doughty, sable,
Jeffersonian yeoman wasn't that different from the desire of Papa's contemporaries to boast descent from Crow princesses or Madagascan roy-
alty. But mine wasn't simply a need to come to terms with the slave past.
(Remember that Ellison quote about slave grandparents and shame.) Born
in the United States, I spent my childhood in Jamaica. Once we returned
to the States, I needed to find a way to belong. It was a craving for "psychic citizenship"—as the Pulitzer-Prize-winning historian David Levering
Lewis put it in an e-mail exchange—that would allow me (finally!) to see
myself as an American.

I think of Dublin as a hero (as well as Sall, Richard, and all the others
whose stories I'll tell), but calling him that's just another way of making
him what I need him to be. He likely didn't think of himself as a hero or
even as an American in the grandiose way I set out earlier. Perhaps he just
wanted Sall and felt incomplete when apart from her, as if missing a leg or
arm. And yet. . . . And yet, that he was so young when he set out to claim
her, that he worked so long and so hard, is evidence of a sacred single-
mindedness. How did he do it? How did he manage to keep faith with himself and his goals? There must have been times when, weary unto death, he
considered running away or slipping back into the stasis of slavery. How
did he summon the strength to go on? Perhaps it was Sall's doing. Perhaps

she wheedled and cajoled, alternately granted and withheld her favors, by turns hectored and encouraged to ensure her man stayed the course.

She must have been some woman.

But to focus on Sall and Dublin ignores all the others whose stories I can't tell because I'll never know them, stories of those who bore the lash laboring from can't see to can't see, stole food to keep their children from starving, then saw those same children sold away, died crippled and bent, damning their white masters with their last breaths.

Saying that Dublin (and the rest of my ancestors) believed in America ignores how much they suffered under a system that saw them as less than. And yet. . . . And yet, the fact that I sit here writing this affirms how much they believed. Even when America did not believe in them.

Image of Dublin Hunter's manumission document. Scan from microfilm copy Laurens County Library.

Transcription of Dublin Hunter's Manumission Document

South Carolina
Laurens District

Know all men by these presents, that I, James Hunter of the District and state aforesaid for and in consideration of the sum of one thousand two hundred dollars to me paid, by a certain negro man called Dublin, about twenty two years of age, black complexion, and about five feet two inches high, have emancipated and set free, and by these presents do manumit, emancipate and set free the said negro Dublin to all intents and purposes and I request every person to treat him according and I do bind myself, my heirs, Executors, or administrators to warrant and forever defend his freedom to the said negro Dublin from myself, my heirs and assigns and every other person whomsoever. In witness whereof I have herewith set my hand and seal this 4th day of January in the year of our Lord, one thousand eight hundred and nineteen signed sealed and acknowledged in presence of

Jas. Hunter

Sophia Lewers
S.B. Lewers
We hereby certify, upon the examination of James Hunter (on oath) the owner of a certain slave named Dublin (in the above deed described) satisfactory proof has been given to us that the said slave is not of bad character and is capable of gaining a livelihood by honest means. Jany 4th, 1819

Chas. Allen QM [?]

Freeholders

Collyar Barksdale
   his
Thomas X. Harris
mark
M Smith
Edward Hix
S.B. Lewers

South Carolina
Laurens District

Before me personally appeared Samuel B. Lewers who being sworn saith that he was present and did see the within named James Hunter sign seal and heard him acknowledge the within as his act and deed for the purpose therein mentioned and that Sophia Lewers with himself were witnesses to the due execution of the said. Sworn to and subscribed before me the 10th January 1819.

John Garlington [indecipherable initials] S.B. Lewers

A true Record of the original March the 12th 1819 John Garlington Register[1]

Mr. Washington
Comes to Columbia

It is the afternoon of March 15, 1909, and about one hundred twenty men (and a lone woman who might be Matilda Evans, a physician and surgeon with an interracial practice who founded two hospitals for colored patients) are gathered on the steps of Columbia's First Calvary Baptist Church to welcome Booker T. Washington. Papa's in the second row near the center, a few feet to the right of Washington. He sports a derby and a luxuriant mustache. Studying the image through a magnifying glass, I detect a small, self-satisfied smile. It's the smile of a man who's made himself up through will, hard work, and no small amount of luck. He's arrived, but there are still places he intends to go. It's probably only happenstance, but Papa's managed to find himself an almost perfect spot. He's near the center of the camera's lens, in focus and out of the sun.

Washington, bareheaded, is in the front row, hands jammed in the pockets of his overcoat. The Rev. Richard Carroll, a conservative Baptist minister dubbed the "Booker T. Washington of South Carolina," is a few feet away, heavy and prosperous seeming, sandwiched between the Benedict College band's cornetist and trombonist. It was Carroll who arranged the week-long speech-making tour by the man he proclaimed "the most prominent and greatest Negro in the world."[1] The tour would take Washington and his entourage zigzagging throughout the state to a dozen South Carolina cities, beginning in Rock Hill on March 14 and ending in Gaffney a week later. Counting those he addressed en route during an equal number of "whistle-stop" speeches from the back of his private car, Washington spoke to fifty thousand Carolinians, Black and white.

When he arrived in Columbia, Washington was met by a delegation at the train station. He dined at Carroll's "mansion" in suburban Kendalltown

Papa in the crowd gathered to greet Booker T. Washington in 1909.
Library of Congress.

before going to a reception at First Calvary. Afterward, he spoke to a crowd
of some fifteen hundred people. The photograph must have been taken
before the speech—otherwise, everyone would have clamored to be part of
the record of the great man's visit.

Many "distinguished African Americans" joined Washington's tour, riding in his "special car attached to the regular train." (The hired car allowed
them to avoid "the humiliation of Jim Crow travel.") Some were from out
of state, but others—perhaps as many as two dozen at various times—were
South Carolinians. Papa was a member of this group, his name thirteenth
on a list of "prominent colored citizens" on Carroll's flyer advertising Washington's tour. The names above Papa's are set in what I think is twelve-point
type, but, as if to show he had not yet quite arrived, his name (with the
honorific "Prof.") and the lines after it are set in smaller, nine-point type.
Worse, his name is given as C. F. (not C. G.) Garrett, though he's identified
correctly as "Editor The Light."

Carroll told *The State*, Columbia's morning newspaper, that Washington had come "in the interest of improving race relations." *The State*,
in turn, quoted the *Charlotte Observer* (Washington had spent a night in

North Carolina) to assure its readers that he intended to study "the progress made by the Negroes along educational and industrial lines and to inspire them to greater efforts and to cement as far as possible the friendly relations between the races."[2] The "Wizard of Tuskegee" had more on his agenda, however. With hindsight stretching back more than a century, one historian contends that, in addition to reassuring "African Americans they had the potential to become vital participants in the economic life of the region," Washington wanted to "counter white racist notions about blacks degenerating and regressing into barbarism after slavery." His guests served as distinguished examples, helping Washington undermine "prevailing notions and ridiculous stereotypes about African Americans by placing black doctors, lawyers, teachers, bishops, businessmen, journalists, college presidents, undertakers, [and] ministers . . . on display."[3]

Perhaps. But Washington would only to have seen *The State* to have reinforced what he was up against. The two stories about his speeches in Rock Hill and Winnsboro appeared on the same page as an article headlined "Some Very Plain Talk on the Negro Question." Celebrating President William Howard Taft's decision not to "appoint Negroes to office in the South where such appointments would be objectionable," the anonymous author argued that white Southerners "are the best friends of the Negro, and that they alone are capable of dealing with him intelligently, politically and otherwise." The same page featured an advertisement for Gold Dust washing powder with an illustration of twins Goldie and Dustie, coal-black, tutu-wearing caricatures of African-American children.[4]

Papa's status as lawyer, college professor, and newspaper editor (the misrendering of his name apart) was the reason he was selected to join Washington in South Carolina. In getting it not quite right, however, Carroll's flyer seems symbolic of Papa's near disappearance from history. If Dublin Hunter was the Founding Father in our family mythology, proof that, though we'd come to America in chains, some of us had had the guts and the gumption to lift ourselves up from slavery, then Papa was the Lost Hero. Like tales of treasure we'd been swindled out of, or faded memories of an usurped title, his story (like Dublin's) was proof of a past to be proud of.

– 3 –

Finding Papa

Papa spent twenty-one years as a teacher and administrator at Allen University and was active for more than twice that long in the South Carolina Republican Party. He was a longtime voice for greater participation by laymen in the African Methodist Episcopal (AME) Church and editorialized against unequal funding for colored schools. Although his wasn't the fame of a Booker T. Washington or W. E. B. Du Bois, it was the kind of esteem enjoyed by thousands of men (and women) who worked to better the Black community during the nadir between the end of Reconstruction and, say, the coming of the Harlem Renaissance. Resolute, stalwart, untiring, they created a parallel world of tailor shops, pharmacies, and newspapers, farms and printing plants, social and literary clubs, schools and churches, institutions that nurtured the community and were largely outside white control. All were means by which these "unknown black leaders,"[1] as one historian dubbed them, readied the race to scale barriers to the larger world.

All the same, though, it wasn't easy finding Papa.

By the time Ruth became interested in his life, Papa's correspondence had disappeared. It's a shame. In addition to teaching at Allen and his AME church activities (which spanned the administrations of sixteen South Carolina bishops), Papa served on Republican Party committees, ran three newspapers, helped run the Colored (later Negro) State Fair for decades, sold insurance, and worked as a notary. He got around, traveling as far south as Florida, as far west as Colorado, and up into Canada. Like his letters, Papa's records of his travels were gone. Gone, too, were his speeches, notes, class lectures, articles, and all but a half dozen or so browning, flaking copies of his third newspaper, *The Light*.

Papa couldn't be faulted, however, except (perhaps) for failing to raise children who were less American in their determination to leave the past behind. When Ruth went looking for traces of him in the 1970s, she asked

Mills, Papa's youngest and the child most like him, if any of his papers remained in Columbia. Mills said no. There'd been a trunk of papers in the garage of the house at 2116 Lady Street, but the garage had been torn down. "I have no idea what became of the things in it," Mills said. "I guess they were all destroyed."[2]

I don't know whether it's better to believe the manuscript of Papa's 1933 memoir, "Reminiscences," was in that trunk or that he lent it to Cornell Alvin Johnson and Johnson's family threw it out. A longtime Columbia educator, Johnson contributed a chapter, "Negroes," to a 1936 history celebrating the city's one hundred fiftieth anniversary. A half-dozen paragraphs from Papa's "Reminiscences" buttress a section on education, enough to make me long for the entire manuscript.

With persistence and extraordinary luck, Ruth did uncover traces of Papa, however. On one of her visits to Columbia, she found a trove of documents on the sidewalk outside Papa's house on Lady Street. They'd been discarded by the widow of Papa's youngest son. His second wife, she'd inherited the house after her husband's death. Ruth called a librarian from the University of South Carolina's South Caroliniana Library. She was already sifting through the papers when he arrived.

By this time, the widow had noticed and called the police. As the officers approached, Ruth drew herself up to her full height of five feet, six inches. She couldn't always stand up for herself, but she could for something greater.

"I am Ruth Nicholson, senior manuscript librarian at the Library of Congress," she announced, "and this is Dr. Johnson from the University of South Carolina. These are papers of great historical importance, and we intend to make sure they are preserved for future generations."

The police conferred. After deciding the papers were on public property, they left them to it.

Many of the photographs that appear in this book were in those boxes. They went, with the papers, to the South Caroliniana Library at the University of South Carolina. There, they were removed from the album that held them. Fortunately, the librarian copied the identifications to the backs before she placed them in the acid-free folders where they'd wait patiently for me to develop sufficient curiosity to go looking for them.

There wasn't anything from Papa in the boxes, but it might not have mattered if more of his papers had survived. The twenty letters to his oldest daughter that remain—a fraction of those he wrote to his children and on business, politics, and church matters—are virtually unreadable. Papa's was the handwriting of a man with things to do and places to go. The words boiled in him, overrunning his ability to set them down, erupting in a proudly illegible, jaggedly rhythmic hand. His writing was like his speech (as imitated memorably one Christmas dinner by his grandson, Bill)— jerky and impatient. So impatient, it's possible to imagine Papa interrupting himself.

But, curiously for a man whose careers required public speaking, Papa had a speech impediment. "He stammered all the time," remembered his granddaughter, Jo. "Until he got up to speak in public." Seven years older than Bill, Jo would have known. She'd spent several summers in Columbia as a child and teenager, taught for two years in Clinton, a small South Carolina city, after graduating from Washington, D.C.'s Miner Teacher's College in 1937. (She was the third generation to teach there—Mama and Mills also taught in Clinton.)

Once he was on his feet behind the lectern to fund-raise for Allen or speak at a conference[3] in some small, backwoods AME church, Papa's stammer "vanished when he warmed up to his subject."[4] After one such conference, the *Christian Recorder* crowed that "just the name of Garrett tells us we had a treat,"[5] though allowances must be made for the weekly AME newspaper's characteristic hyperbole—every speech was thrilling and every meeting an exciting occasion.

And yet, even though his heirs failed to preserve the papers that would have documented his activities, Papa didn't completely lose the place he coveted in history. His nine children told stories about him to their children. Those grandchildren—my mother Ruth among them—in turn told *their* children about this lawyer, college professor, and newspaper editor.

There was so much they'd forgotten, and still more they'd never known. But Papa hadn't been completely forgotten. He was enough of a public man to be mentioned in nearly four hundred fifty newspaper stories between 1885 and his death in 1947. Two biographical sketches were published when he was at the height of his career. Copies of the newspapers he published that survive reveal a fearlessness he never abandoned, even when it cost him.

And then there are the obituaries. The three in the *Chicago Defender* (perhaps the closest thing Black Americans had to a national newspaper), the *New York Age*, and the *Baltimore Afro-American* show he was known outside South Carolina. Another, noting his AME church activism, dubbed him the "Maker of Bishops." None of these is my favorite remembrance of him, though. That one, in the *Palmetto Leader*, Papa's hometown newspaper, memorializes him as "perhaps the most outstanding layman in the AME church," as "one of the most outstanding Professors on the Faculty" of Allen University, and as "perhaps the most respected disliked man in Contemporary Negro life in South Carolina during the early years of the twentieth century."[6]

That last bit's the one I particularly like.

"Tell Them We Are Rising"

A few things to understand about Papa: First, he was an Afro-Victorian, a believer in religion, education, and a right way of being in the world, one of those in that first generation after slavery selected to help uplift the race. Second, he was a poor boy who never knew his father. Fueled by ambition and a need to prove himself, Papa married up. Channeled properly, these drives can make a man. In Papa's case, they proved corrosive. He never understood the need to go along to get along, never grasped that simply confronting injustice wasn't enough. A man had to have power to compel change.

He was born Casper George Washington Garrett in Laurens County, S.C., about fifty years before the state began to require birth certificates. His death certificate gives the year as 1866, some forty-seven years after Dublin Hunter purchased his freedom, but gives no month or date. Another source says he was born in September 1865, five months after the end of the Civil War, which means—Emancipation Proclamation aside—Papa avoided slavery by an accident of birth. But the Garrett family Bible (given to Papa's future wife, Anna Maria[1] Threewitts, in 1874) says he was born in the spring of 1865, which means Papa could have been born as long as a year after the end of the war, or nearly two months before its end. His mother, Martha, had been enslaved, torn (like Sall) from her family, and brought to South Carolina as "a slave when small," too young to "remember her parents."[2] The part about being small is true. The part about not remembering her parents isn't, and Papa knew it.

I say that because, in 1886, Martha joined the many thousands of former slaves seeking long-lost parents, siblings, and children. She couldn't read or write, so Papa drafted the query she sent to the *Christian Recorder*. (Notices like hers appeared in the *Recorder* and other newspapers across the country from before the Civil War until the early 1900s.) Martha's plea ran in several issues of the weekly; it's likely she took advantage of a special offer—placement in twenty-six issues (an entire year's worth) for four dollars:

> Information Wanted—I was born in Virginia. My mother's name was Rebecca (called Becky), father's name Billy, brother's name Washington and sister's name Sady. I was sold to a slave trader named Billy Hunter[3] when I was about four or five years old, or perhaps younger, and brought to South Carolina, where I now reside. I know nothing of my relatives. My name is Martha. Any information of the above named parties will be gladly received by Martha Kennedy. Address C.G. Garrett, Laurens C.H., S.C.[4]

Martha's laconic account obscures the sheer terror she felt at being torn from everything she knew and loved. At least fifty years old[5] when she recounted these scraps of memory, she must have repeated her parents' and brother's and sister's names on that hellish journey south, willing herself not to forget as she cried herself to sleep. Hurt endured, as we'll soon see, remaining long after time scarred over memories of form and faces—surely she hoped to assuage that hurt by finding her family again. There's no evidence she did. And so that echo of loss runs through the generations like the blues. Loss and hegiras of displacement like The African's and Sall's; my grandmother Mattie's when she left South Carolina to join her husband in Washington after World War I; my mother Ruth's when she followed her dentist-husband to Jamaica in the 1950s; and my own when we quit the island after Ruth's marriage fell apart, feeling myself neither Jamaican nor American, but something unnameable and unknowable in between.

The same war that freed Martha left her son, young Casper Garrett, fatherless. As he told it years later, his father, Samuel, "could read and write . . . and hence by writing passes and reading war news to the plantation Negroes he was 'marked for slaughter' by Morgan [*sic*] raiders, who were whipping and killing the free-feeling slaves in that section. To escape the Morgan marauders he joined Sherman's army, but soon fell a victim to the yellow fever epidemic at Memphis, Tenn."[6] Mills, Papa's youngest daughter, told another version of the story. In it, Samuel was "run out of the state for daring to teach blacks to read."[7]

As myths do, Papa's origin story raises as many questions as it answers. Perhaps Samuel *was* among the small percentage of enslaved South

Carolinians who managed, somehow, to learn to read and write. But if Papa meant his father fled to escape Confederate General John Hunt Morgan, Morgan's band of eponymous raiders never came as far east as South Carolina. Even if they had ranged into the state, they would have had to do so before Morgan's death in September of 1864, at least a full year before Papa was born.

It's possible Samuel joined slaves following Union General William Tecumseh Sherman as Sherman pillaged his way through South Carolina in January and February of 1865—there are several Samuel Garretts listed as having served in the US Colored Troops. Sherman and his generals didn't go as far west as Laurens; still, Samuel could have easily walked the sixty miles or so. But Sherman didn't go to west to Memphis. He went north.

And, while there was a yellow fever epidemic in Memphis two years after the war, and outbreaks of cholera in 1866, 1873, and 1878, I've found only one Samuel Garrett in the City Directory, a Black laborer in 1879. He was gone in 1880.[8]

Even if everything about Samuel's story can't be proved, what chills more than one hundred fifty years later is his fear of white cruelty. Outnumbered by Blacks, whites sought to maintain control during the war through ever-increasing repression. Nearly a month after Sherman burned Columbia, Nancy Furman (who'd married into the family that founded Furman University) wrote her sister-in-law about "a great deal of insubordination" among former slaves. They had attempted to seize land belonging to whites, but Confederate soldiers brought "to a swift, bloody conclusion" their efforts to give themselves the means to live independently. "Several," Nancy wrote, "have been shot and a great many severely whipped."[9]

One way or another, Samuel Garrett escaped the fate Nancy recounted, clearly pleased the old order had been restored, but perhaps Martha knew only that he'd up and gone. (She didn't ask about him in the notice she placed in the *Christian Recorder*—perhaps she knew he was dead.) Left to raise a child alone in the chaos of war's end, she wove stories from truths and half-truths, telling young Casper George of his great-grandfather, The African, and his own father, Samuel, as she sought to give him a sense of worth and identity. It's possible Papa made it all up, reluctant to let the facts get in the way of a good story. Whatever the truth, he never stopped looking for Samuel. Wherever he went as he traveled throughout the country on AME church business (a volume of Shakespeare at hand to pass the time on crowded, smoky, Jim Crow cars), ranging as far north as Canada, as far south as Florida, and as far west as Colorado, he made a point of asking after his father.

Jo, my aunt, told that story. But it's another of those that raises questions. Papa named his first child Martha Phyllis after both her grandmothers. He named his first son after the man who'd helped him while he was a student at Allen. His second became his namesake. Two others were given family names as middle names and a third, the youngest, named for Mama's younger brother. But Papa named none of his six sons Samuel.

To become South Carolina's "most respected disliked man," Papa had first to rise from Scuffletown,[10] the aptly named Laurens County place where he was born. It was a daunting proposition for a fatherless child in post-Civil War South Carolina, but Papa was lucky. He had the examples of The African and the father who'd used his book learning to help his fellow slaves. He was lucky, too, in having a mother willing to sacrifice for him. Determined from the beginning that her only child[11] should enjoy a better life, Martha invested him with an aspirational name—Casper George Washington. She struggled to support them, working as washerwoman, cook, and farmhand. "Her greatest ambition was to educate her son,"[12] so she made sure he went to school even though it was eight miles away. Later, she moved to Laurens to be closer to the school. His "first teachers were Northern missionaries;"[13] another piece of good luck. The Northern colored preachers and white New England and Midwestern schoolmarms who came South after the War weren't just educators—they were talent scouts, on the lookout for recruits in the struggle to uplift the race.

Believing Samuel dead or unlikely to return, Martha took a new husband, Cato Kennedy. Though he appears in the Garrett family Bible (his date of birth given as February 8, 1818), significantly he's unmentioned in either of Papa's published biographies. Eighteen years older than his wife,

Cato is listed as a farm laborer in the 1880 census, as are Martha and her son. Whether Cato and Martha were sharecroppers or hired hands, there was tension in the house—one biography says Papa "was held to the farm most of the time."[14] Cato wanted help in the fields and resented the stepson who loved books so much he read while plowing. (It must have made for crooked furrows.)

One biographer called Martha's efforts during this hard-scrabble time "constant coercion." Another (perhaps Papa himself) was more charitable: "Encouraged by his mother, the boy struggled on, studying at night and carrying a textbook in his bosom by day, as he plowed. In the winter he would sell game or work at anything that offered to earn money for college. Later, he taught night school."[15] Papa was just seventeen or eighteen years old when he passed the exam to become a teacher in Laurens County. Likely, he presided over a one-room clapboard schoolhouse with a bare wood floor and a potbellied stove for heat. His students would have ranged from barefoot small children to teenagers and, quite possibly, adults. County treasurer's reports show that he received a total of one hundred dollars in salary in 1884 and 1885.[16] The equivalent of twenty-six hundred dollars today, it was scarcely a living wage. Even so, Martha must have been glad for the extra money.

Years after his graduation from Allen University, his admission to the South Carolina Bar, and his appointment to Allen's faculty, and three years before he rode in Booker T. Washington's private car, Papa went back to Laurens. He wrote about it in the *Southern Sun*, one of the newspapers he edited:

Saturday and Sunday were freezing weather. . . . It seemed much colder to us than in our boyhood days, when we would run over the place dressed in three pieces of thin cotton clothes, a fifty cents hat, a pair of brogan shoes with toes burnt out, and our coat sleeve for a handkerchief. The hat we had on the other day cost more than our whole suit then, but we never got cold in those naked, hungry, starving days and yet we could not keep warm Sunday wrapped up in the best our money could buy. After all, we are almost constrained to feel that we were happier then than now.[17]

Papa's pastor, the Rev. N. W. Edwards, encouraged him to apply to Allen University in 1885. One story has it that Edwards "carried" Papa to Allen. More likely, in view of what happened once he arrived, Papa took the train by himself, probably riding the Laurens Railway to Newberry and then transferring to the Columbia and Greenville Railroad. (They'd later combine to become the CN&L—the Columbia, Newberry, and Laurens or, as some called it, Crooked, Narrow, and Late.) Outside the Columbia depot near Gervais and Gadsden streets, he stood with his heavy trunk, wondering how to get to Allen. The "young country boy" with a "box on his shoulder," must not have looked like a promising fare. All the same, a hackman, or drayer, asked where Papa was going. His name was Anderson Threewitts, and he had the concession to ferry travelers and their luggage from the station. Papa told him he had come to go to school at Allen. Anderson asked if he needed a ride. Papa considered it. The school was about a mile and a half away, an easy walk except for his trunk. But he had only a little money—his meager savings from teaching and the pittance Martha had managed to send him off with, the small collection supporters in Laurens had taken up for him.

"How much?" Papa asked.

Anderson told him.

Papa asked if that was for him and the trunk.

Anderson said yes.

"How much for just the trunk?" Papa asked.

A sensible man who had not built up a business and made himself owner of a comfortable home and other property by entertaining fools, Anderson could have slapped the reins and gone on his way. Instead, he did a quick calculation and named a figure.

Papa didn't have to think about it.

"Let my trunk ride and I'll walk along behind," he said.

Impressed, Anderson said, "Get in. I'll take you."

The two talked all the way to Allen. That evening, Anderson told his wife, Phillis, and his thirteen-year-old daughter, Anna Maria, about Papa and his thirst for education. He made a point of keeping up with Papa, and from time to time, came home with stories about Papa and his doings at Allen. So many stories, in fact, that soon Anna Maria became

Anna Maria Garrett, age 4, ca. 1875. Collection of the author.

"disgusted hearing her father talk about this poor boy to whom he'd formed an attachment."[18]

Like Benjamin Franklin's account of his arrival in Philadelphia, the tale resonates with me. Both he and Papa were poor boys come to the big city with hopes of making good.

Much of Columbia's downtown had been destroyed by Sherman's troops near the end of the Civil War, so a great deal of what Papa saw from the bench of Anderson's wagon was only as old as he was. Well on the way to a "miraculous"[19] recovery, Columbia was becoming a city of pleasant wood-frame houses, with two- and three-story brick buildings scattered downtown. Soon the population would be 15,353, nearly seven times Laurens'. The unpaved streets were lit with gas lamps, but there was public transportation—a "street railway" line with six cars drawn by a stable of twenty-five to thirty horses. By 1891, there'd be a plant to generate electricity. Three years later, electric-powered streetcars were introduced. By the turn of the century, Columbia would boast nine railroad lines, which led to the construction of one main station in 1902.[20]

Allen University, Papa's destination, was founded as Payne Institute in 1870 by the AME church. Ten years later, the school was moved from Cokesbury, S.C., to Columbia, and the name changed to honor Richard Allen, founder of the AME church and its first bishop. Columbians saw it as their Church's flagship educational institution, though its claims to being a "real, fixed university"[21] remained aspirational for decades. True, the school awarded bachelor's and master's degrees, and there were theology and music departments. There was even a law school, with seven students in 1890. But six hundred two of the six hundred seventy students were enrolled in the graded, intermediate, and normal (or teacher training) departments that year, with just twelve students in the college department. The school was chronically underfunded—teachers went unpaid and officials were forced to canvass the state, begging for money from local AME congregations. In one commencement day report, the *Christian Recorder* was at pains to deny rumors Allen was for sale, though it acknowledged the university was "in debt and in need of assistance."[22] Photographs taken fifty years after Allen's founding show unpainted one-story clapboard buildings in the shadow of two imposing, multistory brick structures and expanses of bare ground. It must have been muddy when it rained or snowed.

Papa was twenty years old when he enrolled in the normal department, older than some of the students who were in their early teens. He didn't feel much out of place, however—there were other bright young men from the country his age or older in the three-year teacher's training program. Likely, most were as poor as Papa. Although the 1885 catalog seems not to have survived, five years later tuition was just one dollar a month; room rent, fifty cents; and board, three dollars. It was all students could afford.

That year, first-term students would have taken "Higher Arithmetic," history, physiology, and algebra, with "Physical Geography" replacing physiology the second term. Second-year courses included "Science of Government," physics, zoology, "Elements of Pedagogy," more algebra, geometry, and rhetoric. In their final year, students took English literature, astronomy, chemistry, logic, botany, ethics, "Mental Philosophy," geology, and something called "Reviews, Primary Branches." It must have been a heavy load, but Allen's instructors knew their students needed to be ready to prove themselves to the world.

Allen was a church school, its mission to provide "the advantages of a high course of normal culture and Christian education," thus developing "disciplined and inspired . . . leaders and teachers." They didn't put it this way, but administrators, faculty, and members of the board of trustees aimed to erase the heritage of slavery ("ignorance, superstition and sin")[23] to create a generation of sober, industrious, thrifty, and self-restrained Afro-Victorians who would go out into the world to better the race and, eventually, prove themselves worthy of full citizenship. Morning and evening prayers at the University Chapel were mandatory, as were Sunday school and church services, where students went "in a body . . . accompanied by the Matron or a Professor." The daily schedule was grueling. Morning bell was at six o'clock; breakfast was an hour later. Prayers followed at 8:45. "Recitations" began at nine o'clock and continued until noon. After a half-hour break, recitations continued till 2:45 p.m. Evening prayers were at five o'clock, with supper at six o'clock. Students were expected to be in bed by ten o'clock.

There were rules and a list of demerits designed to ensure order and—like the toothbrush Booker T. Washington celebrated—uplift students newly arrived from humble, rural backgrounds. Students were, for example, reminded that "[b]athing . . . must be faithfully attended to on Saturday." Demerits could accrue for skipping prayers, classes, or church and for unspecified "Improper Conduct." Playing a musical instrument outside of lessons or scheduled practice could earn a demerit, as could "[t]hrowing anything from a Window" or "[s]peaking aloud from a Window." Ten demerits meant that a student's parents would be notified. Twenty meant suspension or expulsion.[24]

Severe as they may seem, these kinds of rules and regulations were commonplace. Rules at Benedict College, Allen's Baptist neighbor (the campuses were across the street from one another after Allen moved to Columbia in 1880), were nearly as strict. All the same, for students like Papa, who'd walked miles to find teachers, read as they plowed, and earned money for books and fees by selling game or kindling (as had William

David Chappelle, the future AME bishop whose time at Allen overlaps Papa's and who would figure largely in Papa's life), the University must have been a welcome refuge, a place that valued intelligence and learning.

Papa acknowledged that Allen was the making of him, with lifelong dedication to his alma mater. If he'd stayed in Laurens, he'd have continued to teach, perhaps even risen to become principal of the local colored school, but no further. Allen opened other possibilities.

◆ ◆ ◆

A. B. Caldwell's *History of the American Negro*, the collection of profiles that includes a biographical sketch of Papa, set out to tell the stories of Black men and women who were "the best element of the Negro race," "the real exponents of Negro life in America." Naturally enough, the book treats Papa's college career heroically: "Only those who have struggled unaided for an education and refused to be defeated," it proclaims, "can know the struggles and the sufferings of his college years at Allen University."[25] The panegyric recalls a story from AME churchman George A. Singleton, Papa's student at Allen, his lifelong champion, and obituarist. One day in class, Papa told his students about a "young man [who had] entered school in rags." Questioned "kindly" by a teacher, he responded, "I will take what money I have now and buy a Greek book. After I have learned Greek, I will get some clothes."[26] Even if the young man wasn't Papa, the story shows just how much he and his post-Reconstruction cohort valued learning.

And the story moves me, in the same way I'm moved poring over nineteenth-century photographs of students at Black colleges, normal schools, and boarding academies. The men wear bowties and cravats and grip the lapels of their long coats in a way they must have learned observing their teachers. The women—wasp-waisted in corsets—wear dresses that fall to the floor. Some look away from the camera, hesitant to reveal themselves. Others confront it directly, the same way they confronted the future.

Papa's time at Allen wasn't all struggle and suffering, however. What the heroic myth ignores is the possibility he and his Afro-Victorian cohort just might have had fun.

Papa hints how much the school meant to him in his *Southern Sun* recollections when he recalls coming across "Doc Cook, our roommate in college, and all our five years of college life loomed up before us and we ran over the past pleasant reminiscences. Doc suggested a reunion of the old boys and their friends. . . ." He goes on to list those friends, men with tall-tale nicknames like "big breaches [*sic*] Sandy," "big doings Smith," "Buffalo Dan Perrin," and "big talking Hawkins," before suggesting that they and "Prof. Morris would enjoy a week's outing in the mountains; catching trout on the French Bend, where all could live over in the pleasures of the mind our happy (past) college days."[27]

At some point during his time at Allen, Papa discarded the second of his middle names. He sometimes referred to himself as C. George Garrett, but most often he was C. G. Garrett. It was the way things were done in those days, but Black Victorians had their own reasons. White men's use of initials and last names in contemporary newspaper accounts marked a divide between private and public selves. First names were for family and friends; initials for the rest of the world. But Papa's use of his initials was also a stratagem to forestall white inferiors from addressing him by his first name.

Certainly, he would soon have much to feel superior about.

Papa received his normal school diploma on June 8, 1887, completing the three-year course in two years. He must have done well—he was one of the graduation speakers (his topic: "What Shall We Do?").[28] A few months later, however, his promising start was threatened. Early in 1888, he was summoned to appear in Laurens County Court to answer a charge of statutory rape. The entire story, as it appeared in the *Laurens Advertiser*: "Last week, under a warrant issued by Trial Justice Miller, Casper Garrett, a colored boy, now a student at Allen University, was brought from Columbia to this place, and giving a hearing on the charge of deflouring [*sic*] a colored maid under the age of sixteen years. The evidence being insufficient, Garrett was released."[29]

Odious as we might find it nearly a century and a half on, the age of consent in South Carolina was ten in 1888. (Eight years later, it was raised to sixteen.) So why was Papa charged? Enough of his grandchildren remembered his reputation as a ladies' man—an aspect of his character that may have led to his downfall—for me to believe something must have happened. It was probably when he went home for the holidays in 1887, full

Robert Ralston Proudfit, Papa's "benefactor," date unknown. Collection of the author.

of himself for having completed his first term in Allen's college department *and* its law school. Was it statutory rape? A willing partner who took Papa to court after she'd been seduced and abandoned? And (assuming the allegation wasn't made up) why on earth did Papa put himself in that position?

Allen officials must have known because Papa was hauled back to Laurens, but they didn't force him to leave school. Perhaps the president (and others) were satisfied no offense had taken place. Perhaps whites who counted back home let them (and the judge) know it would be a shame to ruin a promising young man's future for sowing wild oats. At any rate, Papa went back to Allen, where the unpleasant experience must have convinced him he was right to study law.

I'd always heard that Papa read law with a white lawyer named Ralston Proudfit and that he acknowledged that lawyer by naming his first son after him. But how to explain the law diploma from Allen—which, by the way, is still in the family—and the fact that I could find no Proudfit who practiced law in South Carolina in the 1880s? Again, Ruth found the answer. There

Elizabeth Proudfit, date unknown. Collection of the author.

were photographs of a Robert Ralston Proudfit and his wife, Elizabeth, in the trash on Lady Street. There was also a letter from Elizabeth.

Born in 1836 in New York City, Robert Proudfit studied law at Harvard but dropped out after a year. According to his obituary in the Princeton Theological Seminary alumni journal, he spent "the next three years . . . at his home in New Brunswick in general reading." That last, and what he did next, suggests some sort of crisis. After his time reading, Robert enrolled at the New Brunswick Theological Seminary, transferring a few months later to Princeton. He graduated in 1861, just in time for the Civil War.

He served as chaplain with two New Jersey regiments and was wounded at the Battle of Cedar Creek in Virginia. A few years after the war, he went to Europe for his health. There, in Switzerland, he met Elizabeth. They married in 1872 and returned to the United States that same year. They spent the next twenty-five years in Highlands and Morristown, N.J., until Robert's death in 1897.[30]

I suspect Robert had inherited a tradition of uplift, as he was descended from Robert Ralston, who helped Richard Allen and Absalom Jones establish an independent Black church, the African Episcopal Church of St. Thomas, in Philadelphia in 1791. Later, Allen would go on to found the AME church, making Papa and Robert tangentially connected.[31]

Elizabeth's letter is dated February 22, 1894, four years after Papa received his law degree. In it, she mentions gifts of clothes and a Bible for Papa's oldest son, Ralston Proudfit Garrett, born a year earlier. Some of the passages in the Bible were marked—she'd intended to give it to someone else. The clothes, likely also used, were for Papa.

What did Papa and Mama make of the annotated Bible and the hand-me-downs? He was principal of the Winnsboro Colored Graded School then, supporting a family of four—soon to be five—on a salary of ten dollars a month. Were they poor enough to be grateful? Or did they resent the castoffs but, ever thrifty, pass on the Bible and clothing to folks who needed them more, just as we did that Thanksgiving dinner?

Papa (or Mama) labeled Robert's photograph "our benefactor" and Elizabeth's photograph "our benefactress," so the Proudfits must have provided significant, much-needed, help. They supported missionary work in the South and overseas; perhaps they paid Papa's tuition, allowing him to go full time instead of taking on outside work or even dropping out periodically (as did other students) to earn enough to return. At any rate, three years after finishing the normal school, Papa graduated with first honors in Allen's law *and* classical departments.[32] He was also admitted to the South Carolina Bar on May 23, 1890.

He was just twenty-four years old.

◆ ◆ ◆

The year 1890 also saw another, more personal, marker of how far Papa had come from Scuffletown. On November 26, he married Anna Maria Threewitts, daughter of the hackman who had taken him to Allen when he first arrived in Columbia. Their marriage would last fifty-five years.

Six years younger (she was born May 15, 1871), Anna Maria graduated from Allen's normal department in 1886, a year before Papa. Despite the age difference, they may have been in some of the same classes. Perhaps that was how they became friends. At any rate, when Anna Maria brought him home to introduce him to her parents, she discovered that he was the boy whose praises her father had been singing.

Anna Maria Garrett, date
unknown. Collection of
the author.

Anderson, his wife, Phillis, and Anna Maria may not have been members of Columbia's colored aristocracy, but fragments from the historical record (and family stories) show they were better off than the majority of the city's Black population. He's mentioned several times in South Carolina's General Assembly reports as receiving small payments for unspecified services. In 1873, he was paid twenty-seven dollars for serving on a jury. He owned his own home—Columbia city directories show him living at the same address, 44 E. Taylor Street, from 1875 to 1891. The 1879–80 directory lists him as a farmer; likely he also owned other property outside Columbia. Less than a year before his death, a record of real estate transfers published in *The State* shows his purchase of "a lot on Gervais Street, for $225."

When he died, the newspaper carried this brief story on July 20, 1892:

Died Suddenly.

Yesterday morning at 3 o'clock old man Threewitts, perhaps the oldest [born Jan. 4, 1830, he would have been 62] colored hackman in the State, died suddenly at his home in the city. The old fellow went to bed about 11 o'clock and seemed to be in fine health. He was a noted character about Columbia. At one time he was doing a very successful business. It is said that the old fellow had a presentiment of his demise as on the night before he went and sought his creditors, paying all his bills.

Condescending references aside, Anderson was prosperous enough to leave an estate that required probate after his creditors were satisfied. Notices of Anna Maria's application for letters of administration appeared for two consecutive weeks in *The State* in November and December.

Like Papa, Anderson had married into a prominent family. He and Phillis Peacher wed on April 15, 1855—theirs is the first entry in the Garrett family Bible. Phillis (1836–93) was the daughter of Charlotte and Joseph A. Peacher, "a leading housebuilder" and the "wealthiest colored man in Columbia."[33]

Joseph had purchased his freedom, paying twenty-nine hundred dollars for himself and his family in 1853.[34] He would have been about forty years old then. An enterprising man, he "procured the services of a northern white teacher," who was supposed to have pretended to be Black (I'm not making this up!) so she could "school his children, himself and many of his near relatives,"[35] despite laws prohibiting the education of African-Americans, slave or free.

At some point, Joseph decided to pack it in and go to back to Africa. In 1856, he wrote the Rev. William McClain of the American Colonization Society (ACS) to ask about the possibility of emigrating. Two years later, he and Charlotte left for Liberia. When he arrived, he found no one to show him the land the ACS was supposed to have set aside. He chose a plot anyway, cleared it, and started on a house. Enthusiastic about the future, he told the ACS that Liberia was "a rich country . . . [with] prospects for a man, that is, if he is industrious, to make a handsome living."[36] Joseph started a sawmill and advertised a "Sash, Door and Blind Factory," offering "Ornamental Carpentry . . . warranted inferior to none imported in workmanship and variety of style."[37] The shop, in Careysburg, about fifteen miles northwest of Monrovia, was on the corner of a street named for himself. Death put an end to Peacher's enterprise, though not before he was elected mayor of Careysburg. He was buried in Liberia. In 1863, his wife,

Phillis Peacher Threewitts, Anna Maria's Mother, date unknown. Collection of the author.

Charlotte, returned to the United States. It was the middle of the Civil War; given the risk of encountering Confederate privateers, one trusts she kept her manumission papers close at hand.

◆ ◆ ◆

Papa may have found Anna Maria's status appealing, but in one respect, he knew nothing of what he was getting himself into. Only eighteen when they married, Anna Maria had lived a privileged life, not having to cook, clean, or help keep house. Years later, telling his children the story of their first Thanksgiving together, Papa said, "I taught your mother how to cook! She tried to fry a turkey!" But Mama turned out to be a quick study—Elizabeth Proudfit, Papa's Northern "benefactress," made a point of asking him to thank Mama for "the box of preserves" she had sent. Mama had had some practice by then. A few months before, she'd been singled out at the Fairfield County Colored Fair for her peach pickle. She was also honored in the Category of "Fine Art and Fancy Work" for best painting.[38]

Mattie Garrett as a girl.
Collection of the author.

Papa was in his second year as principal of the Winnsboro Colored Graded School when Mama won her prizes. He'd come to Fairfield County in 1891,[39] after brief stints teaching in Laurens and then at Allen. Their family was growing. A daughter, Martha Phyllis, was born on June 18, 1891. Known as Mattie, she was called "Baby" by Mama well into her adult life (though never more than once by anyone else, including her husband). Her siblings called her "Sister." A son was born two years later on February 25, 1893. Though he named him after his benefactor, Papa showed an ear for language by not giving him the commonplace first name Robert. Instead, he named his son Ralston Proudfit, losing the alliteration but gaining a certain formal dignity. He was nicknamed "Buddie." Years later, after he had become a Pullman porter, he was known as "Nick" because of the Nick Carter detective stories he loved.

The Winnsboro school was founded in 1890, so Papa was there almost from the beginning. According to the state superintendent of education's 1894 report, it was a one-story "building . . . , 45x30, with an L 36x20, blackboard painted on the four walls of the building inside; 3 acres of land attached, value, $350; amount of endowment $600, from special levy and poll tax." There was a total enrollment of two hundred thirty-seven people—one hundred nine male and one hundred twenty-eight female enrollees. Total "running" expenses were "about $650." In addition to Papa, there were two "assistants" and a three-member Board of Trustees.[40]

Mama's not listed among the staff. But two years after their arrival, she received a Fairfield County teaching certificate on the strength of her Allen Normal School diploma. It's dated just seven months after Ralston was born. Remarkably, though she had two children to raise (Mattie was two years old) and peach pickle to make, Mama did teach. The same county treasurer's report that lists Papa's salary shows that Mama received fifteen dollars for teaching. Women teachers were supposed to be single, but Papa was, after all, principal.[41]

The Winnsboro Colored Graded School "made splendid progress under his administration," as Papa "brought [it] up to a high standard of efficiency."[42] It must have been a formidable task: The pupil-to-teacher ratio was seventy-nine to one, the schoolhouse was just two thousand seventy square feet, and the amount spent per pupil was $2.75. That superintendent's report doesn't give figures for the five other Fairfield County schools—a primary school, "collegiate institute," two high schools, and the "'colored' Fairfield Normal Institute"—but figures from other districts show the disparity between how much was spent on white students and on Black. The white Chester Graded School, with an enrollment of three hundred sixteen students, had expenses of thirty-nine hundred dollars, or $12.35 per student. There were two Florence graded schools: Black students went to school in a building worth twelve hundred dollars. The white school, just a year old, was worth nearly ten times as much.

Papa's name appears in a handful of articles from the *News and Herald* of Winnsboro in 1894 and 1895. Most are brief: In September 1894, he called "the colored teachers of Fairfield County" to an organizational Saturday morning meeting. A month later, his name appears among the officers of the County Colored Fair association, an early marker of his lifelong interest in expositions to showcase black agricultural achievement.[43]

By far the longest story, written by Papa himself, appeared on May 2, 1894. Headlined "Colored Graded School," it was an invitation to "our white friends" to attend the school's end-of-year ceremonies, which included a "prize contest," a concert, and a "public examination" of students in the first through eighth grades.

Papa's article was not, however, simply a summary of activities during the celebration. It was an appeal to the whites—"our efficient school commissioner, our accommodating trustees, and . . . the many kind friends and patrons"—without whom the school could not have existed. "We are free to admit that we have not accomplished what might have been done under more favorable circumstances," Papa wrote, "but we hope that such additions will, from time to time, be made to the colored school work here that will enable the teachers to give all instructions available and necessary to make the Negro youth what he ought to be—an honest, upright, intelligent and industrious citizen." Visitors to the ceremonies, Papa advised, would gain "better insight to our work . . . as they are fully competent to judge of such work." He closed professing himself "ever hoping to prove ourselves worthy of continued respect."[44]

The prose borders on the obsequious, overdone almost to the point of parody, which was perhaps Papa's intent. At the same time, for those able to see it, he showed his white readers he was no ordinary colored man. He invited his old teacher, J. W. Morris, to give "the annual address." Morris, he informed his readers, was "one of the most classical speakers anent, and will certainly give his hearers a grand treat." That "anent" (i.e., about or concerning), though misused, probably went over most heads.

Papa began his education in the ways of white folk the day he was born, and the unfortunate truth is that a degree of humility was essential if he was to get at least some of what he needed for his students. It was a wearying struggle, requiring tact, deference, and occasional outright dissembling in the face of a society that disguised its contempt as fondness. Side by side with Papa's announcement of his upcoming graduation exercises is an account of closing ceremonies at the Mt. Olivet School. (Unlisted in the state superintendent's report, it may have been private, perhaps affiliated with Mt. Olivet Presbyterian Church just outside Winnsboro.) Among the "exercises" listed on the program is "The Ungrateful Little Nigger," a brief, two-character sketch from *Beadle's Dime Dialogues*.[45] The *News and Herald* correspondent found it "creditably rendered," and the "Negro character perfect."[46]

Papa probably provoked some ire a year later when he introduced Black congressman George W. Murray. (This wasn't his first venture into politics. In September of 1890, the same year he received his law degree, Papa served as a delegate from Laurens to a meeting of the Republican State Executive Committee and as a delegate to a meeting of the Colored Reform Committee a month later.[47])

Murray, he said, "was canvassing the State to arouse the Negro to the fact that his ballot was about to be taken away from him." Disenfranchisement was not long in coming. On December 4, 1895, delegates to the state convention ratified a new constitution that set so many barriers it struck most Black men from the rolls. Murray would become the last Black congressman from South Carolina until James Clyburn was elected nearly a century later.[48]

At the end of the 1895 school year, the Winnsboro *News and Herald* reported that Papa had resigned because he'd been "elected a professor at Allen." The trustees had selected his replacement—"W. B. Nance," principal of the Newberry graded school. This must have been Butler W. Nance, who graduated second behind Papa from Allen's law school. Papa, the newspaper laconically allowed, had "successfully managed the graded school."[49]

Papa had spoken at Allen's commencement a few weeks before, so perhaps his speech was part of a final review by President John Q. Johnson, and Bishop Moses B. Salter, chairman of the Board of Trustees.[50] If so, Papa passed. He would remain at Allen as a teacher and administrator for the next twenty-one years.

It's likely Papa left the Winnsboro Colored Graded School because he needed more money. The Fairfield County treasurer's report for fiscal year November 1, 1893, to October 31, 1894, shows he was paid a total of one hundred twenty dollars,[51] not much more than he'd earned a few years earlier in Laurens and the equivalent of less than four thousand dollars today. He and Mama had had another child, Casper Garrett, Jr. Known as "Tap" from a younger relative's mispronunciation, he was born on March 1, 1895. Then, too, Mama's mother lived with them at least part of the time—the family Bible says she died in Winnsboro on October 29, 1893. Elizabeth Proudfit's 1894 letter mentions Papa's "good mother,"[52] so Martha may also have lived with him. I suspect, too, that after five years in Winnsboro and perhaps an equal amount of time teaching in Laurens, Papa knew all he needed to about life as a rural schoolmaster. Columbia and Allen promised more opportunities, albeit in a world where possibilities had dimmed since the end of Reconstruction twenty years before.

– 5 –

Papa Returns to Columbia

If there were no good places in South Carolina to be Black in Papa's time, then some were better than others. Columbia was one. The city had grown since he'd come to attend Allen—its population was now 18,405, about ten times that of Winnsboro. The 1895 City Directory touted it as "a beautiful and exceptionally healthful" place with a climate Yankee tourists would find rivaled Florida's. It boasted of streets one hundred feet wide, cotton and cottonseed oil mills, eight railroad lines, a canal, hydropower, public and private schools, colleges, churches of "[a]lmost every denomination," six banks, three newspapers (two morning and one evening), and an opera house that seated six hundred.[1]

Though Black men and women made up nearly fifty-three percent of the population, they received scant mention in the directory's introduction. No matter. Afro-Columbians were creating their own community, separate and hardly equal, but nonetheless vibrant and thriving. The Howard School (Colored) boasted twelve teachers in addition to its principal, Joseph E. Wallace. (He would go on to become president of the Colored Normal Industrial Agricultural and Mechanical College of South Carolina and would head the Colored State Teachers Association.) There were Benedict College and Allen University, where Papa was now a "Professor of History and English Grammar." Worshippers of color could choose from ten churches—Bethel and Zion AME; Calvary, Nazareth, and Zion Baptist; Free Will Baptist; Ladson Presbyterian; Sidney Park and Wesley Methodist Episcopal; and St. Luke's Episcopal. There were two colored militia companies, the Carolina Light Infantry and the Capital City Guards, though both would be disbanded by the early 1900s. Black men and women worked at a variety of enterprises. There were thirteen barbers (some probably catered only to whites); twenty-one men and women operating boarding houses

Mama, Papa, and seven of their children, ca. 1904. *Bottom:* Maceo, Ralston, Colon, Casper George Jr.; *Center:* Papa, Marian, Ruth, Mama; *Top:* Mattie. Collection of the author.

and/or restaurants (for some reason, a "huckster" who sold "fish, game, etc." was listed among the restaurateurs); one carpenter and one furniture repairer; two sellers of fish and oysters; two doctors; nine shoemakers, one saddler; two tailors; and one undertaker. I. J. Miller ran a clothing store, and Samuel Dreher managed one of five groceries. His was called "Our Store," in what may have been an appeal to racial pride.

All of the aforementioned business people were in addition to—thumbing through the City Directory at random—the asylum attendants, bakers, blacksmiths, brickmasons, butchers, butlers, caterers, clerks, cooks, draymen, dressmakers, drivers, farmers, hackmen, house servants, laborers, laundresses, mail agents, moulders, music teachers, nurses, painters, plumbers, porters, railroad firemen, hands, laborers, and waiters.[2]

There was no dentist and no newspaper, but Papa would soon rectify the latter. Within a few years, Aiken-born Matilda A. Evans would return to South Carolina after finishing medical school in Philadelphia. The state's first licensed woman doctor, she would establish a substantial practice that included both Black and white patients, found two hospitals, and open Lindenwood Park, the city's only recreation center for African-Americans. In addition to picnic grounds, it featured a swimming pond with forty-four "bathing houses," an auditorium, and a lunch counter.[3]

In his "introductory" to the 1899 directory, publisher William H. Walsh boasted that "[t]here is probably no city in the South that is richer in the promise of the near future than Columbia. In fact it stands on the threshold of greatness and prosperity." A few years later, he proclaimed, "*Get together; talk Columbia at every opportunity—what you have done, are doing and what you are going to do. . .* [italics original]." The city's newspaper, *The State*, never shied from stereotypes and reminders of white supremacy, characterizing Black children as "pickaninnies" and an event as "dark with Negroes," celebrating the comeuppance given "impudent Negroes" by beating, knife, or firearm. Still, its owners' desire to "talk Columbia" accounts for the generally positive coverage of Allen and Benedict and the activities of Black Columbians throughout the 1890s and well into the new century. Was the city, like Atlanta, too busy to hate? Or did its white citizens regard Blacks with a kind of benign, almost bemused condescension? (They may be only colored folk, but they're *our* colored folk.)

"The people of the two races appear to be in such easy association that they could never be removed," one Black visitor marveled in 1890. "Upon the surface, there is little to indicate the prejudice that exists between the races. . . . The more the matter is regarded the more enigmatical it becomes." All the same, there was his conclusion: "None could think to see the Columbians move about town on Saturdays, that the horrible Barnwell and Lexington outrages could possibly take place."[4]

Memories of those "outrages" were fresh in the minds of Black Columbians—each had occurred within six months of publication of the visitor's report in the *Christian Recorder*. In December 1889, eight Black men had been taken from their Barnwell jail cells, tied to trees, and shot to death. Six months later, and just a month before the article appeared, a white mob broke into the Lexington County jail and shot to death a Black seventeen-year-old named Willie Leaphart.

On the one hand, the *Recorder's* anonymous correspondent wasn't wrong—Richland is one of two South Carolina counties for which there's no record of a lynching, so enterprising Black men and women like Papa and his cohort must have felt relatively free of the threat of racial violence. On the other hand, he wasn't right either. Barnwell is about sixty miles south of Columbia. Lexington is just fifteen miles west.

The lynchings that occurred there were among the constant reminders of the savagery whites used to maintain their dominance and limit Black aspirations. Between 1882 and 1900, there was at least one lynching a year in South Carolina. Overall, as many as two hundred thirteen men and women were lynched from 1877 to 1950; fewer, to be sure, than in Mississippi, where seven hundred five were murdered. Still, murder was murder, and so men (and women) in the Palmetto State could be beaten to death, hanged, or riddled with bullets because they'd been accused of rape, tried to vote, cursed a white man, or simply been impudent enough to knock on a white woman's door.[5]

And while Columbia may have been free of lethal racial violence, Black men and women still faced hazards and affronts. In 1906, *The State* called on police to "promptly and vigorously" suppress offensive behavior at the annual State Fair. Small whips were sold and sometimes used by "a pretty girl to tap a passing acquaintance lightly." But others, inclined to "hoodlumism . . . set upon Negroes . . . [who] cannot retaliate and should have protection."[6] The newspaper's editorial did no good. A year later, it had to repeat its call for the whips to be banned.

Color marked African-American Columbians, even in matters as minor as listings in the City Directory. From 1875 to 1903 (with the exception of 1897), they were included with the rest of the population, albeit with the letter "c" or an asterisk after their names. In 1897, and from 1904 on, they were relegated to a separate section. It was called "Colored Population" in the 1897–98 directory, with a redundant "(c)" after each name, to ensure against mistaken identities. In 1904, that separate (but equal) section was called the "Colored Department," though it was listed in the index as the "Gen'l Directory of Colored Names." Sometimes, the section was printed on orange paper. One edition used an orange divider of heavier stock to separate Black and white. Another used the same paper as for the white section but printed the names in red ink. That the compilers went to such lengths demonstrates their anxiety about maintaining the color line. (Later, poring over microfilmed directories on ancestry.com, I found two or three from the late 1930s where the colored section appeared not to have been filmed. Was it a mistake or deliberate omission? Did the microfilm operator decide on his own to omit half the city's population? These are the kind of uncomfortable thoughts that come dealing with such a complicated history.) The 1950 directory finally did away with the separate section, though Negro residents were identified with (c) after their names. For reasons I'll never understand—wouldn't most people who consulted the directory have known?—the symbol's explained in a section headed "Special Abbreviations." Two years later, it too was gone, all racial identification finally consigned to history.

The almost four hundred fifty articles published in the *Christian Recorder*, the *Palmetto Leader*, *The State*, and other newspapers between 1887 and 1947 show Papa engaged in the same kind of can-do boosterism that the City Directory publisher William Walsh called for, though Papa's served the larger goal of uplifting the race. Never reluctant to sign a petition or loath to attend a meeting, he worked for the creation of a Colored State Fair and to organize a bank.[7] He was active in the Republican Party and the AME church. Blessed with remarkable energy, he gave speeches and wrote

Undated photograph of Papa (top row, right) with other prominent Columbians, including Matilda Evans, the Rev. J. C. White, Dr. L. M. Daniels, Mrs. Walker, the Rev. Mack Johnson, Butler W. Nance, and C. G. Garrett, on the steps of St. Luke Hospital. (South Caroliniana Library.)

articles and editorials (it was sometimes hard to tell the difference) for the newspapers he published—albeit with significant gaps—between 1902 and 1928. The sum of these activities led one writer to include him, late in his career, among the "well-known Negro men and women who make up the [Allen] faculty."[8]

One thing Papa did not do was practice law. The City Directory contains just one listing, in 1897–1898, identifying him as an attorney. It isn't surprising there are no other listings. More than seventy-five African-Americans were admitted to the South Carolina Bar between 1877 to 1915, but few actually practiced. Even fewer made a living at it. Whites were reluctant to hire Black attorneys, and most Blacks too poor to hire a lawyer of any race. And when Black men and women needed to go to court, those who could afford a lawyer hired a white one.[9]

Instead of looking for clients, then, Papa settled in at Allen. His personal listing in the 1895 City Directory gives his occupation as professor of law. Allen's listing in the business section of the same directory has him as a professor of history and English grammar. Six years later, a university advertisement listed him as a professor of mathematics. A few years later, the 1911–12 catalog listed him as "C. G. Garrett, A.M., LL.B. Dean of Law Department, Literature, Rhetoric and Logic." He taught wherever he was needed.

In his time, Papa was so well known that a letter addressed simply "Professor C. G. Garrett, Columbia, South Carolina" could reach him. Significant as it was, however, his Allen connection shouldn't obscure Papa's other activities.

Foremost among those was his work in the AME church. In time, he'd earn the appellation "Maker of Bishops," most notably for ensuring fellow Allen alumnus William David Chappelle's election to the bishopric in 1912. Early on, however, Papa's activities as an AME layman were more mundane. He spoke, often and eloquently despite his stammer, at Sunday School conventions and church conferences throughout South Carolina in the late 1890s and early 1900s. "Language fails us to properly commend the lecture," a correspondent reported on one such occasion, "but be it said that it was sublimely eloquent, profoundly logical and fraught with that kindly advice which our young people so much need."[10]

But that was only one side of Papa. Another, more combative, fitfully prompted him to wield his "pen staped [*sic*] in vitriol."[11] He showed that side in May 1900, a few months after he (and Chappelle, by then the school's president) spoke about "dear old Allen University" at the Northeast South Carolina annual conference in Darlington. His target was one James Dean, who'd also spoken at the conference. A one-time county judge in Florida in 1888, James had become an AME pastor. He did not lack for powerful friends and was soon a presiding elder—a minister who supervised a group of churches within an annual conference—in North Carolina with hopes of advancing even further.[12] (As noted earlier, the word *conference* has two meanings in the AME church. It indicates geographical boundaries as well as meetings on church business. Those include quarterly, district, and annual conferences, and the General Conference, a national meeting held every four years.[13])

Papa's attack came in response to something Dean had written, likely in the *Christian Recorder*. Dean's article is missing, but after reading Papa's, he must have felt as if he'd brought a knife to a gunfight. It wasn't just that Papa's front-page letter criticized him for attacking Chappelle and distorting Chappelle's comments about several candidates for bishop; it was the way Papa did it. In fifteen hundred words, replete with legal terms and classical references and brimming with hyperbole and invective, Papa called Dean everything except a child of God. He accused him of "malicious intention," vilified him as a "briefless barrister," "a cat's paw," "a country judge," "a hired scavanger [*sic*]," and "a zealous minion." He cast doubt on Dean's fitness for the ministry, implying that friends had facilitated his ordination. As evidence of Dean's incompetence, Papa claimed he'd been unable to "preach up a collection, neither lecture out a penny" at that meeting where Papa and Chappelle had spoken about Allen. In the end, Chappelle had been forced to "openly and manfully [come] to the rescue."[14]

The two men's exchange came on the eve of the 1900 AME General Conference May 7–25 in Columbus, Ohio, the first for which I've found a record of Papa as a delegate.[15] Church politicking could be rough-and-tumble as presiding elders, ministers, and laymen advocated for their causes and candidates for higher office. In this case, Dean supported the Rev. Marcellus M. Moore for bishop, and Papa supported Chappelle for head of the Sunday School Union, which published the Church's educational materials.

William David Chappelle
(Centennial Encyclopedia of
the AME church).

Papa obviously hoped to influence delegates, but his letter (and many of his subsequent actions supporting Chappelle) seems too impassioned to have been written out of mere duty.

There's no biography of him, but one admiring historian characterized Chappelle this way: "Without hesitation [he] spoke truth to power, publicly criticizing white leaders for their discriminatory treatment of African-Americans. A recognized leader within the church, Chappelle extended his leadership far beyond it too."[16] During his decades-long career, he was an activist inside and outside the AME church, an advocate for Black education and for Black civil rights, a supporter of Black farmers and Black businessmen, leader of one of the Church's primary printing and publishing operations from 1904 to 1908, and, finally, bishop for thirteen years until his death in 1925.

Existing photographs show a not-unhandsome man who (in some pictures) resembles the actor Clarence Williams III. The down-turned ends of the mustache Chappelle wore when younger give him a dour, forbidding look. In later photographs, clean shaven, hair gray, he looks out from behind wire-rimmed spectacles with guarded aloofness. AME doctrine against gambling aside, he would have made a good poker player.

Eight years older than Papa, Chappelle was born into slavery in 1857, in Fairfield County. He grew up working on the plantation where his parents were enslaved and did not learn to read or write until he was at least twelve years old. He married at eighteen. He and his first wife, Eliza, would have three children.[17] The same year he married, Chappelle joined the AME church. Soon, he was licensed as an exhorter—"a lay helper to the preacher"[18]—and then as a preacher. After graduating from the Fairfield Normal Institute, he began to teach in 1880. A year later, he enrolled at Allen. He continued to preach, walking miles to the Pine Grove Mission in Lexington County every Sunday. He was supposed to be paid sixty-five dollars a month, but his parishioners had trouble raising the money, so Chappelle was forced to drop out of school to return to teaching. Allen's president, Bishop William F. Dickerson,[19] helped by giving him a room to live in (one source says the room was in the bishop's yard),[20] paying him to take care of his horse, and allowing him to ride the horse to his preaching duties. Chappelle was ordained in 1883. Four years later, he graduated from Allen, with "full college honors" and "at the head of his class."[21] It was the same year Papa became one of seven normal school graduates.[22]

Papa's and Chappelle's connection with Allen would continue for decades, though Chappelle's was more prominent. He was elected to the school's Board of Trustees the year he received his diploma and would twice serve as president (1897–99 and 1908–12) and as chairman of the Board of Trustees from 1916 until his death in 1925.

It may be too much to call Papa and Chappelle friends, but it seems too dismissive to dub them mere acquaintances. Papa was Chappelle's staunch advocate for some two and a half decades, and the two men were close enough for Chappelle to baptize Papa's first child, Mattie, in 1891. For much of their time in Columbia, they lived about two blocks apart.[23] Perhaps it's best to describe them as allies in the fight for uplift.

They shared many similarities, not least the same trials as they struggled to surmount early hardship. They fought the good fight over a period that saw one country boy—Chappelle—reach the highest echelons of the AME church and another—Papa—become vice president of their alma mater. In 1916, however, the two fell out, and Papa was forced out at Allen. Cut off from his beloved school for nearly a decade, he devoted his energies to trying to bring down Chappelle, seldom missing a chance to lambaste his illustrious target in the newspaper, *The Light*, he published from his home.

In the end, perhaps, it was their similarities as much as their differences that shattered their alliance.

◆   ◆   ◆

Mama's peach pickle and paintings notwithstanding, Papa's interest in a "colored fair" as a showcase for Black homemakers, farmers, and craftsmen dates back at least two years before the Fairfield County Colored Fair. At a summer 1891 meeting of the Colored State Agricultural and Mechanical Society, he spoke on "The Utility of Invention."[24]

Black South Carolinians had enough energy—and, perhaps, a need to prove their worth after Reconstruction—to form two competing state fair associations. In 1892 and 1893, in fact, J. H. Williams' Colored Agricultural and Mechanical Association of South Carolina *and* Andrew E. Hampton's Colored State Agricultural and Mechanical Society held fairs weeks apart in Columbia. Ego of the organizations' founders aside (the two men had been part of the Association), there was no need for two fairs; moreover, each group was plagued by financial shortfalls and fiscal irregularities. In 1896, when *The State* published an announcement for the "fourth or fifth Colored State Fair undertaking," it also published an editorial calling out Hampton for "his unbroken record of stupid failures." "The colored people are making progress . . . ," the newspaper went on, "but a farce like A. E. Hampton's is a discredit and an injury to them. . . . The tendency of it is to make the race ridiculous and contemptible."[25]

Apart from his name in stories about the fair, I've found little about Hampton. Allen's 1908–10 catalog lists him as a member of the Class of 1887 and says he earned both bachelor's and law degrees. With so little to go on, it's difficult to tell whether he was a charlatan or simply the kind of fast-talking visionary who lacked the gumption (and the money) to see his projects through. He and the secretary of his organization were arrested in 1893 and charged with misusing state funds granted to put on the fair; nonetheless, he continued to put on what *The State* called "fake fairs." After one, the newspaper quoted an anonymous "gentleman" who claimed the exhibits had consisted of "one bottle of blackberry wine, three

Columbia ca. 1901, six years after Papa returned to teach at Allen.
Library of Congress.

chickens—two roosters and one pullet, two quilts—crazy, one pumpkin[, and with] seven Negroes in attendance."[26]

Never one to want to seem ridiculous or, worse, contemptible, Papa in 1897 joined a fifteen-man commission seeking a state charter for yet another colored-fair-organizing organization, the Colored State Fair and Educational Association. The association proposed to sell one thousand shares of stock at five dollars a share. A constitution and by-laws were approved. Soon it was announced that the commission—now a "board of corporators"—would run the organization until stockholders met to elect officers. It was hoped the association would become "the great centerpost of Negro enterprise in this State."[27]

The association held at least one more meeting, but it did not manage to put on a fair. Meanwhile, to the Columbians' chagrin, Black farmers in Seneca, Orangeburg, Rock Hill, Cheraw, and Kershaw County mounted fairs in 1897, 1898, and 1899. Worse, Hampton's "fake fairs" continued. In

1902, he resigned—or was voted out. All the same, Hampton refused to turn over his books, claiming the success of the South Carolina Colored Fair Society was "due entirely to his painful labors of years." When pressed, he said he'd burned the account books. Opponents threatened a lawsuit.[28] Finally, in 1904, a Columbia judge ordered Hampton "the president and founder of—and flounderer in—the State Colored Fair society"[29] to turn over the fair's books to some of his former associates.

Not until 1908, largely through the efforts of the Rev. Richard Carroll, South Carolina's Booker T. Washington, did Columbia host a real Colored State Fair. Noting that there had been "a separate building . . . granted to Negroes" during previous white fairs, Carroll proposed expanding this in 1907, with part of the fairgrounds set aside for Black exhibitors. There would, of course, be a separate gate and separate admission. By 1908, he was ready to propose a separate fair. Despite last-minute misunderstandings about how much the organizers were expected to pay for use of the state fairgrounds, the fair began on November 9. Carroll would later be called the founder of the fair, a tribute to his hard work and the white support he enjoyed that helped make the fair a reality.

Papa would soon become a member of the fair's executive committee and serve as superintendent until at least 1944, when he would have been nearly eighty years old and the fair itself—albeit in different incarnations—more than a half century old.[30]

At its height, the fair was a multi-day extravaganza dubbed the "greatest event for Negroes in the state" "where the colored race shows to great advantage." It included a midway with rides (and girlie show), horse and harness racing, parades, national entertainers such as Joe Williams and his Manhattan Serenaders, animal exhibits and displays of needlework, sewing, and canned goods, fireworks, and as many as three football games. One year, Columbia's Booker T. Washington High played Spartanburg's Cummings Street High, Benedict College took on Bethune-Cookman College, and Allen hosted Morris College of Sumter. When Allen met Benedict, the local-school contest was called the "annual classic."[31]

Fair officials, like Papa, President Arthur J. Collins, and Secretary David R. Starks, worked tirelessly, traveling the state to talk up the fair, coaxing publicity from newspapers, convincing the railroads to offer discount tickets to fairgoers. According to the *Palmetto Leader*, sometimes they even had "to set up exhibits." Collins, a Columbia dentist, remembered that he'd once taken a personal loan to pay rent on the fairgrounds.[32]

The white State Fair officially integrated in 1965, but a separate Negro fair continued until 1970. It was canceled that year, for only the second time; the first had been forced by the 1918 influenza epidemic. In 1971, the colored fair was officially dissolved, an unintended casualty—like so many of the Black community's institutions—of the long-sought opening up of society.[33]

◆ ◆ ◆

Papa was also part of an effort to found a savings and loan, serving in 1894 as "solicitor" for the Savings, Loan and Investment Association of Fairfield County. *The State* reported that the South Carolina Secretary of State had granted the association a charter and that "[t]he required amount of the capital stock has been subscribed and paid in."[34]

The Colored State Fair endured for decades, but there's no evidence the Fairfield S&L ever opened its doors. Still, both were typical of Black efforts at self-improvement in the decades after Reconstruction and more evidence of Papa's support for thrift and "Negro enterprise." Like Booker T. Washington, Papa believed that "the permanent progress of the race"[35] depended on getting an education, owning property, obeying the law, and choosing good leaders. All the same, Papa understood there were limits to the great man's program of accommodation.

After more than twenty-five Black men were killed in the Atlanta Riots from September 22 to September 24, 1906, editor William Jefferson White was criticized for the "downright traitorous" editorials he'd published in his newspaper, the *Georgia Baptist*. Arguing that the city "had no room for such incendiary Negroes," the (white) *Augusta Chronicle* called for him to be forced to leave the state. It wasn't White's first brush with the mob—six years earlier, after he'd reprinted an antilynching editorial, angry whites marched to the newspaper office, which was also his home, threatening to destroy it and tar and feather him.[36]

Papa took Washington to task in *The Southern Sun*, pointing out that his efforts "to solve the race problem" by encouraging African-Americans to open businesses and own property had "failed, it seems, in the case of Rev. J. W. [sic] White [editor] of the *Georgia Baptist*." Atlanta, he wrote, was "a great place for Negro gatherings. . . . [where] the friendliest sentiments are ever expressed by the blacks towards the whites at their public meetings." Nonetheless, he noted, "the race was without sufficient influence among the whites to keep an afternoon paper from incensing the white population to rioting."[37]

What's unfortunate about Papa's editorial, though, is what he wrote next: "Rev. White was intelligent, wealthy and industrious; in fact he is white in color and good, we believe, at heart." There's a tinge of irony and insult in that statement, characteristics ever present in Papa's writing. White was, in fact, fair-skinned enough to pass, but why bring it up? Perhaps there was some disagreement between the two men, details of which are lost. From what I know about each, though, I suspect they were more in accord about how to oppose white supremacy than they were in disagreement.

Both men were seldom loath to test the proposition that pens could be mightier than swords. And Papa, too, would pay the price (albeit a different one) for what appeared in the pages of his paper.

Atlanta was, of course, the city where Booker Washington in 1895 famously proposed that "in all things that are purely social, we [blacks and whites] can be as separate as the fingers, yet one as the hand in all things essential to mutual progress." (He also joked about stealing chickens, but perhaps he was just warming up his audience.) Eminently practical, Washington believed Blacks should seek financial security and material success before going after political power and civil rights. He supported vocational education, farm and business ownership, and a conciliatory attitude toward white Southerners. Papa didn't disagree. But he saw the value in academic *and* vocational education and, because he believed Black progress depended on the right to vote, did not shy away from political involvement.

Five years before he returned to Columbia from Winnsboro, Papa served on the education committee at a meeting of the Colored Reform Conference. The conference adopted a multipart resolution that included this: "That we do not desire social equality, nor demand political supremacy as a race, but as citizens of this State and of the United States we do demand an impartial administration of the government under which we live, and a just and fair share in that administration."[38] Two years later, in 1892, Papa was one of four Laurens delegates to the Republican state convention.[39] And, four years after that, he was a delegate to the state and congressional conventions, this time from Fairfield County.[40] In 1908—when William Howard Taft ran for president against William Jennings Bryan—he joined a "contesting delegation" at a state convention "remarkable for disorder." A white delegate knocked a Black delegate unconscious after he was referred to as a "Royal good Democrat," and "a free-for-all fight seemed imminent." Calm was not entirely restored, however, as some delegates charged they'd been "run over roughshod" by Taft supporters and elected a competing delegation that included Papa.[41] Potential for fisticuffs notwithstanding, Papa's political involvement continued into the 1920s and '30s. In 1920, he was elected to a first district seat on the state executive committee (there were twenty-three members from seven districts); and in 1926, he was chosen as a delegate to the state convention.[42]

One report says Papa was "at one time chairman of the State [Republican] Executive Committee."[43] I can't document that, and the source gives no date. But what can be documented is that 1920 was his second stint on the committee. The first was in 1892. After listing the names of the fourteen members of the committee, *The State* commented, "Among these will be recognized many of the most red-hot radicals in the camp."[44] Papa must have been pleased to have been in such good company.

It seems incredible—after Donald Trump's election gave Republicans license to openly embrace white supremacy—that Papa would devote so much to the Grand Old Party. But his was a different time, a time when many African-Americans understood they owed a debt to the Party of Lincoln because of the Emancipation Proclamation and the war that ended slavery. Awareness of that debt explains why, in 1912, Papa served as a "commissioner" from South Carolina and delegate to the educational congress for the national celebration of the fiftieth anniversary of the Emancipation Proclamation.[45]

Debt or no debt, however, it was not easy being a Black Republican in the decades after Reconstruction. The 1868 South Carolina Constitution that had provided education for all—allowing Papa to go to school in Laurens—also gave Black men the vote. The 1895 constitution, product of the return to white supremacy dubbed the state's "Redemption," mandated separate schools and limited Black suffrage by imposing a literacy test and poll tax. Bowing to the new realities in 1901, former congressman Thomas E. Miller, a Reconstruction-era state legislator and nominee for lieutenant governor who had opposed the new constitution, resigned from the legislature. "I have done with politics," he announced, "and shall devote the rest of my life to the education and elevation of our Negroes." True to his word, he became the first president of what is now South Carolina State University.

Republicans were virtually powerless—one historian wrote that, after 1900, the party got only two thousand votes per election in South Carolina—but Blacks came in for special ridicule. One report of a state convention noted "the fun . . . ten stories high," the "humorous scenes, and . . . a good many instances of Cuffee[46] playing politics. . . ." Another news story felt it worth mentioning that, despite a "strong Negro representation. . . . they were as a rule, away above the intelligence of the usual Negro delegates to Republican conventions." (The writer also couldn't help referring to two delegates as "bright mulattos"—one "of lavish appearance"[47]—but then, Papa couldn't resist punning on the Rev. White's last name.)

All the same, Papa kept the faith. Thirty-six years after he represented Laurens County at the 1892 state convention, the party made him an alternate delegate to the 1928 Republican national convention, held in Kansas City, Missouri, from June 12 to June 15. "Dad leaves in a day or two for Kansas City," Mama proudly wrote Mattie that June. "He is to try his hand at making Presidents now. Can't say if he [will] be as successful as in making bishops."[48]

Mama was—alas!—exaggerating. There were eleven South Carolina delegates and Papa was one of seven alternates. It's likely he didn't do much on the convention floor. And, as with so much else in his America, segregation ruled. White delegates stayed at one hotel, African-Americans at another.[49]

6

The Light

By 1908, Papa had succeeded his mentor, Joseph White Morris, as dean of Allen University's law department. His connection with the school contributed to his renown in South Carolina and throughout the AME church, but Allen lacked the money to pay enough to support his growing family. The school's financial problems were of long standing: In 1892, Thomas A. Saxon, head of the law department, resigned on Christmas Eve because he hadn't been paid.[1] Papa and Chappelle made frequent fundraising trips throughout South Carolina, speaking at small churches and taking up collections. In May or June, the unwieldy Board of Trustees (I count more than one hundred members in the 1911–12 *Catalogue*[2]) met to decide on a budget and on which faculty members would return in the fall. Nonetheless, Papa and his fellow teachers were committed. As George A. Singleton put it, "Whether they received their salary or not they stuck. When they did receive it, they had not received much."[3]

Commitment or not, the uncertainty was hard on Papa and Mama.

Their fourth child, Fleming Maceo, had been born on February 24, 1897, when the Garretts lived at 1500 Harden Street. (Children were often named for relatives, ancestors, or friends who were due particular acknowledgment, but I can't account for Maceo's names.) The house on Harden Street, near Allen, was probably faculty housing. Once Maceo (as he was called) was old enough, the six Garretts posed for a photograph in the Columbia studios of W. A. Reckling. All look intently at the camera, faces stern, almost forbidding, though a faint smile teases on Mama's full lips. Six-year-old Mattie stands shoulder to shoulder beside her in high-button shoes. Their closeness was not feigned for the picture—it would endure until Mama's death. The infant Maceo is on Mama's lap, bare toes visible beneath his gown. Tap (Casper Jr.) is on Papa's lap in a similar gown—it must have been the fashion for younger children—his intent look softened by something almost questioning. Buddie (Ralston) is behind, between Papa and Mama, a scarf knotted around his neck. Well dressed, healthy, and prosperous looking, they pose before a painted backdrop of an idealized bucolic setting—wistful reminder of the rural past Papa romanticized in the *Southern Sun*.

By the time Papa was dean, the family had grown to eight children. Colon (Spanish for Columbus) Hunter was born on April 22, 1899; Marian (a boy, given the name because Mama had wanted a daughter to name after herself) Threewitts, on March 25, 1901; Ruth Eidier, on April 16, 1904; and Naomi Mills, on August 24, 1906.[4]

His growing family explains why, in addition to attempting to practice law briefly, Papa ran a grocery in 1907 and 1908. It also explains why, in 1902, 1904, and 1906, he and Mama were taken to court when they failed to repay bank loans or other debts.[5]

Mama's letters hint that he was paid for organizing and speaking at AME meetings, though he may have been reimbursed only for travel and other expenses. Later, after he left Allen, Papa would sell insurance and act as a notary. Apart from teaching, however, his most consistent activity was journalism. There was the *Southern Sun*, published from 1902 to 1909, which overlapped *The Light*, published from 1907 to 1915. According to his obituary, Green Jackson, a Columbia activist and "man of enthusiasm,"[6] owned the *Southern Sun*. He and Papa edited it. *The Light* was published by Farmers' Union Sun Company and Light Publishing Company, with Papa as sole editor. A second iteration of *The Light* (the paper's motto was "Let There Be Light"), published between 1916 and 1928, was Papa's own: Its publisher, also called The Light Publishing Company, was located at his home, 2210 Lady Street. Newspaper letterhead Mattie sometimes used to write her beau, Alfred Edgar Simons, lists Papa as editor, A. J. Martin as city editor, and journalist and educator I. M. A. Myers as news editor.[7] Like Green, Myers was one of those energetic, civic-minded Afro-Columbians whose deeds deserve to be remembered.

As editor and publisher of *The Light*, Papa also sold subscriptions and ads, collected accounts, set type, and ran the press.

A one-year subscription to *The Light* cost $1.50 in 1918. A six-month subscription was one dollar, and a three-month subscription cost fifty cents. Two years later, the cost of a one-year subscription had gone up fifty

Mama, Papa, and four of their children, ca. 1897. From left, Mattie, Mama, Maceo, Ralston, Papa, and Casper George Jr., "Tap." Collection of the author.

cents.[8] Papa sought ads, charging twenty-five cents per inch for the first run of an ad, and a fee of fifteen cents for each run afterward. There were occasional large or full-page ads, but most were small one-column by one- or two-inch notices for Columbia's Black doctors, lawyers, dentists, and small businessmen like the photographer who called himself Johnson the Picture Man, or B. A. Blocker,[9] who did cleaning, pressing, and alterations and sold secondhand clothes.

A boxed note titled "To Our Subscribers" beneath the masthead of one issue suggests that Papa had a hard time keeping the paper going. It's an interesting mix of Papa's trademark acerbity and faith that, given a choice, most people will do the right thing:

> We have been and are trying to give you a strong, manly paper, touching war and race news, as well as uncovering hypocrisy and black scoundrelism in God's church, and secular news in general. We ask that you pay us what you owe. If you don't want to read it, be honest, pay up and stop. We will not be insulted.
>
> We can not call to see all our subscribers, we have not the time, and the expense is too much, so please send the money you owe us. Our paper is $1.50 a year, paid in advance, if you have paid a part, send us the remainder of a year's subscription. Be fair, don't beat us. Send the money by check, postal order or any way, send it. We need the money to run the paper, which costs us considerable cash every week. DON'T WAIT TO SEE US or to receive a bill, pay us at once and read *The Light*.[10]

Papa had little leverage to force subscribers and advertisers to pay, so the papers probably didn't turn a profit (even a small one), or come close to breaking even. Nonetheless, he persisted for more than a quarter-century, refusing to abandon his forum though financial realities meant that he sometimes published intermittently. In 1925, Columbia's *Palmetto Leader* welcomed *The Light*'s return. Papa, the notice said, was "a trenchant writer and no doubt The Light will add to the gaiety of the newspaper world."[11] There must have been another interruption; in 1928, the *New York Age* welcomed the paper's return after "an absence of three years."[12] This time, however, the *Palmetto Leader* was not so charitable toward its erstwhile competitor. *The Light*, it said, had been "for quite a while in an eclipse" and now "comes forth belching venom and abuse as usual."[13]

All the same, readers valued Papa's paper. One man, quit Columbia and settled in Washington, D.C., even wrote the *Palmetto Leader* to commend Papa for having sent him *The Light* during World War I, "while I was on the firing line in France, fighting my way to German soil."[14]

It's doubtful, however, that the newly resurgent *Light* was any more profitable than it had been before its three-year hiatus. When Mama wrote Mattie that Papa "neglects the paper" because he was spending more time selling insurance, she added that she didn't "much care since there is less expense."[15]

There was another reason for her to be grateful. Without his newspaper, Papa had fewer opportunities to get himself into trouble.

The thing is, Papa was a born crusader. Never reluctant to take others to task, he made *The Light* a "rather iconoclastic newspaper . . . whose Caustic [*sic*] and satirical editorials were the bane of evildoers in Church and state alike."[16]

The paper had few bylines, so we don't know what role, if any, Mama played. She probably wasn't much inclined to help out—after all, they had nine children by 1909. The last, Christopher Threewitts, was born on February 25, 1909, a year after the death of his namesake, Mama's brother. Papa and Mama weren't done, however. After Ralston's out-of-wedlock daughter, Frances, was born on September 22, 1912, they took her in and raised her as their own.

All the same, it's a pity Mama couldn't step in to help run the paper. She had her father's business sense—when she died, her estate was valued at more than sixty-five hundred (one hundred seven thousand dollars today) and included four houses and a 175-acre farm—so she might have put *The Light* on a sound economic footing. She had another quality that would have made her a valuable co-editor: Her letters that survive show she knew what all smart small-town newspaper editors must if they're to prosper— they have a duty to entertain as well as inform.

By contrast, Papa wanted to protest and to persuade. He published tidbits of social news, but most of his space (apart from national and international news of dubious value to the paper's readers) was reserved for attacks on Black complacency and, occasionally, white supremacy. Some read today as justified. Others likely alienated many who might otherwise have supported him.

In one February 1906 *Southern Sun* editorial, Papa observed that South Carolina had just appropriated two hundred thousand dollars for white colleges but only fifty-four hundred for the Black state college in Orangeburg. This, the editorial noted, was manifestly unfair, and Papa posed a challenge:

> If our white friends want to be sincere and prove that their racial and blood traditions make and keep them superior to Negroes, let them put their merits to the test of the survival of the fittest, and give those Negroes who evince competency a partial chance at the millions of emoluments dispensed in political functions, and then it will be time to predict the fatal racial terminations, if the Negroes fail after grappling with advantages that are always lavished on white men. Equal advantages are the only correct solution of the race problem.[17]

Three years later, he wrote criticizing Black physician William D. Crum for lacking "backbone and race manhood" when he resigned as customs collector for the port of Charleston. Appointed by Theodore Roosevelt in 1902, Crum had been opposed by white Southerners, and the Senate failed to confirm his nomination. He was finally confirmed in 1905 after Roosevelt had kept him in office using a series of interim appointments. Four years later, however, Crum chose to resign when William Howard Taft was elected president. Papa thought he should have waited and forced Taft—under pressure from whites—to either stand by the Constitution or "give in to prejudice."[18]

The word "manhood" and phrases like "manhood of the race" occur with remarkable frequency in Papa's writing and that of his contemporaries, often enough for me to intuit that he and other African-American men of his time craved the freedom to "imagine their manliness defined by the same public roles and private responsibilities as those of white manhood." During slavery, attempts to show "public masculinity"[19] were met with lethal violence. Papa was writing more than forty years after slavery's end; nonetheless, he understood the reality of a world where Black men were, all too often, unable to protect those they loved and their property.

It took courage, then, to write and publish opinions like these at a time when Black men—remember the threats the Rev. William J. White faced after the 1906 Atlanta Riots—could be maimed or lynched for challenging white authority, but Papa did not lack courage. In September of 1921, he was attacked twice in a six-week span, the first time by two stick-wielding men as he and Mama were walking home from the streetcar. It was just weeks before his fifty-sixth birthday, but Papa "defended himself briskly," and the two men fled. "The whole town is stirred over the attack on Dad and both white and colored are offering assistance in helping to run them down," Mama wrote Mattie. "We feel that we will soon bring the guilty ones to task." The second time, Papa charged that he'd been struck by a preacher with whom he'd been walking. Neither account says why Papa was assaulted. Both name him as editor of *The Light*, which is how the *Record*'s readers might have known him. But perhaps the editors were also hinting that the attacks were connected to something Papa had published.[20]

Whatever Papa did to provoke the wrath of J. P. Perk, the preacher who was arrested, is long forgotten. But another pastor incurred Papa's antipathy about the same time when he was foolhardy enough to publish, and sign, a statement calling "white people . . . curs" for whom "hell is too cool." Papa responded by calling the Rev. John McClellan, of Elloree, S.C., "a wicked fool" and dubbed his invective "race rot." He accused him of getting "this big talk . . . from his dirty, wicked Bishop [Chappelle]." However white citizens found out what McClellan had said—from *The Light* or an unnamed "church newspaper"—they "ordered [him] not to let the sun go down on him" in Elloree. He packed hurriedly, and he and "his wife left town immediately in his buggy. The last seen of him, it is said, was when he passed through Creston about noon going toward Columbia."[21]

Clearly, there were limits to Papa's philosophy of race manhood. What's clear, though, is that Papa enjoyed infuriating those who, with a little bit of persuasion, might have supported him. A small house ad at the bottom of one page of *The Light* reads, "If you are afraid to subscribe for [*sic*] The Light, play coward, sneak over and read your neighbors."[22] It was hardly a sentiment to win friends and influence people.

Then there were Papa's legal troubles because of what he'd published.

Six years after his *Southern Sun* editorial taking on white supremacy, Papa was sued for libel. After an appearance before a magistrate on November 19, 1912, he was bound over to the Court of General Sessions and released on a bond of two hundred dollars. The complainant, according to a story in *The State*, was "D. M. Magill, a Negro preacher."[23] The *Columbia Record* thought it was "[p]robably the first case to be brought under the new statute for libel,"[24] passed earlier that year.

"Magill" was Daniel M. McGill, an AME presiding elder. He'd graduated from Allen in 1888, a year after Papa, so the two men must have known each other. McGill's sons—Eugene Howard and William Odell—graduated from Allen in 1904 and 1913. If they were not Papa's students, Papa certainly knew them. An AME minister, like his father, Eugene McGill would become an Allen trustee and, in the late 1930s, president of the institution.[25]

Green Jackson and a white businessman named William Cole Swaffield appeared with Papa. Each came up with two hundred dollars to ensure Papa's appearance. Jackson was co-editor of the newspaper, but I don't know why Swaffield came to court—perhaps (though it seems unlikely) he'd invested in *The Light*. When he died of typhoid in 1915, aged just thirty-four, his obituary described him as "public spirited and of a liberal nature." Perhaps that, and the fact that "his charges were numerous" explain why he vouched for Papa.[26]

There's no transcript of the trial and the offending issue of *The Light* has not survived; thus there's no way to know just why Papa attacked McGill. According to the indictment, however, on October 9, 1912, Papa "did unlawfully originate, utter, circulate, and publish, with malicious intent, the statement that D. M. McGill, a minister, 'is following the devil's ambition and the fool's of [lust] and graft,' which said statement, being then and there false, tended to injure the character and reputation of the said D. M. McGill, contrary to the statute in such case made and provided, and against the peace and dignity of that state."[27]

Jackson was listed as one of Papa's defense witnesses, as was William Chappelle. Did Papa represent himself? The court papers don't say. He must have been ably defended, however. He was found not guilty when the case went to trial in January 1913.[28]

Though Papa's may have been South Carolina's first trial for libel, it was not the last time the lawyer who no longer practiced would find himself in court. All too often, Papa's courage seemed almost indistinguishable from recklessness. In the years to come, the forces that compelled him to protest would thwart his hopes for advancement.

7

Martha's Trials

Now to something I've put off writing about—how Papa's new life in Columbia was complicated by the presence of his mother.

Martha had come to Winnsboro from Laurens a year or so before Papa quit the Colored Graded School because he'd been hired to teach at Allen University. Illness may have forced her to leave Laurens. In her 1894 letter, Elizabeth Proudfit (the Garretts' "benefactress" and wife of the man for whom Papa named his first son, Ralston) told him she hoped "your good mother is as comfortable as circumstances will allow," adding she thought Papa must have found it "a great pleasure to you to have her home with you." Cato goes unmentioned, as absent from Elizabeth's letter as from Papa's biographies. Twenty years older than Martha, perhaps he'd died. Or perhaps she'd left him.

Four letters published in *The State* on consecutive days in April 1901 show how wrong Elizabeth likely was. Even if Papa was innocent of the accusations contained in three of the letters, their publication soured any pleasure in sharing a house with the mother whose "greatest ambition" had been "to educate her son."

The first letter, from a correspondent identified only by the initials "D. J. B.," alleged that Papa (misidentified as "a professor in Claflin university") was guilty of neglecting his mother, "an aged and very decrepid [*sic*] mulatto woman." (Martha was about sixty-five years old.) Misidentifying her as Martha Garrett—not Martha Kennedy—the writer claimed she was "much afflicted" and had suffered "three strokes of paralyses." Because Papa "allows her to stay in his house [but] he will not support her," she was forced to go door-to-door "soliciting alms." Worse, rumor had it Papa "beats his feeble old mother." After making inquiries, the writer claimed he'd discovered that "the case is notorious among the colored people."

D. J. B. attempted to cover himself by claiming he didn't want to injure Papa's "good name" and that he didn't know whether any of this was true. Still, he wanted to know if a son who "owned his own dwelling house and lot and also three houses that he rents out," and had only a family "of moderate size," could be compelled to support his mother. (Papa and Mama had six children in 1901, but perhaps theirs was considered a moderate-sized family in those days.) He called for Papa to be investigated by "the State authorities who have control"[1] of Papa's school.

Of course, Papa didn't teach at Claflin, and it—like Allen—was private and church funded. But perhaps D. J. B. believed "State authorities" were in charge because from 1872 to 1896 the state-funded colored agricultural and mechanical institute had been part of the university. They are now separate institutions, and Claflin University is funded by the United Methodist Church. All the same, even though D. J. B. had gotten Papa's affiliation wrong, it's hard to believe Allen's trustees would have ignored a request from lawmakers to look into the matter of how a professor was treating his mother.

Whatever else Papa did to defend himself, we know of only one thing— the letter he sent the same day to *The State*. He began by welcoming the inquiry, though he noted that D. J. B. "would have been better prepared to use the charitable pen had proper information been sought beforehand." His mother had suffered no strokes. Instead, she "was an excessive morphine eater" and had used the drug for nearly thirty years. He had been purchasing it for her for fifteen and continued to do so because he'd been unable to convince her to take "the Keeley or some other cure." (Named after physician Leslie Enraught Keeley, this was a franchised cure based on a "proprietary tonic"[2] and the then-novel idea that addiction was a disease.) Unconcerned about the possibility of injury to his reputation—"I am doing what I conceive to be right"—Papa closed by saying, "I will bear the result of drugs, tattlers and the charitable inquisitors."[3]

I've found just one person with the initials D. J. B. in the 1899, 1901, and 1903 Columbia City Directories—the Rev. Daniel J. Brimm, a professor at Presbyterian Theological Seminary. This doesn't mean he wrote the letter. And, even if he did, it's impossible to know his motivation. Whoever D. J. B. was, he could, as he styled himself, have been a well-meaning

Columbian genuinely concerned about Martha's welfare. But Papa had a gift for making enemies. And so, except for erring in identifying him as teaching at Claflin, his accuser could have been a competitor at Allen or someone he'd offended in the AME church or the Republican Party. Whether D. J. B. wanted to injure Papa's good name or to caution him against ruining it, Papa's urge to defend himself is understandable.

As it turned out, he might have been better advised to leave well enough alone: Immediately beneath his response, *The State* published *another* letter from *another* anonymous correspondent. This one, "L. R. B.," claimed he'd been helping Martha "for some time" because he knew "of the treatment she received from her son—or more specifically her son's wife." When he'd visited Papa "to implore him to be better" to his mother, he had to talk to Mama because Papa was away. Mama's "impertinence" made him so angry he threatened to "call the public's attention to the case." Mama told him to—she didn't care if he did. That must have been why L. R. B. related secondhand testimony from a neighbor alleging that Mama "beat Aunt Martha shamefully, and she was put into a [*sic*] out house to sleep, that was not fit for a dog to lie in."[4]

Whoever L.R.B. was—I've found just one person with those initials, a contractor named Louis R. Boland—the matter wasn't over. Martha's letter appeared in the newspaper the very next day.

The 1880 census says Martha was illiterate, so she must have dictated the letter to someone—perhaps D. J. B. or L. R. B.—familiar with the niceties of spelling and grammar but astute enough to preserve something of Martha's distinctive way of speaking. She accused Papa of failing to do "his part by his poor old mother," thus forcing her to rely on whites "to give unto me what he should have done." Martha claimed that not only had Papa neglected her, but his "companion" had also given her "a great deal of unkind treatment." They'd forced her to live "in a little out house," refusing to allow her "to come into their house." (The 1901 Columbia City Directory says the Garretts lived on Lady Street in the Waverly neighborhood but gives no house number. The 1903 directory gives his address as 2208 Lady. Neither directory lists Martha.) "He never says, 'Ma, here is something to eat,' and they eat in a room near the little coop I stay in and they never offer me scarcely a bite to eat." She lived "on the charity of my friends. . . .

ashamed to beg but [I] have to live." Martha admitted to taking morphine, saying she'd "used it all my life since I was a girl but I don't use more than a bottle every week."[5] But she said that she, and not Papa, paid for it.

Perhaps, as I sometimes think I should have done with the newspaper story about Papa being charged with statutory rape, I ought to have closed the computer window and hoped no one else would come across D. J. B.'s letter, or Papa and Martha's responses. The matter disappears from the pages of *The State*, and I've found nothing else that would help me figure out the truth. Mama doesn't mention Martha in her letters, Papa's are lost, and I've been unable to find Martha's death certificate, which might have listed some chronic complaint accounting for her addiction. That said, I'm inclined to be more sympathetic to Papa—if not outright believe him— than to believe either of his anonymous accusers.

For one thing, it seems unlikely that Allen's president, the Rev. David H. Johnson, didn't call Papa in after the letters were published. (Bishop Wesley J. Gaines, chairman of the board of trustees, lived in Atlanta, but surely someone kept him informed). If Johnson believed Papa guilty of mistreating his mother, wouldn't he have done something? Allen was, after all, a church school that demanded its students live up to the highest standards. Would Johnson have required less of teachers? It would have been easy to fire Papa: Teachers didn't enjoy tenure, and the board of trustees met during commencement week to decide which ones would return in the fall.

Unlike Cato, Papa's stepfather, Martha doesn't go unacknowledged in Papa's life. She's depicted as "a good mother" in one of his contemporary biographies, a woman "who struggled amid the hardship of the homeless and unsettled slaves to make a living for herself and child."[6] If Papa didn't write this himself, he must have provided the information. The absence of a death certificate means Martha probably died before South Carolina began to require them in 1915. Both biographies were published later, so maybe Papa was acknowledging in death the mother he'd mistreated in life. But he named his firstborn Martha Phyllis after his mother and Mama's mother. He'd hardly have done so if he didn't feel some filial tie—after all, remember that he named none of his six sons Samuel, after his father.

I'm guessing, of course, because I've told you everything I know about Martha. Except for one more thing: Almost done writing—I'd printed a

C.G. Garrett, his mother, and three of his children, Mattie, Ralston, and Tap, ca. 1897. Collection of the author.

draft to review and help me compile the index—I came across a photograph of Martha in the files Ruth left me. She's sitting beside Papa and her grandchildren, Mattie, Ralston, and Tap. Someone's written the names above their heads or on their chests. Tap—he's labeled "Baby Casper"—sits on Martha's lap, wearing a dress-like gown. Ralston's wearing one too. Tap looks like he's no more than two years old, so the picture was likely taken in 1896 or 1897, after Papa came back to Columbia to teach at Allen.

One of Martha's hands rests on Tap's waist, as if to keep him from wriggling away. High-button shoes peep from beneath the hem of her long check-patterned dress. Martha looks straight at the camera, eyes unflinching, mouth set. Her hand holding Tap is rough and workworn. Her gaze hints at the iron determination that drove her to sacrifice so Papa could make something of himself. That hand, and the bulging sides of her feet confined in the worn leather of her shoes, hint at how much it cost her.

Perhaps Papa buried his complicated feelings about his mother beneath the Victorianism adopted from his Northern teachers, ignoring a tangle of gratitude and guilt leavened with embarrassment over her country ways. It couldn't have been easy living with the woman who'd sacrificed so much to see him educated. Ready to coerce (the word Papa's contemporary biographies use), she must have had a sense of doing right that was not easily shaken. Forced by illness or the death of her husband to give up her home and rely on her son, she would have expected him to care for her as she had for him. But perhaps she made it difficult by refusing to abandon the notion that she knew best—after all, both knew she'd been the one to put Papa in the position to make something of himself!

Papa referred to his mother as a "morphine eater," a term used in the nineteenth century to refer to those addicted to opiates.[7] Until 1914, he or his mother would have been able to walk into a pharmacy and purchase morphine without a prescription, often in patent medicines advertised for pain and a range of ailments from asthma to coughs, diarrhea, and menstrual cramps. But how had Martha become addicted? If it happened when she was in her mid-thirties (Papa claimed she'd been using morphine since 1874), perhaps she'd been sick or suffered injury working as laundress or farm laborer to keep Papa in school. The drug might have allowed her to keep working and provided relief from a hard life. Martha herself claimed she'd used it since girlhood, which would mean she began taking it while enslaved.

That would have made hers a rare case, as most owners believed their African captives more immune to pain than whites. As a result, slaves' "illnesses and injuries were often left untreated," and they "were rarely given opium."[8] Although morphine was first isolated in 1805, it didn't come into widespread use until the invention of the hypodermic needle fifty-one years later—in plenty of time for the Civil War. Some veterans continued to use the drug after war's end and, because there were more "wounded or shell-shocked" Confederate than Union veterans, more white Southern men became "morphine eaters" or "morphinists." Others, including Southern women with "their own war-related troubles," turned to opiates because of the "enormous psychological impact" of defeat. As a result, "southern whites had the highest addiction rate of any regional racial group" in the decades following the Civil War "and perhaps one of the highest in the world."[9] Black Southerners, on the other hand, were relatively free from addiction. Most freedmen lacked the same access to medical care whites enjoyed,[10] but there was an "ironic benefit"[11] to this absence of medical care: They didn't go to doctors who were likely to routinely prescribe opium or morphine for diseases such as arthritis or malaria.

◆　◆　◆

By the time the letters were published, Papa and Mama had six children. Marian, the youngest, was only three weeks old. The next youngest, Colon, would have been a week shy of his second birthday. (Having a houseful of children to care for explains Mama's "impertinence" when L. R. B. knocked on her door—she had more pressing business). Conflicts about child-rearing aside (both Mama and Martha were strong-willed women), mightn't Mama have welcomed the help? Or would she have mistrusted the mother-in-law who consumed a bottle of morphine a day?

Martha's addiction remains one of those haunting facts I can't forget. She was both Black and a woman, so her drug habit (however she came to it) makes her something of an outlier. Though a grown woman in her mid-forties when she placed that pitiable notice in the *Christian Recorder* asking after her parents and siblings, deep inside, somewhere unacknowledged, she was still the bewildered little girl crying herself to sleep on the long journey south, suffering from what we'd call today posttraumatic stress disorder. And so she stifled her grief with doses of morphine or laudanum. We'd call it self-medicating today.

I have to remind myself to breathe as I study Martha's face in the photograph Ruth left for me to find, marveling at the history I hold in my hand. Her blood flows in my veins, this woman who knew what it was to be a slave. She knew what it was to be a slave.

8

"For Editor of the
A. M. E. Church Review"

By now, it ought to be clear that Papa was as good at alienating others as he was at making friends and winning influence. All the same, despite his penchant for invective and Daniel McGill's 1912 lawsuit (not to mention the allegations about his mother), Papa became vice president of Allen University some time in 1913 or 1914. The university librarians I've talked to say many records were destroyed when a basement storage area flooded, but the earliest mention I've found of Papa as Allen's vice president is in a June 1914 story from *The State*. The paper noted "the annual election of the teachers" at a meeting of trustees after commencement, so it's possible Papa was elected then. However, he's also listed as vice president on official stationery Mattie used to write a letter to Alfred weeks before that meeting—perhaps Papa won the position after the death in 1913 of Vice President Joseph W. Morris. (Morris, of course, taught Papa law and was the professor he remembered in the autobiographical sketch published in the *Southern Sun*.) At any rate, the vice presidency was one of the reasons Papa was listed in 1915 among the "well[-]known Negro men and women" making up the university's faculty. Soon, there'd be talk he might even become president.[1]

Unfortunately for Papa, it was only talk. His two- or three-year stint as vice president turned out to be the summit of his career. He was forced out in 1916, ending his connection with the institution that had nurtured him for some thirty years. His friendship with William Chappelle would also end, and the two men become bitter enemies. Not all the events surrounding Papa's departure from Allen can be documented, but there is enough to make it clear his temperament—and a desire to see more representation for laymen in the church—helped precipitate his departure.

When William ran for secretary-treasurer of the AME church's Sunday School Union in 1900, Papa touted his friend as "one of the ablest scholars, deepest thinkers and foremost champions of the Church and race," and predicted that "his business tact, his indomitable push and energy will enable him to bring the Union to the highest expectation."[2] He was right. William arrived in Nashville to find the union six thousand dollars in debt, its plant heavily damaged by fire, and the white Methodist Episcopal Church, South, printing the AME church's educational materials. By the time he left eight years later, the union owned its own equipment, was printing AME literature, and had a plant worth twenty-five thousand dollars.[3]

With the union on sound footing in 1908, William felt it was time to try for the bishopric. Six weeks before the General Conference in Norfolk, Va., one newspaper called him "prominent among the candidates for the high honor" and said it was "generally conceded that he will be elected on the first ballot."[4] The paper was wrong. Five other men were elected bishops, three to serve in the United States and two abroad. Chappelle had narrowly lost the contest to return to Nashville, so he returned to Columbia for a second stint as Allen's president. The man he replaced, the Rev. William Decker Johnson, became pastor of "the largest Methodist congregation in Charleston."[5] It was all too neat not to have been arranged.

Four years later, William ran for bishop again at the General Conference in Kansas City, Missouri. This time, he was elected on the second ballot. Details are scarce—even if I could find the minutes, I'd have to guess at what went on behind the scenes. Still, AME insiders believed Papa's guidance and support had been essential. "No man," one of Papa's obituaries notes, "did more for Bishop Chappelle's election [in] 1912 at Kansas City than Professor Garrett.[6]"

The falling out between the two men began innocuously enough in March of 1916, when Papa left Columbia for Philadelphia to help prepare for the General Conference that would celebrate a century of African Methodism. Allen's president, the Rev. William Wesley Beckett, stood a good chance of being elected bishop. Papa may have been lobbying for Beckett, but he was also working for himself—he wanted one of the Church's general offices, the editorship of the *A.M.E. Church Review*. In the weeks leading up to the election, letters supporting Papa's candidacy appeared in the *Christian Recorder*.[7] Once the conference began on May 3, he and his allies continued their campaign—the Maker of Bishops knew his way around a general conference.

He did not help himself, however, by bowing to the will of the men who ran the Church.

Two days into the three-week long meeting, the bishops presented the list of delegates they'd chosen to serve on the thirty committees that would work throughout the gathering. Approval was supposed to be a formality —one newspaper called the bishops a "steam roller." A number of laymen had met earlier, however, and "perfected a temporary organization." Choosing a chairman and secretary, they'd passed a resolution demanding greater representation for laymen within the Church. Instead of approving the bishops' committees, the delegates balked, and "one of the leaders of the insurgents" rose to protest.

Little surprise: That leader was Papa. The laymen, he complained, had been left off "the all-powerful episcopal committee, which handles the moneys [*sic*] of the church and dictates its financial policy." This deprived them of oversight and the power to investigate the Church's financial secretary. Others supported Papa's position. Finally, the bishops capitulated, and "the entire list of candidates [was] rescinded for revision."[8]

None of this appears in official accounts, which makes it seem as if the conference ran smoothly, with no deviation from the bishops' wishes.[9] It did not, and Papa's insubordination made him a marked man. The "black princes"[10] of the church would not forget.

The editor of the *Review*, himself running for reelection, was activist and AME stalwart the Rev. Reverdy C. Ransom. On taking office four years before, he'd vowed to publish "the best thought of Negro scholarship in every department of knowledge." Naturally, this included articles on religion, as the *Review* was a church publication. But Reverdy sought—and published—insightful, thought-provoking articles on topics that ranged from politics to the sciences, from art to civil rights. Literary kin to the *Crisis*, the *Review* was often offered in a package deal with Du Bois's National Association for the Advancement of Colored People journal.[11]

The vote to choose the *Review*'s editor was taken during the May 20 morning session, four days before the end of the General Conference.

Before the results could be announced, however, the same Episcopal Committee Papa had made revise its list of nominees interrupted. Reverdy protested that an earlier ruling gave elections priority over other business. The bishops rejected his plea. Any report from their committee, they proclaimed, was always in order.[12]

The candidates were kept in suspense until the afternoon session. When the results were announced, Reverdy had won another term. It's worth noting that the *Christian Recorder* did not publish the vote totals as it did for other races. Two months later, prize safely in hand, Reverdy noted the "surprisingly large vote" for Papa. He himself had believed he'd easily win reelection, but he confessed he'd been mistaken. Papa "had almost caught [him] napping." And all because he'd forgotten his grandmother's advice— "Son, remember that it is always dangerous to be safe."

Unfortunately for Papa, Reverdy didn't stop there. Unable to resist ridiculing him in the pages Papa had hoped to make his own, Reverdy wrote, "Prof. Garrett is neither a contributor or [*sic*] subscriber to the *A. M. E. Church Review*. We have no means of knowing whether he has even seen a copy of it in years. This literary and pecuniary detachment may have had much to do with whetting the edge of the keen enthusiasm with which he conducted his campaign."[13]

A hundred years later, when Black men serve as generals and CEOs of corporations worth billions, the stakes (as is sometimes said of academia) seem too trifling for Papa's enthusiastic campaign. But the *Review* was a prize worth having. There were far fewer opportunities for Black men and women in Papa's time. Denying their ability, white Americans barred the advancement of Black people in business, politics, and education. Most Black men were employed as laborers or farm workers. Black women worked as domestics or washerwomen. A lucky few taught or found government work delivering or sorting mail, or cleaning federal buildings. Election as an AME general officer meant a salary of thirteen hundred fifty dollars a year (thirty-three thousand dollars today), as well as reimbursement for church-related travel. There would be opportunities to dispense patronage and build alliances, invitations to give paid speeches. Equally important, general office also brought the respect and acknowledgment the white world refused.

With so much up for grabs in elected offices (there was also sectional competition between North and South), AME general conferences could become raucous affairs, with accusations of impropriety, occasional fist fights, and, on one occasion, a delegate "leaping the room across the tops of the benches, pen knife in hand."[14] But there were also more sedate machinations that would have done credit to any smoke-filled back room.

Passed over for bishop in 1920, Ransom himself lamented the "combinations and organizations," "political machines," and "campaign methods, primaries and headquarters 'induced to win delegates whose moral sense [have] already been perverted by being schooled in these decadent methods.'"[15] And Richard R. Wright Jr., a staunch AME churchman, remembered he was told "it was impossible to be elected without spending money" when he ran for bishop in 1928. Asked to give "the leaders of large delegations . . . $500 each, to help needy delegates pay board and lodging," he declined and failed to win election.[16]

Clearly, there was as much politicking and horse trading as there was prayer and hymn singing at the quadrennial AME general conferences. Any machinations would, of course, have taken place behind the scenes, but it's just possible the delay in announcing the vote was part of a plot to keep Reverdy as editor. Papa made no accusations, but one anonymous supporter, identifying himself as Papa's "old friend," lamented that "it took all they could to keep C. G. Garrett from being elected editor of the *AME Review.*"[17]

Did the bishops thwart Papa's ambitions because he'd led the laymen's revolt that forced them to withdraw their nominees? Did they intervene because they'd considered Papa's reputation for combativeness and decided it would be asking for trouble to turn over to this insurgent one of the Church's public voices?

The *Christian Recorder* and other contemporary publications are silent.

Papa returned to Columbia, smarting from his loss in Philadelphia but hopeful about the possibility of Allen's presidency. Elected bishop at the General Conference, Beckett had been assigned to West Africa. He stepped down at Allen in June. Three men were touted as candidates to succeed him: Papa; the Rev. Robert Weston Mance; and the Rev. Sandy Simmons, an AME pastor who'd attended Allen with Papa. The boy from Laurens who'd been too poor to ride *and* have the drayman carry his luggage might now lead the institution that had helped make him.[18]

When Allen's Board of Trustees met, the members chose Mance.

Given his journalistic background, perhaps Papa himself provided the list of candidates that had appeared in *The State* before the General Conference. It's also possible the story was written by I. M. A. Myers, who worked with Papa on his newspapers and occasionally contributed to *The State*. Regardless, Papa's chances probably were never good. Of eleven Allen presidents during the half century between 1881 and 1932, only one—Joseph W. Morris—was a layman.

And, while Papa may have made bishops, he hadn't worked his way up the AME hierarchy as had Mance. Born in 1876 to more advantages and with better connections—a grandfather "was a prominent political leader during . . . Reconstruction"[19]—he was a second-generation AME minister who'd proven himself as a preacher and fundraiser, been a trustee of Allen and Wilberforce universities, and active in the governance of the AME church.

Given this record, Allen's trustees must have believed he would make a better leader, but there's a titillating family story that offers another possibility.

Despite their personal and professional relationship, and despite how tirelessly Papa worked for his election to the Sunday School Union and to the bishopric, there's no evidence William Chappelle supported Papa's quest for the editorship of the *A. M. E. Church Review*. Nothing if not savvy, perhaps he acted behind the scenes using intermediaries. And perhaps he stayed neutral—a bishop only four years, he may have felt it prudent to conserve his political capital. Still, if the race was as close as Reverdy implied, how much effort would William have had to make to help elect the man to whom (some thought) he owed his position?

And what about the presidency? As presiding bishop of the Church's Seventh District, William was also chairman of Allen's board. If he'd wanted Papa as president, the trustees would have had a hard time defying their bishop.

It was an article of faith among older family members that the last thing William wanted was to see Papa leading Allen. It wasn't that he thought Papa unqualified—William's opposition was personal because Papa had

Rosena Chappelle (Centennial Encyclopedia of the AME church).

had an affair with his second wife, Rosena. Just forty-one years old in 1916, she was eighteen years younger than the bishop. (Papa himself was about fifty years old.) Did anything really happen? Impossible to say: All of the parties involved are gone, and the bishop's descendants say his papers were destroyed in a fire. Still, even if both men's papers had survived (and they'd kept journals), I doubt that Afro-Saxon Methodists of their kind maintained records of their conquests and cuckoldry.

All the same, there's a part of me that would like the story to be true: It might mean I'm related to the comedian Dave Chappelle—*his* grandfather was William and Rosena's son.

What is true is that Papa "loved the ladies" (as his granddaughter, Jo, put it) and that more than a few reciprocated his affections. "Do you make many trips with your beloved husband now?" a family friend wrote Mama in 1937. "You had better keep up with him as you know how fond the ladies are of him."[20] Perhaps she was joking. All the same, while Jo and others of her generation didn't know about Papa's 1888 legal troubles, they remembered excursions with him to the country outside Columbia. Chauffeured by a young Allen student, they stopped at out-of-the way farmhouses where women (husbands conspicuously absent) welcomed Papa. Children were directed to stay with the chauffeur while Papa disappeared inside. He stayed far longer than might be explained by a simple exchange of pleasantries.

In 1935, when Jo was eighteen, Alfred and Mattie sent her to Columbia for the summer because they were afraid she might have tuberculosis. She was on the porch with Mama when two women and a little boy approached, the boy dressed up as if the women were determined he make a good impression. Mama ordered Jo into the house. Curious, Jo listened at the door. The women had come to ask for help because, they claimed, Papa was the boy's father. Mama would have none of it and sent them away.

Whatever her troubles with Papa, Mama kept them mostly to herself. When she complained in her letters to Baby, it was because he couldn't find work or didn't help out at home. She hinted at no improprieties. Still, one curious, very specific part of her will makes me think there were aspects of her marriage she'd reluctantly come to terms with, accepting them as the price of being Professor Garrett's spouse. The Lady Street house was in her name, but when she died, Mama didn't leave it outright to Papa.

Instead, she provided that he could continue to make it his home. There was one stipulation, however. To stay there, Papa, her "beloved husband," could not marry again.

◆ ◆ ◆

In mid-July 1916, the *Christian Recorder* published William Chappelle's screed condemning "Church politicians." In a piece that took up most of a front-page column, the bishop called out the laymen for their "lack of respect for those who [they] had exalted and consecrated as [their] leaders."[21] He was referring, of course, to the insurgents who'd forced the bishops to revise committee assignments at the General Conference. Papa responded two weeks later in a letter that appeared inside. Complaining that the bishops had left laymen off important boards that oversaw church business, Papa declared, "Such treatment is about what the South gives the Negro."[22]

That last bit of hyperbole must have been particularly irksome to the leaders of the haven of Black autonomy that was the AME church.

Both men toured the state to raise money for Allen during the summer,[23] putting aside their differences for the sake of the school each loved.

Despite that shared commitment, matters came to a head in October, when William invited the former South Carolina governor Coleman "Cole" L. Blease to speak at Allen's opening exercises. "Coley," as white admirers called him, was an incorrigible racist, a man who opposed Black education, claiming it would "ruin a good field hand, and make a bad convict," and who announced that "marital infidelity seems to be their [Blacks'] more favorite pastime."[24] Allen alumni protested.

At bottom a pragmatist—he once said he'd "follow anyone, even the old devil himself part of the way,"[25] who could give Blacks the balance of power by splitting the Democratic Party—William reasoned that Allen might benefit from supporting Cole. For his part, Cole had been defeated recently in the state primary and was considering a challenge to the Democratic candidate in the general election. He may have wanted to assess his chances of attracting Black support. At any rate, when William introduced him, the bishop said he'd carefully gone over the records of the state's former governors before deciding who to ask for "the protection for our people." And, he said, more bluntly: "We want the friendship of our white people. I want money. I am going to ask him for it to help lift up our people."[26]

Around the same time, Papa published a series of "scurrilous articles . . . against the bishop"[27] in his newly resurrected newspaper *The Light*. Those issues of the paper have disappeared, but he must have attacked the bishop for giving Cole a forum. It would explain why Chappelle took time for a jab at his former ally. "Who are they, anyway?" he asked of those who dared "to dictate the policies of a great church." Answering himself, he said, "They aren't known outside of their own backyard."[28]

The sally must have hurt. In the months and years to come, Papa would attack Chappelle again and again with all the fury of a spurned lover, accusing the bishop of graft and corruption and of insufficient patriotism in the war the nation would soon enter.

When Allen awarded "65 diplomas and certificates" in 1917, it marked the first time in more than thirty years that Papa had not been part of the festivities at the school whose "defense and advancement" he'd made "the pride and purpose of his life."[29] Reverdy Ransom—*The State* misspelled his first name as Beverly, though it described him correctly as editor of the

A. M. E. Church Review—preached the baccalaureate sermon. Surely Papa must have known and been filled with chagrin.[30]

He had to work, but what he did right after he was let go isn't clear. Papa's not listed in the 1917 Columbia City Directory. The following year, he's listed as "principal" of the Mayesville Institute, a school fifty miles east of Columbia.

Known as "Little Tuskegee," the Mayesville Educational and Industrial Institute was founded in 1886 by Emma J. Wilson, a former slave so determined to get an education she walked seven miles to school once Reconstruction began. She attended Scotia Seminary in Concord, N.C., hoping to go to Africa as a missionary. Instead, she returned home to Mayesville to start her own school and "found Africa at her own door." Like Booker T. Washington's Tuskegee Institute, Mayesville offered some academics, but every student was expected to learn a trade such as carpentry, masonry, blacksmithing, or dressmaking. In addition, students operated a farm where they grew their own food as well as produce and cotton sold to support the school.[31]

By 1915, classes included algebra, chemistry, and psychology in addition to the reading, writing, and arithmetic tradesmen would need, so Wilson may have hired Papa as part of an effort to broaden the school's curriculum. After his time at Allen, however, he must have felt as if he were starting over, slipping back decades to the Winnsboro Colored Graded School he thought he'd left behind. There were just five hundred students and only twelve teachers. The budget was about six thousand dollars, and Wilson was constantly on the road raising money. One sign of the school's lack of resources came in a notice Papa printed in *The Light*, advising that winter weather had burst pipes and damaged the school's heating plant. Opening had been delayed till February 4.[32] Initially, Papa must have approached the job with his customary energy and enthusiasm, but he wound up staying only a year or two. He understood the value of knowing how to do for oneself, but he was not convinced industrial education was the only way to uplift the race.

9

Change and the Great War

The loss of salary and status that came with Papa's exile from Allen University marked a downturn in the Garretts' fortunes, but it was only one disruptive event in a time of downturn and loss. Millions of African-Americans had begun to flee the South, heading north, to the Midwest, and out west in search of greater opportunity. Their departure would come to be called the Great Migration. When it began, ninety percent of Black Americans lived in the South. By the time it ended some six decades later, a little more than half did. And then there was the upheaval of the Great War that America would join in April 1917. Both turned the world, and the Garretts' lives, upside down. Like all sons and daughters, Papa and Mama's children wanted to make their own lives. Driven by the war and the African-American exodus, they'd soon begin to drift away, abandoning Columbia for Washington, Philadelphia, and New York.

The first harbinger of change came in 1913, when Tap, Mama and Papa's second son, left for New York to study at Columbia University. Eighteen, he'd just graduated from Allen's College Department. Two years before, older sister Mattie had become Allen's first female college graduate (she'd also been salutatorian)[1] and was teaching in Allen's elementary school. Older brother Ralston had abandoned college after the birth of his out-of-wedlock daughter. Which made Tap the new hope of the family—years later, Mama would recall him as "especially favored"[2] among her children. As she and Papa watched him board the train to go north, their sadness at his departure was tempered by pride.

Tap, too, must have anticipated a glorious future—he scrawled his name boldly on the flyleaf of his copy of *The Poetical Works of William Wordsworth*, above the inscription "Student, Columbia Univ. New York." The *New York Age* even took notice in a column headed "News of the Churches" (Tap had joined Bethel AME), noting that he'd come to the city

Casper Garrett, Jr., Tap, ca. 1913, when he went to Columbia University. Collection of the author.

to do "post-graduate work."[3] This wasn't true. Even though he'd finished Allen's College Department, Columbia's 1914–15 catalog lists Tap as a freshman. It's the only time I've found his name in the records. Years later, his younger sister, Mills, would decide she was going to get a master's degree, even if it took years of graduate summer school. Tap wasn't as hungry. Perhaps he gave up or flunked out because he was too young to resist the attractions of the big city.

Still, even if he didn't get a degree from Columbia, Tap maintained his connection with Harlem. Though he went home to teach at the Howard School, he'd return during the summer. Tales of his Harlem sojourns must have helped three of his brothers decide that, in time, they too would also venture north.

◆ ◆ ◆

Ralston and Maceo were the next to leave home, although it took Ralston a while. After graduating from Allen's normal department in 1909, the same

Ralston "Nick" Garrett, undated. Collection of the author.

year Tap had, Ralston went to South Carolina State, at least according to family stories—I've found no record of his attendance.[4] Three years later, however, he'd fathered a daughter, Frances Peacher Garrett. She was called Frank. Her mother's name was Sarah Francis, but I know nothing else about her. Ralston remained in Columbia for a few years working as a tailor, which suggests he tried to shoulder the responsibilities of fatherhood. By 1917, his draft registration card shows he'd moved to New York, where he worked as a Pullman porter. Mama and Papa raised Frank as their own.

Ralston's draft card included a question about dependents—parents, wife, child, or siblings under twelve years old. He answered: "one sister." Surely he couldn't have meant Mills, who was eleven and Mama and Papa's responsibility. But if he meant four-year-old Frances, why didn't he call her his daughter? Perhaps he thought the Army might deny him the chance to serve. But then why not just leave the space blank, as Frank was also his parents' responsibility?

And then there was Fleming Maceo, whose erratic life gave Mama and Papa cause for despair, even unto his untimely death.

There's something a little, well, askew about him in a family picture from 1904 or 1905. Just seven or eight, he sits blank-faced, eyes cut to one side, folded hands between his knees. Had he just been chastised by Papa? Did he not want to be there? Was he upset because older brothers Nick and Tap got to wear ties, while he'd been forced to wear the same kind of doily-like Little Lord Fauntleroy collar his four-year-old brother, Marian, sports in the picture? I wonder sometimes if there isn't some other, more profound, reason for Maceo's off-kilter affect. Others who've seen the picture wonder, too.

The letters of his I've seen are rife with spelling and grammatical errors, the handwriting rounded and suggesting a child's tongue-between-lips effort. Perhaps Maceo's teachers thought he was slow or (worse, from his educator parents' point of view) stubborn. Today, he might have been diagnosed with a learning disability. That's just speculation, though. All I know for certain is that while Maceo attended school at Allen (as did the rest of the Garretts), I've found no record of his graduating. That's not surprising—of all their children, only Maceo (and Ruth) caused Mama and Papa so much worry.

He was the first to wed, marrying a woman named Jimmie Bethea in Marion County, S.C., on February 23, 1916. For reasons unknown, Maceo told the probate judge who married them he was twenty-three years old. Actually, it was a day before his nineteenth birthday. Jimmie was seventeen. Mama dutifully recorded the union in the family Bible, but Maceo's listed just after Mattie, who'd married Alfred E. Simons, son of a farmer and Baptist preacher, the Rev. Isom Wesley Simons. They courted for four years before finally marrying on December 27, 1916. Did Maceo wait ten months to tell his mother? Or did she want her Baby to appear first? Both entries look like they were written with the same pen, but—make of it what you will—a careless ink blot partially obscures the city "Marion" in Maceo's entry.

◆ ◆ ◆

For colored Americans of Papa and Mama's time, "[p]atriotism was as Afro-American as religion,"[5] so Papa's three oldest sons—Ralston, Tap, and Maceo—would serve once war was declared on April 6, 1917. Single, with no dependents, Tap was the first to go, registering for the draft on June 5th.

He lied about his age, giving his date of birth as March 1, 1894. He'd actually been born in 1895, but perhaps he thought making himself a year older would better his chances of serving.

Tap's teaching contract had been renewed for the fall, but he was done with the classroom, fired up by the same patriotism that motivated South Carolina's whites.[6] A troop of Boy Scouts telegraphed President Woodrow Wilson to offer their services; a girls' marksmanship class accepted the invitation of a city "machine gun company . . . to become its auxiliary"; and a group of women formed a "Red Cross society unit," which promptly began making pillowcases.[7] Surely, however, Tap and other Black Columbians understood why W. E. B. Du Bois called for Negro Americans to "close ranks," "forget our special grievances," and join the fight for democracy.[8] They needed to do so to claim their rights as citizens.

Two days before war was declared, Blacks held a "mass meeting" at First Calvary Baptist Church and voted to tell Governor Richard Irvine Manning they wanted to support the war effort. Not everyone favored the resolution. One man declared that white people would not "ask you whether you want to enlist. They'll just take you out and shoot you, if you don't." He was shouted down. Order returned only after physician Matilda A. Evans mounted the stage and began to sing "My Country 'Tis of Thee." Richard Carroll urged Black men to enlist, even though they would serve in segregated units. "We've had . . . jim crow street cars; jim crow cemeteries, churches and schools," he said. "Now let us have a jim crow regiment, surgeons and hospital corps."[9]

Carroll understood the limits of Black activism and understood, too, that incremental progress was better than none at all.

Papa was part of the delegation of about a dozen Black men who met with Manning to assure the governor of Black Carolinians' loyalty and to ask for "military training and instruction" and "the organization of a colored regiment" with "Negro officers."[10] Later that year, he and "a few representative colored men" met with Manning again. (William Chappelle was not present at either meeting, which must have pleased Papa.) The governor pronounced himself delighted with the participation of Black South Carolinians in the war effort, saying that he "felt sure they would continue doing their part whether on the farm, in the work shop or rank of battle."[11]

Tap was aware of the discrimination Black men faced in the armed services when he registered. How could he not have been, especially since Papa had written the Navy (traditionally, the most segregated service) to ask what kinds of assignments Black men could expect aboard ship. A Lt. Cmdr. L.B. Porterfield[12] replied that there was "no legal discrimination shown against colored men in the navy." However, Porterfield said, "as a matter of policy . . . and to avoid friction" Black men were assigned as "cooks, stewards and mess attendants, and in the lower ratings of the fireroom; thus permitting colored men to sleep and mess by themselves." When the *New York Age* printed Porterfield's response, it concluded that "little opportunity will be furnished the Negro to become gunners in the Navy during the present crisis."[13]

◆ ◆ ◆

Patriotism and a young man's desire for adventure aside, Tap must have had more personal reasons for wanting to serve. He was twenty-three years old and lived at home with Papa and Mama. For all that Allen, Benedict, the many churches, clubs, businesses, associations, and secret societies provided to make Columbia something of a haven for Afro-Carolinians, it was still a small town where a man saw the same faces day after day in church, in school, on downtown sidewalks, and on the streets of Waverly. To be sure, he was active in that community, serving as secretary of the local branch of the NAACP.[14] Still, what fulfilled Papa must have been confining for a vigorous young man in the prime of his life.

Though the *New York Age* called him "vice-principal of the Howard public school, Columbia, S.C.,"[15] Tap was only a teacher, just one of twenty-four.[16] He likely had nearly fifty students in his classes—there were 1,174 students at the school in the fall of 1916.[17] And if he'd hoped for promotion, he must have noted that Principal Nathaniel J. Frederick was nearly forty years old, young enough to occupy the position for years to come. From time to time, then, Tap must have looked out the window as his pupils droned on, dreaming of another, better, life.

That opportunity came in late May, when Capt. J. M. Graham of the South Carolina National Guard appointed three prominent Black Columbians—Bishop William Chappelle, the Rev. Richard Carroll, and physician John H. Goodwin—to help select fifty-two candidates for officer

Tap in his World War I uniform. Collection of the author.

training at the Fort Des Moines Provisional Officer Training School. Subject to the same rules as whites, Black candidates were expected to be college educated, "of good moral character,"[18] physically fit, and between thirty and forty-four years old.

Within a week after he'd registered, Tap was accepted for training as an officer. He and the other men left June 15, traveling in "a special coach"[19] on the Carolina Special, which ran from Charleston (with a stop in Columbia) to Cincinnati. "[A]n abandoned cavalry post"[20] near Des Moines, Iowa, the fort had been chosen for "this most important . . . historic, . . . military experiment"[21] after the NAACP and the Central Committee of Negro College Men pressured Woodrow Wilson and the secretary of war to provide Afro-American officers for Afro-American soldiers. (One man who was part of the effort described it as "[c]olored men . . . fighting the Government in order to wring from it permission to fight for it."[22]) The generals and the secretary of war believed Black men would make poor officers, but they agreed to provide a segregated camp, placing it far out of the way in the hopes the experiment would attract little notice should it prove a failure.

Training was supposed to last until September, but officials decided to extend it another thirty days. "[A] few . . . faint-hearted fellows" left, "giving as a reason that 'the War Department never intended to commission colored men as officers in the army.'"[23] Tap seems to have been one of them. His name is not on the list of officers commissioned at Fort Des Moines, and his "Final Statement" pay record says he received an honorable discharge on September 14, 1917.[24] But Tap's service record lists him as a second lieutenant, with service dates from December 1917 to January 1919, and his name appears on at least a half-dozen "muster rosters" in 1917 and 1918.

Clearly, Tap returned to the Army, though he didn't serve with the 92nd or 93rd Infantry Division, the two all-Black units that saw combat and gave the lie to white canards about Black inferiority. Instead, he remained stateside, spending the war at Camp Sherman in Chillicothe, Ohio, with the 158th Depot Brigade. It was a unit that trained new recruits and processed returning soldiers for discharge.

Ralston was next to enter the Army. Four months after registering in June of 1917, he was inducted and sent to Camp Upton, N.Y., as part of Company L, 367th Infantry. Six months later, he was promoted to corporal—"Ralston says address him as Corp. R.P. Garrett next time as he is no longer private Garrett," Mattie informed Alfred—and then to sergeant five months after that.[25] On June 10, 1918, he sailed for France aboard the USS *America*. Originally, the SS *Amerika*, a German passenger liner, it was seized when the United States entered the war and used to carry troops across the Atlantic.

After two months of combat training in France, the men were sent to fight in the St. Dié sector, Vosges, as part of the 92nd Division. The division, whose men wore buffalo shoulder patches and called themselves "Buffalo Soldiers," in tribute to the famed nineteenth-century Black cavalrymen, suffered thirty-four wounded and four killed. At one point, the Germans bombarded the men with shells containing leaflets asking them "to throw their guns away and come over to the German lines where they would find real friends."[26] None did.

Four months into his stay in France, Ralston was promoted to mess sergeant—a separate rank then and the equivalent of staff sergeant today.

He doesn't seem to have seen combat, but his rank likely allowed him to avoid the work given most Black servicemen—"loading and unloading supplies, clearing roads, digging trenches, removing disabled equipment and barbed wire, and burying dead soldiers."[27] He remained in France for several months after the November 11, 1918, Armistice, sailing from Brest on February 8, 1919, and arriving in Hoboken, N.J., nine days later. Ralston was discharged on March 8 at Camp Meade, Md.

That December in Philadelphia, he married Corinne Bellamy, daughter of a D. S. D. Bellamy of Florida.[28] What little I have found suggests an AME connection—Corinne's father's identified as a professor, abbreviating the title "Prof.," in a list of pastors and laymen attending an AME conference in Marianna, Fla., and he served as state superintendent of the AME church's Sunday schools. He was also "vice president and manager" of Jacksonville's Afro-American Investment Company.[29] According to the 1930 census, he owned his own home worth two thousand dollars and was a manager of real estate sales. Like Papa, he was one of those religious, civic-minded leaders important to their communities in their time but now forgotten.

◆ ◆ ◆

By contrast with his brothers', Maceo's was a blemished Army career. He registered for the draft on January 5, 1917, in Fayetteville, N.C., where he worked as a "garment cleaner" for W. T. Collier's Service Cleaning Company. Seventeen months later, he entered the service. He served just five months, much of it with the 153rd Depot Brigade at Camp Dix, N.J., before he was discharged on December 19, 1918.

Most of Maceo's Army records were destroyed by fire—as were Nick's and Tap's—so I have only his final pay voucher. Two notations suggest that the Army was ready to be shut of him, even if the war hadn't been over. Neither is dated, but one states that Maceo was "[t]o forfeit $7.50 of his pay per month for three months." The reason was not given. The second note states that Maceo was docked "$5.26 for Trans. of guard fr Camp Dix NJ to Atlantic City NJ and return to Camp Dix NJ." Again, the infraction is unstated but, given that Maceo was stationed at Camp Dix, he must have gone AWOL in Atlantic City.

– 10 –

Patriotism at Home

World War I gave Papa's sons—even Maceo—a chance to prove their patriotism by enlisting. It gave Papa a chance to buttress his by attacking the man who'd forced him out at Allen.

In early 1918, almost a year after the United States entered the war, he accused Bishop William Chappelle of "saying he was with the Germans, they would whip the world, [and] he hoped they would come over here and f[l]og America."[1] Papa didn't stop with that attack on the bishop's patriotism. He went on to allege that William had voted against recommending Tap to become an officer. Richard Carroll, who chaired the committee that helped assess candidates, denied anything untoward, declaring that the three members had all striven "to do our duty impartially." Moreover, he said of the bishop, "I have never seen a man act fairer."[2]

In the end, it didn't really matter. If William did vote against Tap, the other two members (and the white National Guard captain who likely had final say) supported him, and so Tap *had* gone to Fort Des Moines and received his commission. Papa knew this when he published Carroll's letter; in fact, he'd run a story in *The Light* two weeks before, reporting that Second Lieutenant Casper G. Garrett, on leave in Columbia, had married Cornice Gertrude Christie on December 13, 1917. (She was the daughter of the Rev. David A. Christie, the AME minister who'd married Mattie and Alfred the year before.)

Another man might have let matters rest. Papa was not that man.

As he saw it, William's opposition to Tap was just one more example of how the bishop had "carried [their quarrel] to our family." He claimed William had slandered him by charging that he had used church funds to take Mama to the 1916 General Conference. And, he said, the bishop had "refused to pay our daughter her salary for teaching in Allen and her husband sued him for it, won the case, and then Chap looking like a sick mule

Tap's wife, Cornice Christie Garrett. Collection of the author.

with the botts in his nose, had to pay the claim. Then he carries his animus to young Garrett and Mister Simons—and he will carry it to us in the other world."[3]

"Mister Simons" was my grandfather, Mattie's husband, Alfred E. Simons. In June or July of 1917, he, too, had put in for officer's training school. His application was supported by letters from prominent Columbians, including one from Mayor L. Ashby Griffith, though the mayor showed a notable lack of effusiveness when he attested that he'd known Alfred "for several years and as far as my knowledge goes his moral character is good."

Ashby's lukewarm endorsement—not William's animus—may have had more to do with why Alfred wasn't accepted as an officer candidate. (Having failed to qualify, he'd soon leave to seek work up North.) Papa told the truth about Mattie's salary, though. She'd continued to teach at Allen after his departure, at least until the end of 1916. She may have resigned because she and Alfred had finally decided to marry, though it's possible she was let go because she was Professor Garrett's daughter. At any rate, early the next year, now Mattie Garrett Simons, she sued the school for "sixty-five dollars, balance on salary for the previous term."[4]

By April 1918, William had had enough of Papa's attacks. When Papa denounced him "as a 'would-be Kaiser of the negroes and self-styled black German,' and declared that he is 'encouraging slackers, traitors, and cowards among his race by his indiscreet talks on the war,'"[5] the bishop sued for libel. Given that Papa continued to attack the bishop, he must have been acquitted or the case dismissed—I've found no court record. It's just possible, though, that Papa was foolhardy enough to continue to indulge his animosity even if the court had found him guilty.

Most of the wartime issues of *The Light* are gone, and with them whatever William said to lead Papa to dub the bishop a "would-be Kaiser." In the weeks before the United States entered the war, he'd advocated American neutrality, protesting "the hypocrisy of attempting "to make other people do right when we ourselves are guilty of violating the very rules" for which the nation was about to ask its young men to fight and die. William was speaking, of course, of Black Americans, "whose rights are abnegated and to which she [the United States] pays no attention whatever." (Lest he offend powerful white Columbians, he quickly assured them that Afro-Carolinians were "just as true to 'Old Glory' as any man who treads her soil," and would "follow her to conquest or defeat."[6])

Once war was declared, William would declare that "[t]he president of these United States and the [C]ongress have spoken, and there is no position for me to take, but [to] follow their lead."[7]

By contrast, Papa never wavered in his support of the war. Too old to serve at age fifty-three, he backed the war with the same "patriotism and fierce loyalty"[8] most Black South Carolinians professed. Small American flags appear at the top of the front page of surviving issues of *The Light* well into 1920.

In addition to urging his readers to volunteer, Papa used his newspaper to press them to buy Thrift Stamps. Aimed at those who could not afford the cheapest fifty-dollar Liberty Bond, these twenty-five-cent stamps were sold at the post office or by letter carriers. Once purchasers had sixteen of them, they could exchange them for a five-dollar certificate redeemable after five years. Twenty certificates could be pasted onto a savings card, valued at one hundred dollars after five years.[9]

South Carolina officials hoped to raise thirty million dollars,[10] and Papa exhorted his readers to participate: "Every loyal Negro must buy a Thrift Stamp. Only slackers and cowards will refuse to aid in this struggle. . . . Every stamp puts the [K]aiser farther from victory. Hit him a lick."

The *Columbia Record* reprinted Papa's summons approvingly, concluding that Negro "leaders are patriotic and are giving wise counsel."[11]

It's doubtful, however, the *Record*'s editors thought Papa's counsel wise when he declared that "[a] man who fights for a country's flag should vote for its rulers."Urging the soldiers to pay the poll tax, Papa noted that, although they were "registered as soldiers and must take a man's place in this mighty conflict," they weren't "full-fledged citizens unless they pay their poll tax, which enables them to be voters."[12] Whites understood they needed Black Carolinians' support to win the war. Once it had been won, however, they had no intention of weakening their own control by granting them the right to vote.

The thing is, white South Carolinians had always been ambivalent about enlisting Blacks as soldiers.[13] The first time Papa and his cohort met with Gov. Manning, Manning "stressed the fact that they [Negroes] could serve the country in the present time in other capacities than soldiers." He even asked Papa and the other members of the committee "to use their influence" to stop Blacks from leaving the state because "the South was the place for the Negro."[14] Later that year, the governor went to Washington to join the state's congressional delegation in opposing the training of Black and Puerto Rican troops at Camp Jackson, the new Army training facility near Columbia. The prospect of thousands of armed Black men so close to the city must have provoked much white anxiety. In the end, the War Department sent the Puerto Ricans elsewhere and placated white Columbians by assuring them that Blacks would be trained separately at Camp Jackson.[15]

All the same, Black men did their part. More than twenty-five thousand Black South Carolinians would serve in the war—"one-seventh of adult black males."[16] Three months after the Armistice, Columbians turned out to welcome back members of the 371st Regiment and their white officers. "White people were as numerous as Negroes along the line of march" that began near the State House and ended at Benedict College. For once, though, they gave way so Afro-Columbians could celebrate their heroes. "[B]y common consent, the Negroes were given places of vantage along the curbing," although "the whites were not less cordial in their welcome, filling windows in office buildings, standing on tip toe on the streets in order to see over the heads of the Negroes. . . ."

Even so, the newspaper couldn't help speculating that the presence of so many African-Americans likely meant "that more dinners were left uncooked and more babies left unnursed than at any time since Sherman invaded the city." And whites who followed the parade to Benedict must have bristled at the speakers who made it clear that the men who'd fought, and died, in France were owed a debt. The Rev. Nathaniel F. Haygood, pastor of the Sydney Park Colored Methodist Episcopal Church[17] (CME), called for the veterans to be given "a man's chance" and the opportunity to serve as jurors and police officers. Bishop Chappelle demanded the vote, declaring, "We want freedom; we want a part in our government and a place on the juries, and we will not get our due unless we get it."[18]

White Carolinians did not intend to honor that debt, something Mama understood a month later when she came across a poem in *The State* by former Columbia mayor Wade Hampton Gibbes. He called his poem "Our Soldiers at Home," a title that suggests he'd written a paean welcoming back the men who'd fought so bravely. He had—but only the white ones.

As for the rest, he put Haygood, Chappelle, and the returning Afro-American soldiers on notice—nothing would change. Whites would maintain their supremacy.

The poem's too odious and too long—thirty lines—to quote in full, but after three verses celebrating those who "did their duty . . ./To save the world from a German Hell," Wade issued the returning colored soldiers a direct warning:

> The Negro still the Negro must be;
> He may fight the hordes of Germany.
> He may follow his leaders beyond the sea,
> Yet if in the South he choose to dwell
> He must keep to himself and bear him well;
> No race shall rule the Saxon free[19]

When she'd finished reading, Mama was so incensed she picked up her pen to respond. Unlike his doggerel, her response is worth quoting in full. (The struck-out words are hers.)

To the editor of [The] State;

~~I trust you will not deem me too bold in this attempt~~ Please grant me the privilege of making just a little comment on the poem of Mr. W. H. Gibbes which appeared in the columns of your paper on the 25th inst.

On reading these lines, I was reminded of something which happened to me when a small child. My mother had some sugar[-]coated pills and being overly fond of sweets, I took three or four of them and sucked the sweet coating off. After which I was made na[u]seous by the bitter substance which was the real pill.

As I am very patriotic, I read everything I see about soldiers and when I saw the heading or subject of this poem ("Our Soldiers at Home"), I knew there was something worth reading.

Well, I began and enjoyed it immensely. And thought how gracious and good of him to speak thus of "our boys." Meaning, as I thought, all the boys. Imagine the painful surprise when I found he only meant a part of the boys to be included in his good wishes, while the other boys—just as brave, just as true—were threatened and told "to keep to yourselves."

I know Mr. Gibbes didn't stop for one moment to think of the harm which might follow such words as he ended his verses with, neither did he consider how deeply he would wound the feelings of those same Negro boys who "had fought the hordes of Germany and had followed their leaders to the sea." They each and all, as the records show, played the part of men.

Can you not, in this hour of rejoicing accord them their ~~same~~ rights to live as men? How much better it would have been to have ended your beautiful poem thus:

> And the slackers spawn be the spawn of hell
> The Negro now our brother must be
> He has fought the hordes of Germany
> He had followed his leaders beyond the sea
> And if in the South he still chooses to dwell
> We must help him to bear himself up well,
> One race shall all Americans be.

Then ponder the problem and ponder it well,
We must lift them up inch by ell,
Then there'll be no servile rebels to quell.
None must be under bond, all must be free
To win this fight so none must flee
What tale of you shall history tell?[20]

Mama had heard the speeches and sermons about the responsibility of colored men and women to support the war effort, heard the arguments that service was the path toward full citizenship, as well as the counterclaims that nothing would change and that Blacks should expect to return to their subordinate status once the war was over. But these weren't simply abstract discussions to her. Three of her sons had served and, in fact, Ralston just been discharged about two weeks before Gibbes's poem was published. Mama was lucky—all her boys had returned home safely. Others were not so fortunate. Although only twenty percent of the Black men who served in France saw combat, they died at more than twice the rate white soldiers did.[21] Mama must have known mothers who'd lost their sons, witnessed the aftermath of the sacrifices Black men had been willing to make for the country, the price they might pay in their quest for equality.

In the end, however, she didn't send her letter and poem to *The State*—she must have known it unlikely the newspaper would publish either. Indeed, *The State*'s editor, William Watts Ball, would soon tell a correspondent he'd "concluded that with increased black activism and protest for political rights, it was 'highly necessary that white solidarity be unbroken.'"[22]

Perhaps Mama kept her poem to herself because she understood the viciousness white people were capable of. Indeed, Black veterans had already been the victims of mob violence by the time Gibbes published his poem on March 25, 1919. One Black man had even been beaten to death because he continued to wear his uniform.[23] The violence was a bloody prelude to a bloody season of white-instigated carnage the NAACP's James Weldon Johnson would dub Red Summer. In Charleston, martial law was imposed after white sailors began a riot that led to the deaths of three Black men. In Elaine, Ark., at least one hundred were killed when Black sharecroppers tried to organize a union. (Some estimates put the total at more than twice that.[24]) In Washington, D.C., white servicemen rioted for four days and Black men took to the rooftops with rifles to defend their homes and families. But the violence wasn't confined to the South. More than twenty incidents of white-provoked violence occurred in thirteen states from "Texas to Nebraska, Connecticut to California." Clashes, and deaths, occurred in New London, Conn.; Syracuse and New York, N.Y.; Philadelphia, Coatesville, and Scranton, Pa., and Chicago, Ill. At least fifty Black people were lynched, "[h]undreds—most of them black—were killed" and "[t]ens of thousands were forced to flee their homes."[25]

Knowing the brutality that whites were capable of, Mama abandoned the draft of her poem and her letter, leaving them for me to find a hundred years later.

But perhaps there was another reason she folded the letter and poem and put them away. The Richland County Board of Education would soon vote to hire her as supervisor of its rural colored schools. The prospect of a job that would allow her to support her family led Mama to conclude (as Papa too often did not) that sometimes it was better to keep your own counsel.

11

Mama Comes
into Her Own

The bittersweet time of loss and of change continued with Mattie's 1916 wedding to her longtime beau, Alfred. Soon, the war would take Papa and Mama's older sons from home. Younger ones would leave for college. But if 1916 marked the start of a time of inexorable change, it also marked the beginning of Mama's coming into her own. With Papa out of work, the pampered drayman's daughter who'd once tried to fry a Thanksgiving turkey launched her own career, first as a teacher and then as supervisor of Richland County's rural colored schools.

Forty-five when she went back to work, Anna Maria Threewitts was a remarkable woman, though I didn't always see her that way. Even before I began searching through archives and poring over issues of old newspapers for evidence of Papa, I was predisposed to like him more. It was a predisposition formed in the 1970s and '80s, when books by Black women like Alice Walker and Gayle Jones tarred Black men as nasty, brutish, and shiftless. Some were, of course; far more were not. Determined to celebrate the achievements of Black men little noted (and long forgotten), I saw writing about Papa as part of that celebration.

It was easier, too, to find out about him. Papa's children and grandchildren may have failed to preserve his letters, speeches, and copies of his newspapers, but the world took greater notice of him than it did Mama. She was a woman, of course, and she wasn't a public person, so her name appears in fewer than a hundred newspaper stories, often as an adjunct to Papa. Twice, she's even referred to as his "queenly wife"![1] With fewer opportunities to enter the public sphere, she labored in relative anonymity, much of her life until her death in 1944 escaping public notice.

Mattie Garrett, photo given to Alfred during their courtship. Collection of the author.

It's one of history's unhappy oversights: If Papa's AME church activism is the history of the laymen's quest for a greater voice in church affairs, then Mama's in the Richland County schools is the history of separate, and unequal, education in South Carolina.

She'd taught before, of course, in Winnsboro in the 1890s, when Papa was principal of the graded school. That was only briefly, however. This time, now the sole support of her family, Mama was in it for the long haul.

She began in Laurens County in November and December of 1916, a month or two after Papa left Allen, timing that suggests she wanted to help pay for Mattie's wedding to Alfred. She was paid just $12.50 a month, the equivalent of about three hundred dollars today. The following year, Mama returned to Laurens County for three months—January, February, and May.[2] The superintendent's ledgers don't say where she taught, but according to family stories, it was in Clinton, a small town of about three thousand people sixty miles northwest of Columbia and nine miles east of Laurens.

Within two years, Mama had been appointed supervisor of Richland County's rural colored schools. She continued as supervisor from 1919, when she would have been forty-seven, to 1925. Afterward, she taught into the 1930s and was still working in 1941.[3] The 1922 Columbia City Directory lists her separately, just above Papa, as "superv Rural Schools," as does the business card I found in the papers Ruth left me. Mama must have been proud.

When she was hired in October 1919, the County Board of Education specified that it would contribute no more than four hundred dollars a year to her salary. A few years later, the Board recommended increasing Mama's salary to one hundred dollars a month, making the increase contingent on an increase to fifty dollars a month in a grant from the Jeanes Fund, a Northern philanthropic institution dedicated to improving Black education. Founded in 1907, it provided money for the hiring of Black "supervising teachers" like Mama.

As supervisor, Mama was responsible for more than sixty schools. Many were one-room, one-teacher schools in remote parts of the county. Her job kept her away so that, she told Mattie, "I'm only home Saturday and Sunday and if your letter doesn't reach me by Saturday it is a week before I get it." She traveled "on the train or streetcar to my first stop and then from one school to the other through the County. I don't have much trouble to get around but must go every day—must spend every day in someone's schoolhouse. As I said before, I like it all but being away from home so much."[4]

In April of that same year, 1920, Mama provided a summary of her activities: "My work is quite strenuous just now, what with school closings and speechmaking, tests, reports, recommendations and such like I am kept constantly on the go. I am now down in the [S]andhills looking after a building project which I'm trying to put on foot for the summer. I hope to build ~~three~~ [strikeout original] two houses, between now and October."[5] Two years later, Mama was in the midst of another "building campaign": "We put up four buildings this year," she wrote, "and hope to put up four more by the end of the year. That means *work*."[6] [emphasis original] Her labors didn't go unrecognized. When the cornerstone for the two-teacher Rock Hill Colored School was laid on Labor Day in 1925, Mama's name was on it.[7]

What Mama omitted from her list of activities were field days, which involved lessons or demonstrations in "domestic science" (home economics)—an important part of the national effort to lessen the drudgery of farm women's lives and to improve farm families' diets[8]—as well as games, performances, and speeches. At one field day, abandoned by two teachers who stayed home because of bad weather despite their promises to come, Mama reported that she'd "taught twenty-two lessons Saturday 'all by myself.'"[9] It wasn't unusual for her to work weekends. One Sunday was spent at four church services and a parents' meeting. She left home at eight o'clock that morning and did not return until eight o'clock that night.

And, as if all that were not enough, Mama was a joiner, like the tens of thousands of Black men and women who flocked to fraternal and sororal orders after slavery. Next to the church, these organizations were an important part of African-American life, providing insurance coverage, wages for employees and, later, a focus for civil rights activity. Most important, though, as one organization put it, these groups were "your own and not second-hand."[10] By the 1920s, they boasted more than 2.2 million members and twenty million dollars in property that included hospitals and "social-welfare institutions."[11] Mama was active in at least three—the Heroines of Jericho, a Masonic women's auxiliary; the Order of Good Samaritans and Daughters of Samaria, founded in 1847 to work for temperance reform; and the United Order of Tents. She was particularly active in the last institution, rising to the post of president of the executive board. Incorporated in 1867,[12] the women of the Tents were active at least twenty years earlier in helping runaway slaves. (The name, according to some accounts, came from the tents in which those slaves sheltered.) By the time Mama became active, the organization's social welfare mission including caring for the sick and providing burial insurance. Members' dues were $6.50 a year, according to an undated leaflet Mama wrote. The dues included insurance premiums, and the organization paid sick benefits of two dollars a week and death benefits of one hundred dollars. In addition, "There is a home where old, sick or broken-down sisters are cared for and where dependent orphaned children are cared for during childhood and given a start in life."[13]

Always indefatigable, Mama even found time to enter her handiwork in the Colored State Fair, winning first place for her asparagus fern and second place for her canned peaches, canned beets, and blackberries in 1925.[14]

◆ ◆ ◆

The pace of what she called "the work," as if it were a mission or calling, took its toll: If Mama hadn't been born with the stoic optimism character-istic of her generation of Black Victorians, then surely she would have had to develop it. "This is my busiest season," she told Mattie one year as spring approached, "trying to get ready for the state Association [teachers' meet-ing], looking after two buildings, teaching industrial classes and 1001 other things all at once. Maybe I'll survive it, if I do, I'll be a 'good one.' The only way I keep up is by going to bed as soon as I get in, if I feel the least jaded from a long drive. I am in bed now, with books and papers all around me. Everyone else is asleep save me; I still have lots to do."[15] In another letter, Mama confessed that she "had been sick, didn't work for a whole week. The doctor says I'm about broken down and must stop trying to take such long walks."[16] (Walking must have been how she got from school to school when there was no other way.) But she continued to work—the family needed the money she brought home.

As Mama established herself, Papa did what he could, publishing *The Light*, working as a notary, selling insurance, and organizing occasional AME conferences. None of this likely brought in much, so Mama's was the Garrett family's sole regular income for more than a decade.

"Whenever money runs short, I can't help but get blue,"[17] she told Mattie in 1923. A few years later, Mama complained that "Dad is down and out, with no money, no work."[18] Things were no better at Christmastime in the early 1930s: "Money was scarce," Mama lamented, "and we tried to stretch it over so much ground, but it was a seeming impossibility to make ends meet or to get worthwhile things."[19] And yet, throughout, she was adamant she would find a way. "I know we have absolutely nothing, but I should starve before I beg," Mama proclaimed. "I have some plans on foot for a little money and if they do not materialize I shall go into service somewhere but shall ask no man for a penny as long as I have health and strength."[20]

Indeed, for a few months on the eve of the Great Depression, Mama did go into service, caring for a seventy-eight-year-old woman who was "crip-pled and cannot get about much except in her rolling chair." The work was pleasant enough, apart from having to be away from home at night. Later,

Mama would ask Mattie to help her find work "as a nurse-companion to an aged or invalid person" in Washington. "I want something for the last of April or 1 May. My school will be out then and I want something light for the summer. If I could get a place which suited me I'd give up teaching altogether."[21]

Mama's declaration that she'd abandon teaching was the result of some momentary frustration, but the can-do spirit that would have allowed her to accept a job as a caretaker explains why she exploded when she found out that Papa had asked Alfred to lend him ten dollars "if you have it." He needed, he explained, "a little lift for a few days to meet an urgent demand."[22] Alfred sent the money, perhaps enjoying some satisfaction in having his father-in-law beholden, but Mama was furious.

"[Dad] did not let me know he had written Alfred for money because he knows I would not approve of it," she told Mattie. "I am much humiliated that he writes begging letters to you children and to others. . . . I am humiliated beyond words and shall let your Daddy know it."[23] (A few years later, she'd changed her mind. "Give Dad all you could spare," she told Mills. "He needs it. They haven't paid any money at Allen in a long time and folks have many obligations to meet which they cannot meet."[24])

Further humiliation came when Mama and Papa were sued again by creditors in 1922, 1925, and 1926.[25]

Still, despite her complaints about the "gaps under which I am struggling,"[26] somehow Mama managed, and well enough so that I wonder sometimes if she exaggerated her penury.

Though it's possible to detect a whiff of envy (as well as pride) in Mama's account of a visit from friends "touring South Carolina and Georgia"[27] in their chauffeur-driven car, she and Papa had an automobile, too. They'd gotten "a little Ford touring car"[28] in 1923 to ease the burden of Mama's "long walks" to her schools. Likely, given her complaints about money, it came used. Columbia's Southern Motor Company listed two new 1923 Ford Touring Cars in an ad in *The State*—one was three hundred seventy-five dollars, and the other was three hundred dollars. (List price seems to have been a little less than four hundred dollars, about sixty-six hundred dollars today.) Older models were cheaper. A 1922 "tourer" was two hundred fifty dollars, and a 1921 model was one hundred fifty dollars, about twenty-five hundred dollars in 2022. Advertised as "the lowest cost transportation for five passengers," Ford claimed that its Touring Car "can go anywhere a motor car can be driven, at the lowest possible cost, and with the comfortable certainty that it is built to withstand the hardest usage."

The little tourer had front and rear bench seats and three doors, one on either side for rear-seat passengers, and one on the right side for the driver. (The floor-mounted emergency brake was on the left side, smack in the middle of where the driver's door would have been.) A cloth roof folded down behind the rear seat. It had no windows, but there was a sloping windshield. "When we drive it in the rain," one modern-day car collector quipped, "the inside of the windshield is like a waterfall." A 177-cubic-inch engine delivered about twenty horsepower, and there were two forward gears and one reverse. The top speed was close to forty miles an hour. I'd be surprised if Mama drove that fast.[29]

South Carolina didn't require drivers' licenses until 1930, so she taught herself with Papa's help. "I am learning to drive it," she wrote in 1923, six months after her fifty-first birthday. "I've made two trips to the country driving myself, but Dad goes with me. He won't trust me to go alone yet. Guess I will go alone in a week or two."[30] Papa went with Mama, but he preferred to let others drive—two weeks later, she was chauffeuring him and teaching Mills "so that she can drive Dad sometime[s] when I am away or busy. She did very well for the first trial, but will have to continue much practicing before she is able to handle it alone."[31] (Mama's faith in Mills's driving abilities did not change. When she told Mattie that Mills had written "of her achievements as a driver," she made sure to add "I tremble each time I think of it.")[32]

There were just "26 miles of roads" in and around Columbia and the surrounding county in 1920, many "still unpaved and all . . . unmarked." It was worse in the country, where "buggies had cut deep ruts," making the roads "practically impassable for automobiles with their narrow 'pneumatic' tires." "Sometimes the trip is so rough," Mama said of one sixteen-mile drive, "but I grit my teeth and go on."[33] One hopes the copywriter didn't exaggerate the Ford's ability to survive "the hardest usage."

Alas, Mama's little Ford seems to have lasted less than a year. Shortly after they bought it, Papa found himself in court again when fourteen-year-old Christopher was charged with "reckless driving" after he collided with a vehicle driven by Fred B. Shackelford, owner of a women's clothing store. Shackelford claimed "painful injuries." The jury awarded him one thousand fifty dollars in damages. "Of course we are not worrying over it because the car will be sold and whatever it brings in is all the man will get," Mama reported. "A judgment can only be collected where one has something and Dad hasn't."[34]

◆ ◆ ◆

The Ford may have been gone, but no one could take away Mama's new skill. When a friend asked her to share the driving on a trip to Tuskegee, she leapt at the chance. It's a five- or six-hour drive today; the two women did it over two days in 1928, leaving Columbia at five o'clock in the morning on Sunday, May 27, and driving to Macon, Ga., where they stopped for dinner with friends. They continued on to Columbus, where they arrived at seven o'clock in the evening. They'd "made it in good time," covering three hundred twenty miles in fourteen hours, an average of about twenty three miles per hour. The next morning, they left at seven o'clock and arrived at Tuskegee by nine-thirty that night. "We made the same or better time coming back," Mama reported.[35]

I marvel every time I think about these two genteel colored women on the road nearly thirty years before interstate and state highways. The South Carolina State Highway Department's 1926 "Condition Map" shows no paved roads between Columbia and Aiken, a small city about thirty miles east of Augusta, Ga. Instead, roads are marked "other types under construction" and "open to traffic."

Mama and her friend (she doesn't name her) were lucky. They had no breakdowns or flats, but Mama would have known what to do. "You should have seen us patching an inner tube yesterday," she reported after another trip. "We did it nicely."[36]

Still, it was eight years before the first edition of *The Negro Motorist Green Book*, which listed hotels, gas stations, restaurants, and other businesses that catered to Blacks. That lack of accommodations explains why the two women broke up their journey by stopping with people they knew. It was safer than depending on the kindness of (white) strangers. Years later, Jo thought it possible the force of Mama's personality was such that when they were hungry she "just walked up and went into the front door and asked for food in such a way that they brought it to her on a tray."

Perhaps. More likely they packed box lunches and lemonade and drove so long the first day because there was nowhere for them to stop. Nonetheless, they enjoyed their adventure. "It was a lovely trip," Mama reported afterward. "There was a drive over Pine Mountain between Macon and Columbus. This in itself was worth quite a deal."[37]

In the same 1923 letter in which Mama announced the purchase of the Ford, she also told Mattie about her new house. She and Papa had purchased a lot at 2116 Lady Street and were building the house that would be home for the rest of their lives. Colon, Ruth, and Mills were still in school—Colon probably at Meharry Medical College's dental school which, with Howard University, produced most Black dentists until well into the twentieth century—so she accepted that "I won't yet be able to get what I want in a house."[38] Later, she'd tell Mattie that "I am not having but seven rooms, four bedrooms, an entrance hall which will serve as both living room and parlor, a kitchen, dining room and back." Once the plumber began, Mama crowed that she was "getting one of my life-long desires, a bathroom, with hot and cold water."[39]

Ever practical, Mama built a "tenant house first" because it was "a good investment."[40] It turned out that she'd inherited Anderson Threewitts' gift for making money. "No matter what, you must manage to save something," she once advised Ruth, the daughter who probably most needed to hear it. "Remember, it is terrible not to have a dollar laid down."[41]

In time, Mama would own four rental properties in Columbia, advertising in the *Palmetto Leader* when she needed tenants. In 1943, they brought in $62.50 a month—the equivalent of more than twelve hundred dollars today. And when Papa wanted a farm, she bought more than three hundred acres of land outside the city. "I've always wanted money and city property," she explained, "but Dad has had his heart set on a farm for years and since this was a bargain and close [to] home I let him get it."[42]

The house on Lady Street had something else dear to Papa's heart—room for floor-to-ceiling bookshelves on a second-floor landing. Passing them as she walked up- or downstairs during her Columbia sojourns, Jo promised herself that one day she'd have a library like Papa's.

Like his papers most have disappeared, but I'm lucky enough to have a few, though not his copy of *The Souls of Black Folk*, which wound up at S Street after his death. When Jo told Du Bois's daughter, Yolande, that her family owned a copy, Yolande said, "Don't let my father know. He'll want it—he gave away all his copies long ago."

Many of Papa's books—histories of American literature, *The Merchant of Venice*, an anthology of Milton's "lesser poems," a study of drama—must have been texts for classes at Allen. Others show the range of his interests and give the lie to the notion that interest in Black history and literature was a phenomenon of the 1960s. I cherish Papa's copies of an anthology of the work of Paul Laurence Dunbar; *Masterpieces of Negro Eloquence*, edited by Dunbar's widow, Alice Moore Dunbar; an autographed copy of AME minister and professor Charles H. Wesley's biography of Richard Allen; AME Bishop Charles S. Smith's account of a voyage to Africa in 1894 and Bishop Levi J. Coppin's account of his tenure in South Africa; Maude Cuney Hare's biography of her father, Norris Wright Cuney, a Texas politician and businessman; and a collection of poems by Josephine D. Heard, wife of AME clergyman and diplomat William H. Heard.

All bear Papa's distinctive angular signature on their endpapers.

Mama took pride in her willingness to do whatever was necessary to support her family, but there was something else in her determination as well. Papa's misfortune provided the reason, but Mama welcomed the chance to leave home and enter the world. "I'm so glad you are able to get out," she told Mattie when Mattie wrote that she'd found work, perhaps as a maid or waitress. "It means a lot when one is not confined to home all the time. Home becomes a prison when one is tied there by the constant grind and drudgery. Then[, too,] the little money you make helps defray expenses and allows you to put by a dollar now and then."[43] An early feminist, though she wouldn't have described herself that way, Mama once argued that "it was not right to address married women by their husband's initials"—i.e., Mrs. C. G. Garrett—"even though it was conceded by custom and grammar to be proper."[44] Instead, she preferred to be called Anna M. Garrett, addressed as a person in her own right, not as an extension of her husband.

She enjoyed the responsibility and the power—a modicum, but power nonetheless—that came with being supervisor of Richland County's rural colored schools. She oversaw construction of school buildings, hired and fired teachers. "I could get you a place in this work and $80.00 per month," she wrote in one of her periodic attempts to lure Mattie home, "as these people will take anyone who I recommend."[45]

The work also allowed Mama to go away for summer continuing education classes. These were often at Benedict or at Allen, but sometimes they were farther away, at Hampton or the "State College for Negroes" (now South Carolina State University). The summer institutes exposed her to new ideas, provided respite from children and home, and allowed her the chance to renew ties with women friends from across the state and throughout the South.

The sessions at Hampton or in Orangeburg also provided other opportunities for travel. One letter mentions a "class trip" to Jamestown, as well as plans for a Baltimore jaunt with a friend. They, and "the work," also gave Mama a forum for activity in the State Teachers Association. At one meeting, the members "offered a resolution to give me a rising vote of thanks for the help I had been." But, Mama reported, "I was so busy, they had to call me and tell me they were doing the honor."[46] With something of the same not-altogether-convincing modesty (a trait she shared with her daughter, Mills), Mama called her invitation "to deliver the annual address at the commencement exercises of the training school at Moncks Corner. . . . the biggest joke of the season, to me."[47]

As personally and professionally fulfilling as these honors must have been, Mama was driven by a sense of mission as she joined the "common cultural project . . . of racial uplift"[48] that engaged the unknown Black leaders of her time. Early on, about three years after she was appointed supervisor of colored rural schools, she went to Orangeburg to "take the short course in Home Economics." She'd been offered a job performing home economics demonstrations. She wasn't going to take it—it paid less than she was earning—but she'd decided she needed the course so "that I may be able to help my people more."[49]

These kinds of sentiments occur rarely in Mama's letters—she was too practical and too much a realist. Still, her fifty-first birthday put her in a reflective mood. She wondered if her life had "been for any good. . . . [I]f

I've been any help to humanity. . .," before concluding, "You know I believe each of us has a mission to—or a duty to perform while passing this way and that we will suffer eternal regrets if we fail to do those things for which we were made."[50]

It was good she had that sense of mission—the lack of state support for colored education made it as necessary as the summer courses at Hampton or State. Searching for signs of her in the Richland County directory of teachers and schools on my first trip to the State Archives in 2011, I was surprised to find handwritten directories compiled in dime store note-books until 1968. Did a tradition-bound school board prefer to do things as they'd always been done? Or was there simply no money for luxuries like typewriters and printed directories?

If the latter, Black South Carolinians suffered unequally from the lack of resources. Though there'd been progress in the decades since school attendance was made mandatory during Reconstruction, salaries were low and many teachers barely qualified. Whites controlled local school boards that set the length of the school year, allocated funds, and hired teachers. The result was that ninety percent of "colored schools" were one-room and one-teacher, and many Black children went to school just three months out of the year. Most high schools were white-only—Black Columbians did not get their own until 1918.[51]

"The Negro schoolhouses are miserable beyond description," the state's first supervisor of rural schools wrote in 1911, just eight years before Mama was appointed supervisor of Richland County's rural colored schools. "Most of the teachers are absolutely untrained and have been given certifi-cates by the county board not because they have passed the examination, but because it is necessary to have some kind of a Negro teacher. Among the Negro rural schools I have visited, I have found only one in which the highest class has known the multiplication table. Just three years later, the state superintendent of education said, "It is not a wonder that [Black stu-dents] do not learn more, but the real wonder is that they learn as much as they do."[52]

Mama's plans for a "write your name" week one December need no explanation. More telling was the state teachers' meeting attended by eigh-teen colored school supervisors. Their "splendid" reports showed "that the state has become aroused and is trying to help the poor ignorant Negroes," but the reports also showed how much remained to be done. One woman, Mama wrote, "reported finding four children who had never been outside the confines of their own farm and had never seen any other children. One is 14 yrs. old."[53]

Reading through two decades of Richland County School Board meeting minutes and superintendent's ledgers, I noted mentions of school improvement association prizes, reading contests, and provisions for teachers' libraries. All were for white schools. In April 1917, the board authorized summer school for Black teachers, as long as it did not cost more than one hundred dollars. White teachers were given three times that. In July, the board reported that "the summer school for Negro teachers opened . . . with seventy-five present. By contrast, forty-five white teachers had enrolled in their separate summer course and "regular attendance was about thirty." Two years later, the board allocated five hundred dollars for the white teachers' summer school. There was no mention of summer school for Black teachers. A year later, in June of 1920, the Board minutes noted that "[i]t was found necessary to dispense with the colored summer school."[54]

When the Richland County Board of Education voted to rehire Mama as long as the Jeanes Fund paid half her salary, the Board decided to pay African-American teachers half the salary of white ones. Trustees of individual schools were free to pay more, but "at their own expenses [sic]." The school system reported almost equal numbers of Black and white students the following year—9,887 and 9,661—but only one hundred seventy-nine Black teachers as compared with three hundred forty-one white teachers. Black teachers taught an average of fifty-five students, whereas white teachers taught only twenty-eight.[55] In other words, Black teachers were expected to teach twice as many students for half the pay.

Mama never complained, but her letters reflect the unfair allocation of funds.

"The city school situation is becoming serious," she wrote in 1921. "There will be two or three classes conducted in the basement of Zion Baptist Church to help relieve the congestion." In an undated letter, she reported that since she had been given no vacation, the county superintendent had told her to take off until after the first of the year, presumably because he could not pay her.[56]

Things were no better in the 1930s.

"We began our eighth month tomorrow," Mama wrote in April 1937. "Our people have raised their part but the trustees still haven't said definitely what they will do. However I think our folks will raise the balance if necessary." A year later—the letter is undated, but I believe it to have been written in the spring of 1938—Mama reported that "[w]e are heading toward our last weeks, maybe days. The State Board is cutting all Negro schools in the state so we expect to be cut also. Can't say how much till the P.T.A. Committee sees the trustees. We were hoping for eight months the same as last year but when any cutting is made we are the ones to feel it most."[57]

12

"We Are as Well as Common"

As Tap and Ralston made ready for war, their younger brother Colon finished Allen University's normal department and entered Lincoln University in the fall of 1917. Known as "the Black Princeton" because many of its early white teachers were graduates of that Ivy League institution, the school (then all-male; it now admits women) was about two miles north of Oxford, Pa. (Its founder, and first president was the Rev. John Miller Dickey—more than a century later, one of his great-great-nephews would be my classmate at Sidwell Friends.)

A year later, Marian, the son Mama had named after herself because she'd hoped for a daughter, would leave for South Carolina State in Orangeburg after finishing at Allen.

Both boys would prove disappointments.

Colon did well at first—he's listed in the second freshman honor group in Lincoln's 1918–19 catalog.[1] After that, though, he disappears from the records. Minutes of the University's faculty meetings from his time at Lincoln are missing. Surviving minutes often note the names of students dismissed for various offenses, so I suspect the missing ones would show Colon was asked to leave because, sometime in 1919, he'd married a woman named Henrietta Duckett.[2] Lincoln required "[m]oral and gentlemanly conduct" and warned that "[s]tudents delinquent . . . in character, and of bad influence" would be "dropped from the roll."[3] Perhaps Colon's marriage to Henrietta was enough for him to be expelled. Or perhaps it took something more—the birth of their son, Colon Hunter Jr., on November 1, 1919.

If she is the same Henrietta Duckett I found in the 1910 census, she was from Scuffletown, where Papa was born. But she must have had some

Marian Garrett, undated.
Collection of the author.

connection to Philadelphia—she and Colon were married there and Philadelphia is only fifty miles from Lincoln. Later, after she and Colon had moved to South Carolina, she'd visit Philadelphia from time to time, and the two would eventually settle in the city.

Mama must not have been pleased that Colon had left school to take a wife. She'd have been hard-pressed to come up with the one hundred fifty-three dollars in tuition and fees Lincoln required each year, even if Papa had still been principal of the Mayesville Institute. It also probably didn't help that Colon married a woman whose father was a farmer who didn't own his own land. Anyway, Mama dutifully recorded her children's marriages in the big family Bible—all except Colon's and Marian's (and Ruth's second), as if ignoring them meant they hadn't happened.

And, as for Marian, whom Jo remembered as "the nicest uncle," if it weren't for a letter he wrote Mattie, I might not know he'd gone to South Carolina State. The 1940 census says he only finished high school, the same census that says Tap made it only through eighth grade and that Maceo finished four years of college (I suppose he could have lied). In April 1918, however, Marian wrote Mattie from Orangeburg to assure her he was coming home "to put in a full summer's work so as to be fully prepared for next year." He added that "if I have ever liked a place it is this one; and, I'm trying to make good use of my time here or at least I have tried to do so."[4] The 1918–19 catalog shows why Marian needed to put in that "full summer's work." Although he's listed as part of the Normal department's senior class, there's an asterisk by his name. He'd been suspended.[5] That September, he registered for the draft hoping, I suspect, to prove his worth to Mama and Papa by going overseas as had Ralston.

Unfortunately for him, the war ended in November.

Two years later, Marian married a woman named Mary Evelyn Fisher. (She was known as Evelyn.) The news came as a surprise to Mama. "Had a letter from Tap telling of Marian's marriage, the first I knew of it," she informed Mattie. "He didn't give any particulars only said that 'in a way, it was a sad affair.' I have answered Tap but asked no questions. I do not care."[6] And just to show how little she did, Mama didn't record that marriage in the family Bible either.

◆　◆　◆

By 1920, Marian was living in New York, as were four of his brothers. He and Colon worked as Pullman porters. Ralston and Maceo were tailors, though Ralston would soon join Marian on the railroad.[7] Mattie, Mama and Papa's oldest, would also leave home, but as with her courtship and marriage, it took a while. She stayed in Columbia when her husband, Alfred, left to go north in 1917. A year later, she went to him, taking their firstborn, Jo. She stayed seven months, long enough to get pregnant, then returned to give birth to their second child, Alfred Jr., in 1919. She'd leave again when the boy was old enough to travel, come back ten months later in May 1920 to give birth to a second son, named Casper after his grandfather.

Mattie would depart for good in the spring of 1921, leaving Mama with Ruth, age sixteen; Mills, age fourteen; Chris, age twelve; and Frank, age nine. In addition to her teaching and work with the Tents, Mama kept house and took care of her four youngest. She had help, of course; Allen boarders who worked for their keep, much as William Chappelle had for

Colon, Ralston, and
Tap Garrett, undated.
Collection of the author.

Bishop Dickerson when he came to the school in the 1880s. (One hopes
Papa and Mama provided more comfortable accommodations than the
shed the bishop offered William.) The women cleaned and did laundry; the
men chauffeured Papa once the Garretts had a car.

Once Mattie was gone, though, Mama just couldn't seem to find good
help. "I can't get anyone here to stay in the house who will make themselves
solely responsible for the kiddies,"[8] she complained. She went once with a
friend to try to get a girl from an institution she didn't name, perhaps the
Fairwold Home for Delinquent Colored Girls, but had no luck.

Two years after Colon left Lincoln, his wife, Henrietta, came to stay
on Lady Street. The 1922 Columbia city directory gives Colon's occupation as teacher—he'd received a one-year Richland County certificate on
the strength of his normal school diploma. "Henrietta is coming to stay
with the children," Mama reported, "and I am so glad. I wish she was here
now."[9] But Henrietta had her own two-year-old to care for and likely didn't

believe her marriage vows required her to take over her mother-in-law's household. Within a year, Mama was looking forward to Henrietta leaving and hoping she could "get someone . . . to move in who will take an interest in things."[10] Four years later, in 1926, Mama's youngest, Chris, married. He was just seventeen years old; his wife, Charlisena, a year younger. They, too, lived on Lady Street. Despite the presence of another daughter-in-law, however, Mama confessed, "My home keeps itself now. . . . [T]hings 'just go.' I push back the worst of it when I go home some weekends."[11]

But Mama didn't just lose a babysitter and help around the house when Mattie left Columbia to make a life for herself with Alfred in Washington—she lost her Baby and her confidante, the oldest child that she was closest to. Mama's loss was, however, our gain. Accustomed to talking every day, the two women now wrote to maintain their closeness despite the five hundred miles that separated them. The earliest of Mama's letters is dated March 25, 1918, when Mattie departed for the first of her Washington sojourns. A few of Mama's letters survive from each of Mattie's times away, but their correspondence flowered once Mattie was gone for good in March 1921. They continued to write for the next twenty-two years—the last of Mama's letters I have is dated December 16, 1943, two months before her death at age seventy-one.

Family lore says Mama wrote Mattie on a Monday and expected a letter from Mattie by Friday. If she didn't get a letter, Mama wrote immediately to ask what was wrong. Only two hundred letters survive of the more than one thousand letters Mama could have written. I'd like more. Still, with the one hundred additional letters from Mama to Mills between 1939 and 1943, they're enough to give us a picture of her life and the Garretts' doings in the 1920s, '30s, and '40s.

Mama and Papa operated in their separate spheres, but surely Mama, "the bedrock and guiding star of all his efforts and of every success in his married life,"[12] was Papa's equal. It wasn't just her knack for making money, one that helped fund his activities (including *The Light*) from 1916 on. Papa wrote for the world, and so his was a public voice. More private, Mama's writing was more vital. She enjoyed putting words on paper, stealing a few moments at the end of long days of work to order and set down her thoughts. It was something of a ritual. Mattie was her audience, and so was Mills, once Mills also left home. So she speaks to them, her voice closer to her own than Papa's in the surviving fragments of "Reminiscences." There, dignified and aloof, he wrote to prove himself (despite more than forty years as teacher, lawyer, newspaperman, and AME church leader), hoping to ensure his life and work were not forgotten. Mama's letters are relaxed and informal, her voice as intimate as if she's rocking on the Lady Street porch in the cool of a summer evening, exchanging hushed confidences with Mattie and Mills.

She wanted to keep Mattie up to date, of course, even hoped one day to lure her Baby back to South Carolina. Occasionally, as she and Papa grew older, Mama allowed herself to express that hope openly. She must have known it was only wishful thinking: With each passing year, Mattie and Alfred settled into the lives they'd made for themselves in Washington. But whatever her secondary motives, Mama wrote because she was driven by the impetus all born writers share: She knew a good story when she heard one, and she found it impossible to keep the good stories to herself.

And so Mama wrote Mattie about births and deaths and marriages. She wrote about heat, drought, hard rain, and winter storms; about drunkards, fools, and adulterers; about friends escaping north with eager optimism, and the return of some shamefaced in failure. She wrote about the comings and goings of friends and neighbors to Washington, Philadelphia, New York, Cleveland, Detroit, and, somewhat exotically, Colorado or Los Angeles. She wrote about the successes and failures of the Colored State Fair, Benedict and Allen's openings and commencements, and summer teachers' institutes in Columbia, Orangeburg, and Hampton. She wrote about organizing school field days, her sororal activities, church meetings and the AME conferences and Sunday School conventions she and Papa attended. She wrote about the younger children who remained at home, a smaller brood that included her adopted granddaughter and, later, other grandchildren who came for the summer.

The letters reveal a woman of intelligence and a mordant wit that must have been the equal of her husband's. She had a wicked sense of humor, one inherited by the "Three Graces" (as their father dubbed them): my mother Ruth, and the sisters who bracketed her, Jo and Phyllis. Pungent and playful, Mama's language reminds me of her fellow Southerners Flannery O'Connor and Eudora Welty. I have her poem correcting Wade Hampton Gibbes. And I have her lyrics—"God bless the founder of our school/While yet she lives, we pray./And when she's gone, her memory/ Will live in Founder's Day"—set to the tune of "Auld Lang Syne" for the Anna Boyd School Founder's Day.[13] Taken with her letters, they're enough to make me wish Mama had tried her hand at fiction.

Noting that an acquaintance "did finally die," Mama concluded "and so the devil has one of his best lieutenants."[14] When Alfred wrote asking for a seven hundred dollar loan, she asked how he'd gotten the idea she had that kind of money. "I would," she said, "have to sell all of my entire family in order to realize that amount of ready cash."[15] When Mattie reported that she and her family were down with the flu, Mama chided her for wanting to "keep the monopoly" on it. "Turn it loose," she advised, "and let someone else have it."[16] A Baptist convention threatened to bring ten thousand visitors to Columbia one June, which led Mama to write that, "I guess we will all be dead when it's over. If that number of Negroes comes here at one time they will swamp us."[17] Evangelist Billy Sunday's visit prompted this: "Columbia is gone mad. . . . His hell-fighting campaign began today and he is expected to convert every white man, woman, child, and their possessions."[18] And when a woman she and Mattie knew found work "in a little one-teacher country school," Mama predicted that "the children will obey her through fear" because she "is so ugly."[19]

And then there was the phrase with which she ended many of her letters and that I considered for the title of this book—"We are as well as common." It's an antique phrase with the laconic fatalism of the blues—more effusiveness might tempt fate—something a dirt farmer might have written, eying the sky and contemplating the months before harvest. Times are hard, but we're still here.

Perhaps Mama vented her frustrations about school budgets and difficult local trustees, evenings when she and Papa sat in the parlor reading and listening to the radio. She did so only occasionally, however, in her letters. Complaining about a difficult field day, Mama wrote, "The group handled that day is the hardest in the County—the group around Hopkins [an unincorporated community in Richland County]. I sometimes despair of ever being able to help those people at all. They are ridden and ruled by a set of ignorant Baptist teacher-preachers who do not help them at all yet will try to keep good influences away from them. However, I still try to do my best."[20] Another time, similarly frustrated, she wrote, "I am getting settled down to my work now, and feel more and more like cussing these 'low down niggers' than ever. Only I 'cuss' them by ignoring them."[21]

It's the only time the word appears in Mama's letters, though Jo remembered that she sometimes dismissed people as "scrub niggers." But perhaps she didn't—Jo quickly corrected herself: "Scrub pines," she said, leaning forward in her wheelchair in the high-rise apartment at the assisted-living center where she lived after she'd given up her home. "She called them scrub pines." Whichever phrase she used, Mama meant to connote flawed character as much as caste (or color) superiority.

Her letters show a particular ire for William Chappelle and family, but the Chappelles weren't her only targets. When rumors spread that the Rev. T. H. Wiseman, pastor of Bethel AME church, had gotten a young woman pregnant, she was furious: "Columbia is all aglow [*sic*] over the reputed condition of Seretha Cannon with Wiseman as the cause. The men of the city are speaking of running him out of town, if she will openly confess. The poor girl is teaching at B.T.W. That dirty skunk should be killed, and he would be if Columbia's Negroes had any spunk." Four months later, she gleefully reported that Seretha had played and "Mrs. Wiseman led the dance at Julia Saxon's wedding." (The daughter of Columbia teacher Celia Dial Saxon, Julia Saxon married James Woodbury.) In December, Mama wrote that Wiseman was returning to Bethel. "Some of the folks are fussing but none of them have the manhood to rise up and demand his dismissal."[22]

Though I found very little about Wiseman and nothing about his alleged dalliance with Seretha Cannon, I did learn that he was a gospel singer as well as a preacher. Some of his recordings with the Bethel Jubilee Quartet—about which he corresponded with none other than W. E. B. Du Bois!—have been digitized and preserved at archive.org.[23] I listened to a few, marveling at the technology that allowed his ghostly voice to echo across the decades, nearly one hundred years after the recordings were made.

Mama wrote about disasters natural and manmade—the deaths of nearly one hundred people when the roof of Washington, D.C.'s Knickerbocker Theater collapsed after a two-day blizzard in 1922 (Mattie, I'm sure, had been nowhere near the theater); her "first wreck. . . . nothing but a 'turnover' caused by another car running into us"[24]; and the woman who lived nearby who "killed her common law husband last week."[25] Her letters mention about ten suicides or suicide attempts. She called them an "epidemic . . . among our people" in one letter, describing a woman who killed herself, her son, and unborn child; a boy who poisoned himself "because his name was not called on the honor roll at commencement time"; and attempts by "[t]wo young girls."[26] After a woman "went out into the back yard and shot herself in the head," Mama lamented that "we are getting more like the white folk everyday."[27]

She would have made a good police reporter or gossip columnist—she had the requisite appetite for the peculiar and the sensational. But what really underlay her complaints about Wiseman, the Chappelles, and even the unfortunate suicides was her disappointment that some people were unable to observe the essential proprieties. It wasn't simply good manners; it was necessary to maintain order in the world she and Papa had made.

Of all Mattie and Alfred's children, Jo might have known Mama best. She spent time with her and Papa during visits to Columbia as a child in the 1920s. Though Jo believed Mama "never approved of me because I was flip-tongued like my father," Mama had a special liking for her because she was the oldest of her Baby's eight children and a daughter to boot. Later, after she'd finished at Washington's Miner Teachers College in 1937 (she was just twenty years old), Jo came to South Carolina to teach in Clinton. Mama had taught there years before, as had Mills, the aunt Jo came to consider almost a sister.

Jo remembered Mama as a remote, reserved figure, "proud and persnickety," with a precise way of speaking. "She was," Jo said, "the most proper lady I have ever met." Her children called her "Queen Anne" and "Miss Damn" (for "Damn Peculiar"), though certainly not to her face. Out running errands one day, Mama stumbled on Main Street and broke an ankle. She hobbled back to her car, "too proud to ask for help or accept it from anyone," and drove home because "it wasn't anybody's business that she had broken her ankle." Another version of the story makes it clear Mama was one tough old lady—in it, she took the streetcar home.

Unfortunately, unless Mama had the misfortune to fracture her leg twice, neither story appears to be true.

But she did break her leg, and it did happen on Main Street. Walking near Lorick & Lowrance Hardware, located between 1527 and 1529 Main, early in the afternoon of May 19, 1932, Mama stumbled and fell. A Mrs. F. A. Baker[28] saw it happen and called a doctor. Mama had fractured her leg—she lay in Good Samaritan Hospital for six days. I know all this because Mrs. Baker filed an affidavit in support of Mama's claim against the city, noting that she'd seen several people fall at the same spot and had even almost fallen herself once.[29]

Phyllis, Mattie's third and youngest daughter, provides the only other firsthand glimpses of Mama. There's a caveat, though: When Phyllis and her younger brother, Mac, spent about a month on Lady Street in July and August of 1943, Phyllis was sixteen and coming of age in the turbulence of World War II and a changing world. Mama and Papa were in the twilight of their lives; she was seventy-two, and Papa was almost eighty. Small wonder, then, that Phyllis depicts Mama as reserved—"the coldest person I have ever seen; she talks in one tone all of the time"—and a stickler for formalities. When the daughter of an AME minister visited, Mama told Phyllis and her cousin, Marian, that they "were ignorant, ignorant of the finer things of life. [She] came to see you and you have not repaid her visit. You must do so this very day."[30]

Phyllis had looked forward to four weeks free of Mattie's constraints and the chance to get to know her cousins Marian and Christopher Jr.—the children of Mama's youngest, Chris. At home, she had to abide Mattie's strict rules—Jo, Ruth, and Phyllis could go to parties as long as Mattie approved of the hosts' parents and an older brother was willing to bring them home on the streetcar afterward. Phyllis hadn't counted on finding herself chafing under the same restrictions in Columbia. Like Mattie, Mama refused to let Phyllis go out unless she approved of the people Phyllis wanted to visit. Unlike Mattie, however, Mama wouldn't have allowed her to go to parties, especially if she suspected there'd be dancing. A few years before, when she hosted fourteen of Mills's senior Benedict College classmates, the *Palmetto Leader* reported that there'd been "dancing and the playing of games." A week later, the newspaper issued a correction.

"[T]he word 'dancing' was an error, for there was none."[31] Surely Mama's concern prompted the correction.

Mama's belief in the proprieties was the reason she noted, with ill-concealed disapproval, a girl who "ran away and married last summer to a boy she only knew about a week."[32] Another woman married and then went back to school without revealing her marriage until Christmas.[33] "Secret marriages is the fad now," Mama observed. "Several were pulled off this year amongst the public school teachers."[34] Mama was passing on gossip, but another story was the unconscious expression of her deepest fears about what might happen to Baby, or any of her daughters: "The terrible thing of which Honey Punk [yes, that's what Mama called her] wrote is that Ethel has a child, and it seems that she won't tell whose it is nor do they know where she had been. She just got off the train, went by and ordered the doctor and went to her aunt's house in Orangeburg and the child came in a few minutes. . . . I wrote her not to worry over things she couldn't help but you know how keenly she must feel the disgrace and just the two of them."[35]

It's not surprising, then, that when her adopted daughter, Frances, got pregnant in high school in 1930, Mama sent her away to join her father in New York.

The circumstances of Frances' birth explain Mama's ambivalence. On the one hand, Mama had genuine sympathy for the motherless child she affectionately dubbed Frank. On the other hand, given her faith in the proprieties, Mama must have felt Ralston had let her, and the family, down.

In the end, Frank's is one of the saddest stories in Garrett family history.

Looking back on what happened, I have to wonder whether Frank truly felt wanted. In 1922, Mama sent her, Ruth, Mills, and Chris to spend the summer with Mattie in Washington. Mills and Chris came home in September. Frank stayed for another year with Alfred and Mattie and their three (soon to be four) children. Ruth stayed, too—there was a boy Mama wanted to keep her away from; I'll tell you more about that soon.

Almost ten, Frank was old enough to know Ruth had fallen from Mama's good graces. And, watching Mills and Chris board the train for South Carolina at Union Station, perhaps even thought that they got to go home because they were the good ones. She and Ruth had been exiled for being bad girls.

The thing is, Frank didn't know what she'd done to be so black and blue.

Though Mama confessed that "[h]ome doesn't seem like home with Frank away,"[36] once her youngest returned to Columbia she announced that she was sending Frank to New York. "I feel that Dad and I have done our share by her," she told Mattie, "and if [Ralston] was not able to care for her I would keep her to the end. This doesn't mean that we relinquish our claim to her. Whenever she gets dissatisfied he must send her back."[37] Two months later, Mama still intended to give up Frank, "if Buddie [her nickname for him] sends for her. Somehow, while it will be awfully sad to give my baby up, still I will feel relieved from the expense of her care." Though Ralston had promised to send money, he had not. "Maybe he will yet,"[38] Mama said.

By August of 1923, it was clear Frank would have to stay in South Carolina. Mama took her along to a summer institute at Hampton—likely because she had no one at home to look after her. She paints a charming picture of eleven-year-old Frank in one letter, "out on the swing now, swapping experiences," with Celia Dial Saxon. Saxon was sixty-five then and had taught in Columbia's public schools for forty-three years. She was a formidable figure—her obituary noted her lack of "sentimentality"[39] in the classroom and a photograph I've seen shows a woman with a down-turned mouth and forbidding eyes behind round-rimmed glasses. But, Mama said, "Frank doesn't seem to fear her nor to mind her cranky ways one bit, but jokes and plays with Mrs. Saxon just as she would with you or me." Still, Mama was at a loss about what to do with Frank. She was paying $2.50 a week for Frank's room and board, "a big item out of my salary." "I don't know what will become of her," she told Mattie. "I've written Ralston about her but he fails to answer. I can't send her back to Washington at my expense, as I don't feel able to pay regularly and won't send her on Alfred. [In addition to his four children, Alfred was responsible for a cousin, Alice Sightler, after the death of Alice's mother.] So she will have to stay home and do the best she can unless Ralston does something. I am somewhat disgusted."[40]

Nothing in Mama's letters—I have none from Ralston—explains why he didn't take in Frank or contribute to her upkeep.

Though he'd soon become a Pullman porter—which meant he'd be away from home for days at a time—Ralston was working as a tailor when Mama pleaded with him for help. His wife, Corinne, doesn't seem to have worked, which meant she'd have had to take care of Frank. But they'd been married just four years, so it wouldn't be surprising if she wasn't enthusiastic about welcoming his soon-to-be teenaged daughter.

Poor Frank! The chat with Mrs. Saxon aside, just about the only happiness Mama depicts is Frank's "big time" at a "fishing party." "Wish you could have seen her run each time she would catch fish. She caught an eel and almost ran into the river."[41] Most of the time, though, Mama writes with low expectations barely concealed. "As you know, she's not a brilliant scholar but we hope she gets by," Mama told Mattie in 1926. Mills was at Benedict and Colon in dental school at Meharry. Once they finished, and Frank graduated from high school, "we shall draw long breaths of ease."[42]

Mama continued to worry. In June 1929, when Frank would have been sixteen, she flunked chemistry and geography and was told she'd have to repeat tenth grade. "You know how I feel about it,"[43] Mama said. She didn't have to say she was disappointed.

I'd tell you the facts of what happened next, only there aren't many.

That summer, Mama and Papa sent Frank to spend some time in Clinton. It's near Laurens, so she likely stayed with relatives or family friends. Frank was seventeen and in the throes of adolescence: Perhaps Mama thought she needed some time in the country away from the distractions (among them, a boyfriend) that had led to her poor grades. At some point, probably after Frank came home when school started, Mama made up her mind. Frank was going to her father in New York.

And then that Thanksgiving, Mama discovered Frank was pregnant. She must have been some months gone. "I noticed she was wearing a coat every day," one of her Booker T. Washington classmates told me in a letter, "but I did not know what was going on nor did I ask."[44] Only Chris and his wife, Charlisena, knew. But once Mama discovered Frank's "condition" (as Mills primly put it in a letter to Mattie), she decided to send Frank to Ralston "at once."[45]

I can't help thinking of the "colored maid" Papa was accused of "deflouring" in Laurens forty years before. Whoever the father was, Frank must have been drawn to him by her need for love, her need to be valued. Once her secret was out, she was angry and afraid, sad because she'd disappointed the only mother she'd known. Chris told Mills "all that he knew about it" at Thanksgiving, but if he knew the father's name, he didn't say or Mills chose not to put it in the letter. But it doesn't matter if Frank refused to divulge his name, just as it doesn't matter if his parents refused to allow him to get married because he was too young, or if he was an older man with a wife and children.

What matters is Frank's shame at disappointing Mama by failing to live up to her expectations.

It's tempting to see Mama's actions as cold and self-serving—she wasn't just protecting Frank from gossip by sending her away from Columbia; she was protecting her own reputation. She and Papa weren't just Victorians; they were *Black* Victorians—religious, abstemious, and occasionally censorious (Papa's foibles notwithstanding), ever determined to prove their worth. Papa had had help from his mother and from his Laurens neighbors. In the end, however, he'd had to make his own way in the world. Mama enjoyed advantages he had not, but her letters show her familiarity with what he, too, must also have known: They and others like them—the "better" people of Columbia, the doctors, lawyers, and teachers, the carpenters, painters, and plasterers, domestic workers and post office janitors—walked a knife's edge of respectability. The climb upward had been arduous—how easy it would be to slip backwards; how hard to regain lost ground.

Still, if Mama felt betrayed and angry, I hope she also felt a kind of helpless longing as she watched the northbound train leave. She must have, after caring for Frank for so many years, after worrying about her, after coaxing and cajoling her through school.

Frank fell ill on the train; fortunately, a family friend was with her. They made their way to New York, where Ralston took her in. At long last, he and his daughter reconciled. Frank wrote Mills to tell her "that Ralston was so nice to her, giving her all that heart could wish for and waiting on her as if she had been a baby. She said she was just beginning to know real happiness. . . ." All the same, Frank wasn't entirely happy. "In every letter," Mills wrote, "she begged me to come to see her this summer and to try to get Mama to write to her and forgive her. She was planning to send Mama something nice for her birthday to try to make up for the wrong she had committed."[46]

Whatever happiness Frank enjoyed with her father was short-lived. She died on March 9, 1930, shortly after giving birth to twins. Mama recorded her death in the Bible, as well as the names of her children—Edith Cornice and Francis Conrad—making Frank part of the family again. Perhaps it was her way of saying she was sorry. According to Jo, the boy was taken in by Marian and Evelyn, and the girl was taken in by Tap's girlfriend. (A note at the bottom of a page labeled "Memoranda" in the Garrett family Bible says the girl was adopted by a "Mrs. Maynard.") The adoptive parents renamed them Barbara and George.

None of this paints Mama in a very good light, so I was surprised when I came across her sympathetic remarks at a church service she and Papa attended in Aiken: "I was singing ever since I was 12 years old," she told the congregation and youth choir, "but I did not have the opportunity these young people have today. I had to sing with the older members of the church, which I did not enjoy. These young people are grouped together where they can sing and talk together. I think this is wonderful. Somebody was doing some sensible thinking for this is one of the finest arrangements it has been my privilege to see."[47]

And she did have her emotional side. Christmas 1939, she found herself overwhelmed. She'd received greetings from all her children except Ruth—even ne'er-do-well Maceo sent a card! But she had a house full of grandchildren, thirteen-year-old Christopher Jr., who was "just in and out"; his eleven-year-old sister, Marian, who must have been sulky because she "couldn't play much by herself"; and nine-year-old George, Frances's son, who was coming down with the flu but wanted to ride his bicycle and play with the football he'd gotten for Christmas. "I had almost primed myself for a good cry as dinnertime neared," Mama confessed. And then two friends came. They stayed to eat, so "I couldn't get it out—I'm glad to say."[48] Later, after Mills had made the difficult decision to give up a teaching job, Mama told her, "A good cry clears up a foggy mind wonderfully. I should know. You wouldn't call me a cry baby by any means but all through life I've taken time out and indulged. Always behind 'closed doors,' however, because a woman can't or won't always tell why she cries."[49]

Stiff upper lip aside, Mama was also something of a romantic, keeping Mattie posted about a boarder's courtship. "Vance has gone to Jenkinsville today to see Elizabeth Harper," she told Mattie. "I think he likes her fairly well and means to put marrying right up to her. I had a long talk with him last night and I think he really hopes to 'fix things.'"[50]

Elizabeth was from Jenkinsville, a small town in western Fairfield County, so she must have gone home to teach after graduating from Allen's Normal School in 1915.[51] Vance was George Vance Henry, a minister listed as one of three boarders at 2210 Lady Street, in the 1920 census. He continued to pursue Elizabeth, and Mama continued hopeful. "From present indications," she told Mattie, "I think Vance will make it with Elizabeth Harper. He went up to see her last Sunday and staid till Monday and was in the seventh heaven of bliss when he came back."[52]

In the end, despite Mama's advice, Vance failed in his courtship. In December of 1920, he married a woman named Annie Amelia Bethea. I don't know either's relationship (if any) to the Garretts, but Mama included Vance and Annie Amelia in her list of marriages in the family Bible. Alas, there was no happy ending. Sometime in 1925, Mama got the news that "Vance is down in bed. He has about lost his health, has been sick nearly all the year."[53] He died of Bright's disease later that year. And Amelia . . . Several years later, she began to show signs of mental illness and was committed to the state asylum.[54]

◆ ◆ ◆

Mama's letters include the years 1928 to 1941, but there's nothing in them about the Great Depression. She and Papa were used to hard times, had always managed despite them. And they had resources others might have lacked—Papa's farm outside the country with woods for hunting game and timber to sell; a vegetable garden and chickens at home on Lady Street.

Like the Depression, race receives scant attention. It seldom figures in Mama's letters, just as it seldom figures in Mattie's or Alfred's, or any of the hundreds by and to other family members that I've read and transcribed. There's nothing about the day-to-day privations of segregation, nothing about Red Summer, or lynchings in South Carolina and elsewhere. One letter, from Tap to Mama, mentions the Harlem Riot of 1935, which began March 19, after rumors spread that a Puerto Rican boy accused of shoplifting had been severely beaten. Three people were killed, more than one hundred injured, and property damage estimated at two million dollars. Tap assured Mama, however, that the one-day disturbance "did not amount to much. Indeed, it was not a race riot, as many whites were aligned with the colored, but supposedly an economic disturbance." And, he added, "Much of it was downright looting."[55]

I'd like to have known what Mama and Papa thought about these events that loom large looking back. I'd like to have known what they made of Cole Blease, the race-baiting South Carolina governor William Chappelle invited to speak at Allen; one-eyed white supremacist "Pitchfork" Ben Tillman, who served in the US Senate; and the segregation of the federal workforce under Wilson. And then it hit me: As the comedian Godfrey Cambridge tartly reminded white folk, none of us looks in the mirror each morning and exclaims, "Oh my God—I'm black!"

The community Mama and Papa nurtured, and that Alfred and Mattie bequeathed to their children, was "complex and diverse . . . too busy loving, marrying, dancing, worshiping, dreaming, laughing, arguing, playing, working, dressing up, looking cool, raising children, organizing, performing magic, making poetry to be worried about what white folks thought."[56] The dancing and magic-making are more Zora Neale Hurston than Mama or Mattie, but the point's well taken. Like those who'd come before and those who'd come after, Papa and Mama and their offspring, friends, and in-laws did what they could with what they had, instead of worrying about what they couldn't and didn't have.

All the same, Mama was loath to accept white condescension and brooked no insults. Her sons (Tap in particular) lived in fear that one day she'd shoot a white man. She came close at least once.

Looking out the window one afternoon, Mama saw two white men approaching the rental house behind hers. A young couple lived there but the husband was away, leaving the wife alone. Papa was away, too, but Mama retrieved his shotgun and went outside. As soon as they saw her, the two men fled. Another story has Mama sitting on her porch when a passing white man nodded and said, "How are you this evening, Aunty?"

"I'm well, thank you," Mama is supposed to have replied. "And how is your mother, my sister?"

Honesty compels me to note that a similar story appears in the World War II autobiography[57] of Charity Adams Earley, daughter of AME minister Eugene Avery Adams and a neighbor of the Garretts. Perhaps the Garretts appropriated the story. Perhaps both Mama *and* Charity's father really did say it. And perhaps neither Mama nor the Rev. Adams said anything, and the story's really about the kinds of things people wished they'd said but didn't dare. After all, there were some lines too dangerous to cross.

Charity's autobiography is mostly about her time in the States and overseas as one of the first Black female officers in the Women's Army Auxiliary Corps. She left the service after the war as a lieutenant colonel. Surely it was no coincidence that her son, Stanley, was a year or two behind me at Haverford College. Like me, he came from a line of "unknown black leaders."

13

The Editor and the Bishop, 1917–25

Whether he was fired for publishing an angry editorial chastising William Chappelle or resigned as a matter of principle over the bishop's giving Coley a pulpit at Allen University, 1916 marked the zenith of Papa's career. Like Dublin Hunter's, Papa's life until then showed it was possible to rise through hard work and self-sacrifice. Like Richard Hunter's ordeal, Papa's after 1916 showed how easy it was to slip and fall.

Three years after Papa left Allen, Mattie told Alfred her father was still in the doldrums. "Dad isn't doing anything now but running the paper," she said. "I don't suppose he will ever do much more. He doesn't keep well and is complaining all the time. Mama wants him to leave here, but I don't suppose he will, not as long as Chappelle is here."[1]

Without his life's work, all that remained to Papa was a kind of grim pride. He and Mama struggled to make ends meet. Humiliatingly for a former university vice president, Papa even worked as a laborer for a time—if the 1928 Columbia City Directory can be believed. The Garretts continued to take in boarders, and Papa remained involved in politics, even occasionally trying some wheeling and dealing of his own. In 1922, for example, he met with US Sen. Nathan B. Dial to offer information about Black Carolinians' dissatisfaction with Joseph Warren Tolbert, the white leader of the state's multiracial Black and Tan GOP faction. Dial thought Papa might "give some very valuable information,"[2] but Papa wanted a patronage appointment, and President Warren G. Harding wasn't going to appoint any Blacks in the South. Dial didn't tell Papa that, hoping, I suspect, to keep him coming back. Their interaction doesn't reflect well on the senator, who wanted to maintain white supremacy. As for Papa . . . well, hard times had made him desperate.

Despite Mattie's prediction that he'd never "do much more," Papa hadn't given up, however. Instead, he found new purpose in savaging William. The bishop was not entirely innocent in their war—mostly of words, though it came to fisticuffs once. Mutual friends such as I. M. A. Myers may have brokered peace from time to time, but it was not long before Papa or William inevitably broke it.

"Thought Dad and Chappelle had come to peace terms," Alfred wrote Mattie, responding to news of the latest skirmish. "Think I'd have to punch a fellow in his mouth if he agreed to play quits and then wrote me up again like the last one. It should have been worse, though, if possible. If I were a Methodist . . . durned if I'd stand a bishop's bull ragging and woman wrestling like he does. Some good consecrated Methodist ought get a stout two[-]hand pole and wallop him."[3]

No matter who was responsible for breaking the truce, Papa must have welcomed its end. Seeking to bring down his one-time ally gave him reason to live during his exile from Allen, the vehemence of their quarrel so all-consuming it might, for Papa at least, have been a full-time occupation. Their dispute would endure nearly a decade, Papa's animus sometimes expressed in language so coarse the churchman might, in an earlier age, have challenged the editor to a duel. Matters would come to a head in 1920, when Papa joined an effort to have the bishop removed from South Carolina. He failed, but his enmity did not end. Papa continued to hound William, even as the bishop lay on his deathbed in 1925.

In stories indistinguishable from editorials by their lack of objectivity, Papa used *The Light* to criticize the bishop and other churchmen for "grafting, robbing and hogging the poor people" and "abusing and brow beating the poor people in the house of God."[4] William himself was a "black[-]hearted, scary bishop with a blustering, roguish mouth,"[5] "a tyro and gosh bully."[6] Papa even accused him of indulging in the kind of graft the bishop had righteously claimed to oppose earlier in his career, when he had cried "long and loud against church graft."[7] Now, Papa charged, "slipping" the bishop fifty dollars was all a pastor had to do to get the church he wanted.[8]

I want to give Papa the benefit of the doubt by believing his crusade wasn't entirely personal and that he was sincere in wanting to see greater accountability within the church. It was the continuation of his populist fight, begun at the 1916 General Conference when the bishops were forced to give the laymen greater recognition, part of a lifelong quest for transparency because he was convinced that "we little Negroes would catch the very devil at the hands of the big Negro [i.e., men like William] if the government and management of affairs were in their hands."[9] Papa was not without support—pastors and parishioners wrote to *The Light* alleging questionable financial practices at their churches and praising him as "an instrument in God's hands to expose dirt in high places."[10]

William was Papa's primary target, but others came in for collateral damage. Chief among them was the Rev. Edward Philip Ellis (1876–1954). Referred to as E. Philip in contemporary accounts, he was a 1900 graduate of Allen's Normal School. Licensed to preach at age nineteen, he worked as a sales agent for the AME Sunday School Union when William was in Nashville. He's identified as William's "foster son"[11] in a *Palmetto Leader* profile, which likely means the bishop was his mentor. That closeness meant Papa would savage Ellis almost as often as he did William, calling him "a rusty, red-eyed pimpy preacher" and the bishop's "dog washer and carriage driver."[12]

Despite segregation and the lack of voting rights, Black Columbians—at least those able to afford lawyers—felt comfortable turning to the courts when they felt sufficiently aggrieved. Ellis didn't take Papa to court, but then perhaps he didn't have the money. Not so with others.

Papa was sued at least twice more in 1918, posting five hundred dollars bond when Allen's secretary, the Rev. David H. Sims, filed papers alleging that he had "willfully and maliciously slandered the faculty"[13] in *The Light*. As the year neared its end, Papa again found himself in court, this time charged with defaming another AME minister. The case was dropped.[14]

The cases show Papa's propensity for getting himself into trouble, but they also illustrate the shifting nature of alliances within Columbia's AME community. One of those who posted bond in the second libel suit was Carrie E. McGill, wife of the Rev. Daniel McGill, who'd sued Papa for libel in 1912. And Papa must have reconciled with Sims—fourteen years later, in 1932, he would support the Allen secretary's candidacy for bishop.

Papa never reconciled with William, however, and at the 1920 General Conference, held May 2–18 in St. Louis, he led an unsuccessful effort to have the bishop sent anywhere but South Carolina.[15] At least twenty ministers and laymen opposed the bishop, charging he'd threatened them and was "out of harmony with a large part of the ministry and laity." They faced considerable headwinds, however: The state's five conferences had voted unanimously for the bishop's return, leading William to boast that "no power" could prevent his returning to South Carolina.[16]

Six charges were filed against the bishop, but all were dismissed "for lack of evidence or irregularities."[17] Later, Papa would claim he'd brought evidence with him on the train to St. Louis, but "some dirty thief had rifled it [his 'grip'] of all the records and evidence." He blamed "some of Chappelle's henchmen."[18]

Though Papa had predicted the "bishop would be handcuffed as soon as he got to Columbia," William "was given a royal welcome" on his return to South Carolina. In the months that followed, he consolidated his hold, forcing those who'd opposed him "to go before their respective annual conferences and make apologies."[19] The 1924 General Conference kept him in South Carolina, and he continued as bishop and chairman of Allen's board until his death the following year. Meanwhile, Papa's connection with his beloved institution was all but severed. He was listed as an alumnus in the 1923–24 catalog, his profession given as "Editor." The name of his paper was conspicuously absent.[20]

◆ ◆ ◆

William David Chappelle has been dead for nearly one hundred years; and Papa, for more than 75. Though the two men's enmity has been largely forgotten, it was probably inevitable despite their decades-long alliance and shared commitment to Allen. The thing is, they were too much alike. Both were born in humble circumstances and triumphed over early adversity. Both were committed to racial uplift through education, Republican politics, the Colored State Fair and, of course, the AME Church. Both were strong-willed and convinced of the rightness of their causes. Still, though their lives followed the pattern of heroic ascension common to many members of a generation born in the shadow of slavery—*History of the American Negro* called them "fine stories" that, compiled, "would read like a new Arabian Nights"[21]—William would climb higher. The difference in their ages—eight years—meant William enjoyed a head start and, perhaps, a maturity Papa lacked.

I wrote earlier that there was no biography of the bishop, but that isn't quite true. Puzzling over his role in Papa's dismissal from Allen, I began to research his life. He soon took over mine. A few years later, I had a five-hundred-page manuscript (one hundred ten thousand words long) that ended just short of William's death. Close to the end, I abandoned the project—I just didn't like the man enough to see it through.

His contemporaries called him a natural leader, "strong willed, daring, and insistant [*sic*],"[22] a man who "worked along definite lines and got results."[23] There's no gainsaying this, just as there's no gainsaying the strength of character and force of will that allowed William to lift himself from slavery, poverty, and obscurity to the heights of the AME church. He possessed a talent for winning friends and influencing others, inexorable drive and a certain ruthlessness, a tendency toward pragmatism that bordered on hypocrisy. And there was this that allowed him to go further and rise higher than Papa: Reconstruction had ended by the time both men began their careers, thus South Carolina's return to white supremacy meant each faced strict limits on what he might hope to achieve. Whether or not he had greater innate ability, William made the wiser choice in becoming a preacher than did Papa in choosing the law. Aware of the disparity between their achievements (and of how much he'd helped in William's rise), Papa must have resented his compatriot's failure to reach back to lift him toward his own goals. But the bishop was a tireless worker with wide horizons and broad interests. Perhaps he declined to help because he saw in Papa a man who could not always be relied on to serve those interests.

Though remembered as "a bold reformer" who "spoke truth to power, publicly criticizing white leaders for their discriminatory treatment of African Americans,"[24] William spoke to power in language that balanced militancy and meekness, never causing permanent offense. Offending powerful whites would have weakened his influence. One writer saw his political leanings—Democratic in national matters; Republican in local— as showing "his independence."[25] I see them as a canny politician's aversion to being pinned down. In the speech William gave in 1919 when Columbia welcomed its Black soldiers home, the bishop called for "the chance to go to the ballot box. . . . and a place on the juries."[26] A few months later, he was denouncing "Bolshevism as being our greatest enemy" and calling on preachers to counsel "patience, such as that which we have exercised and with which we have won glory in the estimation of the thinking world."[27] There's something shrewd and reserved in the man's gaze in the photographs I've seen, as if he'd long understood it was to his advantage to let others reveal themselves before tipping his hand. He was a realist. Papa, on the other hand, was an idealist. Believing things ought to be a certain way, he dared to risk despite the consequences for himself. In this Papa was true to the legend of the father he'd never known.

◆ ◆ ◆

During the nine years between Papa's departure from Allen and William's death, the two men lived within easy walking distance of one other. In a larger city, one might have moved or each might have found separate circles sizable enough for his ambition and urge to do good. Black Columbia was small, however, and insular enough for the two men to continue to get in each other's way.

Early in November of 1922, the "warfare that has been waging between *The Light* and the bishop for years"[28] came to a head when Papa struck William at a meeting of the executive committee of the Colored State Fair. It was the day after the fair ended, and Papa had submitted a bill for advertising. During the argument that followed, the editor slugged the bishop.

One account says that Papa was arrested, but there was nothing on the docket when William went to court the next day. A policeman said he was told that there'd been a fight, but, according to "several Negroes that appeared to be informed, 'that there was nothing to it.'" The bishop insisted he wanted charges brought.[29] He had witnesses and his own lawyer, but they weren't needed. Papa pleaded guilty. Acknowledging the two antagonists' status in the community, Judge Charles J. Kimball said he intended to "treat them as he would prominent white men that happened to be connected with such disorders."[30] (Fittingly, given the two men's behavior, he was a juvenile court judge.) Kimball fined Papa ten dollars before suspending it and chastised both men (and William's witnesses) for conduct unbecoming "leaders of their race." Afterward, the bishop "repaired himself to an oculist and bought a new pair of glasses to replace those broken in the fray."[31]

The story of Papa's fisticuffs outlived both men, though perhaps (given Papa's pugnaciousness), the one handed down concerned another man who wore glasses. In the late 1950s or early '60s, Jo went to a teachers' training conference at Hampton University, the same kind of conference Mama had attended decades before. A man approached and asked if she was Papa's granddaughter. She said she was, and he asked about an assault Papa was supposed to have committed decades before.

"Is it true," he asked, "that your grandfather took the man's glasses off before he knocked him to the floor?"

◆ ◆ ◆

William would die June 15, 1925, but Papa continued to attack the bishop even as he lay helpless on his deathbed, "unable to talk and utterly incapacitated." Calling him a "'nigger driver' prelate" who had "destroyed his usefulness by giving away [*sic*] to wicked and ungodly ambitions," Papa urged William to "humbly and prayerfully step down" and "seek reconciliation with the men he has slain and butchered."[32]

The crudeness of Papa's language is troubling, but if he was right about William's condition, then William should have retired. Ill for "more than a year,"[33] the bishop was "unable to talk and utterly incapacitated for any episcopal work or supervision."[34] He was well off, so moving to the ranks of the superannuated (as the church dubbed its retired clergy) wouldn't have caused his family financial hardship. He would continue to receive a reduced salary—two thousand dollars a year. After his death, his wife would receive a pension.

In that same issue of *The Light*, Papa went on to allege that Allen was one hundred thousand dollars in debt. Though he doesn't say it, he implies that the trustees had taken on the debt (more than $1.6 million today) to build a monument to the dying bishop. Looking at pictures of the campus from 1920 and 1922,[35] when construction of the Chappelle Administration Building began, it's easy to understand Papa's concern. Two multistory brick buildings, Arnett and Coppin Halls, dominate the campus, but the grounds are dotted with modest, one-story wood-frame structures. The new administration building, brick with stone trim, was three stories high. By some estimates, it cost "an astounding $165,000,"[36] the equivalent

Allen University, 1920, clapboard buildings with Coppin Hall in background. University of Virginia Libraries.

of $2.7 million today. Designed by John A. Lankford, the AME Church's "Supervising Architect"[37] (and the first licensed Black architect in America), it undoubtedly inspired pride among Allenites, AME parishioners, and Black South Carolinians. Still, mightn't it have been better for the trustees, forced to go begging each year for funds to pay teachers and operate the school, to have erected two or three smaller buildings to replace hut-like structures that look as if they date from the University's founding forty years before?[38]

In the end, I can't know whether Papa was right when he charged William with soliciting gifts for preferential appointments, and using his office to create "fat jobs" for his wife and "worthless and inefficient children."[39] Nearly a century later, those involved are long gone, together with any evidence to prove or disprove Papa's allegations. Still, there are strong suggestions that what we now call "pay to play" took place, if not between the bishop and the ministers he supervised, then elsewhere in the church. A year before William's death, Richard R. Wright gingerly approached the subject of involuntary contributions by ministers, venturing that "where there is much smoke, there may be some fire."[40] An AME churchman of admirable integrity, Wright once refused an honorary degree "because of the conviction that no man under forty years of age should receive" one.

Elected bishop in 1936, "he disposed of all business interests"[41] except a bank directorship.

William's contemporaries praised his "fine business acumen,"[42] noting that he'd "been able to handle his own personal resources and investments in such a way as to put him in the class of the well-to-do men of his race."[43] Two years into his first term as secretary of the Sunday School Union, when his salary was thirteen hundred fifty dollars a year, he owned property in Columbia and Nashville valued at ten thousand dollars.[44] As bishop, his salary ranged from twenty-five hundred dollars a year to thirty-five hundred dollars[45] (as much as seventy-two thousand dollars today), with a housing allowance and expenses for travel. After his death, his estate was valued at about sixteen thousand four hundred dollars, almost two hundred fifty thousand dollars today.[46]

A man who sleeps in a shack and earns his keep taking care of a bishop's horse—at the same time going to college *and* teaching *and* preaching to support himself, his wife, and their children—surely must learn thrift and self-denial or perish. It would be surprising, too, if such a man did not vow he'd never be poor or go hungry again. Whether Chappelle's success was due to his frugality and sound business instincts (as those who admired him asserted) or helped (as Papa charged in *The Light*) by his practice of accepting "gifts" from preachers and presiding elders remains a mystery. Like the Rev. Richard R. Wright Jr., however, I suspect that there was a little too much smoke for there not to have been some fire.

14

Beginnings and Departures

Papa had high expectations (even if he didn't always live up to them), and so did Mama. They took it as a matter of course that their children would finish high school and then go on to normal school or college. Afterward, they'd lead moral, productive lives.

Most did, though not in the way Mama and Papa would have wanted.

Mattie graduated from Allen, as did Tap, before his brief stint at Columbia in New York. Ralston finished normal school. Colon went to Lincoln University and then, a few years later, Meharry Medical College to become a dentist. Marian attended South Carolina State. Mills went to elementary school at Allen. Afterward, likely because Papa had been banished from the university, she went to Columbia's public Washington and Howard schools. Tap was one of her teachers at the latter. (Mattie had been one of her teachers at Allen, so Mills was spectacularly unlucky in having older siblings as teachers.) Chris, Mama's youngest, finished high school, and Frank finished tenth grade before Mama banished her to New York.

Only Maceo, of Mama and Papa's natural children, seems not to have followed the path his parents laid out.

Maceo and Ruth, who Mama managed to send to Hampton Institute despite her money worries, hoping she'd graduate, get her certificate, and settle into the security of teaching. Instead, Ruth went her own way for much of her teens and twenties.

Just two years older than her sister, Mills, Ruth was—some said—the "pretty baby." When Mama took them out together, people would ooh and aah over her, ignoring Mills. Later, Jo would say "Ruth wasn't boy crazy. She crazed the boys." Perhaps it all started when she looked up from her pram into the adoring gaze of her admirers.

Looking closely at a picture I've seen of Ruth when she was the object of Mama's concern—I don't know when it was taken, but she appears to be

Ruth Garrett, undated.
Collection of the author.

in her twenties—I see a wistful diffidence that belies the stories of her escapades. If family stories can be believed, Ruth, "attractive and fly," ran away
with the "high school principal" when she was in her teens. Papa chased
her down and brought her back. Mama was mortified. She must have been
exhausted, too, having Ruth to contend with, as well as Papa's AME feuds,
overseeing schools and construction work, and running the house on Lady
Street.

Ruth's escapades were why Mama sent her to school at Hampton. Ruth
didn't like it at first—"You know what a time I had last year because I made
her stay at Hampton," Mama told Mattie—but she soon found a boy who
sparked her interest. "She says she wants to go back, do you think it's for
love of Hampton or that boy?" Thinking it was love, but not for Hampton,
Mama sent her to live with Alfred and Mattie in 1921. It was supposed to be
just for the summer, but later, Mama asked if she could stay and go to Armstrong High, Washington's "colored manual training school." Mama and
Papa would pay "for her [Ruth's] board just as regularly as I would have to
send it Hampton."[1]

"[T]hat boy" may have been Ira B. Valentine, as the 1920 census shows him enrolled at Hampton. If so, Mama's fears were in vain—he was already in Washington when she was trying to decide what to do about Ruth. In time, he'd become Ruth's first husband.

Mama's expectations that Mattie would keep Ruth out of trouble made her a kind of surrogate mother. For that reason, Ira wrote Mattie "a letter of explanation" after committing some unspecified offense, perhaps trying to visit Ruth, or even waiting outside Armstrong to walk her home. Despite Mama's admonitions, Mattie must have been sympathetic to her younger sister. After all, she and Alfred had courted for four years under Mama's watchful eye.

Ira told Mattie he understood he was "liking a girl that is not allowed to receive friends," and thanked her "for the special privilege which you gave me this evening when you permitted me to speak to her."[2] He assured her he'd continue to see Ruth only with Mattie's permission.

In assuring Mattie of the purity of his intentions, Ira said Ruth wasn't the only reason he'd come to Washington. He'd come "for the purpose of working, and not for what you think." All the same, he admitted he was "exceptionally fond"[3] of Ruth. Which explains why he'd found a place to live just five blocks and a ten-minute walk from Mattie and Alfred's.

It was the following year that Mama sent her other children, Mills, Chris, and Frank, to join Ruth in Washington. By that time, Mattie must have known she was pregnant with her fourth child, my mother, whom she'd name Ruth, after her sister. That November, Ruth Esther Simons became the first of Alfred and Mattie's children to be born in Washington. The addition of three more siblings meant nine people in Mattie and Alfred's little house. Located at 50 L Street, NW, it boasted three rooms upstairs and three down. But Jo once said there were only two rooms on each floor, which would have made it even more crowded and unpleasant in a hot, humid Washington summer long before air conditioning. Four rooms or six, the house had a backyard outhouse. In fact, there was no indoor plumbing until Alfred ran a line and installed a sink in the kitchen. All the same, crowded as she knew it would be, Mattie couldn't say no, unlike Colon's

Henrietta or Chris's Charlisena, the daughters-in-law who'd declined to keep house on Lady Street while Mama was away at her schools.

From her perch hundreds of miles away, Mama continued to try to keep Ruth from harm's way. Ruth and Mills wanted to go to New York to see their brothers. Mama decided Ruth could go—Mills was too young—but she urged Mattie to "[t]ell Ruth to be very careful." And, she added, "There are so many ~~places~~ [strikethrough original] phases of danger both to person and mind. Of course she will be with her brothers and sisters but still I want her to be careful with herself."[4] Mills and Christopher went home at the end of the summer, but the two sisters' sibling rivalry continued at a distance. Ruth wrote boasting about her clothes, which made Mills "upset" and "dissatisfied." Mama didn't want Ruth "to get the idea in her head that dress is 'all.'" And, she reminded Mattie, "You know how I feel about schoolgirls and dressing."[5]

Though still arguably a schoolgirl (she was seventeen), Mills was already a freshman at Benedict College. Ruth, though, was nineteen and already a young woman. She was ill at least twice during her Washington sojourn, seriously enough for Mama to write in June 1923 that she was coming up unless Ruth's condition improved. Mama's letters are cryptic, but one orphan page suggests Ruth was having fun instead of paying attention to her schoolwork. Soon, Mama decided her errant daughter needed to go to a "nice place" Papa had "found . . . in Philadelphia with friends of his where she would be under the direct supervision of the principal of the school so much like Miner [Normal School in Washington]."[6] As a last resort, Mama was considering sending her to live with her brothers in New York.

"We shall be certain of her fate within the next 10 days," Mama went on. And, she added, "I do not blame you one bit for Ruth's delinquencies. I know you did your duty but maybe they see and hear too much from your neighbors. Or perhaps it is just the. . . ."[7] The page ends there, and the rest of the letter's lost, so I don't know what Mama went on to say. Still, the word "delinquencies" gives me pause. When I asked Jo—who would have been only six years old in 1923—if Ruth had gotten herself into what used to be called "the family way," she laughed knowingly but said nothing.

As for what Ruth might have heard or seen on that narrow street lined with flat-fronted two-story houses—some people worked as government clerks, but most were laborers, maids, laundresses, and chauffeurs. A few men worked for the railroad—Union Station was a short walk away. Likely, Mama was right about at least some of those neighbors, though. There were bootleggers (Prohibition was two years old)—including one who sold his wares from a shack in the alley just behind Alfred and Mattie's house. In summer, when everyone kept windows and doors open, there must have been plenty to see and hear.

By August, Ruth was back in Columbia, "very sorry that she gave trouble" and "anxious to finish school." However, Mama said she wasn't going to ask Mattie "to take her back, for fear there may be more trouble. If you and she can agree, good and well. Otherwise she must stay home. . . . I am through with the matter now. Shall tell her of my decision when I go home Saturday evening."[8] Later, Mama told Mattie that her sons had "promised to help with Ruth so maybe there will be a little relief with her. She left for school today. We are keeping her destination quiet until she gets settled, for fear of what busy-bodies may do."[9]

Mama's letters in the 1920s and '30s are full of examples of headstrong boys and girls leaving home for Washington, Philadelphia, and New York. Surprisingly, given her penchant for adventure—if she really *did* run away with the high school principal—it was years before Ruth finally quit Columbia for good. Perhaps she wasn't that defiant (nor her "delinquencies" that dire). But it just might be Mama's formidable nature that explains why, when Mama allowed her to go to New York, Ruth didn't decide to stay with her brothers. If her sojourn there was anything like Jo's years later—when Tap, Ralston, and Marian took Jo to nightclubs and shows and introduced her to the pleasures of good Scotch—Ruth must have thought about it.

Colon and Marian worked as Pullman porters. Tap did too, though only briefly. Maceo worked as a tailor, and so did Ralston. Partners with Enoch H. Clark in a "tailoring emporium" called (naturally enough) Clark & Garrett, Ralston touted their "Choicest Fabrics, Guaranteed Woolens [and] Snappy Styles" in the *New York Age*. Their shop was located at 222 W. 135 Street, a five-story building constructed in 1920 and now gentrified into a "boutique condominium building."[10]

Clark was also from Columbia, so perhaps he and Ralston had known each other there. It's also possible that, like other newcomers from the South, they found each other through a network of migrants. Common in big cities during the Great Black Exodus, these networks helped newcomers find jobs, housing, churches, clubs, and schools and showed them where to shop and even how to use public transportation. The Garrett brothers were their own network—the 1920 census shows Colon, Henrietta, Maceo, and Jimmie all sharing the same apartment. Ralston and Corinne lived with Tap and Cornice and a roomer from back home. Only Marian lived apart from his brothers but in a household that included nine others from South Carolina. Like Marian, one of the other lodgers also worked for the Pullman Company.

While Clark kept up his tailoring business, Ralston was working only as a Pullman porter within a few years. (Mama may have called him "Buddie," but his fellow porters called him "Nick," because of the Nick Carter dime-novel detective stories he liked to read.) At some point, Colon went back to school and Tap became a bookkeeper, leaving only Ralston and Marian working the railroads.

I sometimes wonder if they didn't inherit Papa's restlessness, his need to keep moving. On the other hand, what seems like a menial occupation now (remembered only for the genial, rotund, subservient porters that Black actors played in movies from the 1930s and '40s), was then considered a "prestigious position" in the Black community. Porters enjoyed "steady income, an opportunity to travel across America, and a life largely free of heavy physical labor." They played an important role in the fight for freedom, literally carrying the news from town to town in the form of copies of the NAACP's *Crisis* and newspapers like the *Chicago Defender*. And the porters themselves, far from being the movies' jovial, sexless nonentities, were "role models for young men"—"good looking, clean and immaculate in their dress, their style" and "quite manly, their language . . . very carefully crafted, so that they had a sense of intelligence about them."[11]

The six editions of Caldwell's *History of the American Negro* I've found—Georgia; North Carolina and South Carolina; Virginia; Washington, D.C.; and West Virginia—include profiles of dozens of professional men who worked as porters before becoming preachers, principals, lawyers, doctors, and dentists. Many of the latter went to Meharry. Perhaps Colon conceived his ambition to become a dentist after talking with men who shined shoes and made ready beds between semesters in medical or dental school.

The former porters Caldwell profiled characterized work in "the Pullman service" as "a liberalizing and helpful influence"[12] and an opportunity for growth and personal enhancement. Thus, one man's months on the railroad "took him into every State in the Union and into parts of Canada, giving him a rare opportunity of seeing every part of the country and added much to his store of personal experiences."[13] It sounds almost like a grand tour.

The reality was different and more complicated. Tips made up a substantial part of a porter's income, so they were obliged to maintain "a constant smile and courtly service," no matter the humiliation—and there were many affronts. Passengers made free with racial epithets or called porters "George" (the first name of the founder of the Pullman Company). In addition to shining shoes and "making down" the Pullman beds at night, duties included cleaning spittoons. But those duties could also include "delivering a telegram, mailing a letter during a station stop, running a bath, serving food or drink, delivering a card table or aspirin, and carting baggage."[14]

It was a lot of work—in 1926, porters labored three hundred forty-three hours a month, on average, for salaries of $78.11 and $33.82 in tips. The total is the equivalent of about seventeen hundred dollars today. But porters also had to pay for their uniforms, lodging away from home, meals, and shoe polish. Required to show up at the station early to prepare their cars, they weren't paid for that time or for the three or four hours they were allowed to sleep on overnight trips. When the Pullman Company finally signed a contract with the Brotherhood of Sleeping Car Porters in 1937, minimum salaries increased to $89.50, with overtime after two hundred forty hours, three hours sleep guaranteed for trips twelve hours and under, and reimbursement for the time spent preparing cars.[15]

Family lore says Marian worked the run from New York to Chicago and, possibly, all the way out to California. (This contradicts the National Registry of Pullman Porters, which says he went from New York to Miami.[16]) Mama's letters have Ralston running from New York to Florida, with at least a brief stop in Columbia. She prepared a home-cooked meal, and she and her youngest son, Chris, went down to the station. "There is a long wait generally as the train is always late," she told Mills. "No one gets tired waiting for we are well repaid when the jolly face appears looking out the train pulls in. Then his gags and such when he sees his lunch. . . . So you see how joyous it all is."[17]

Ralston was also a staunch supporter of the Brotherhood. It may, or may not, be coincidence, but in 1924, he lived in the same apartment building as union head A. Philip Randolph.[18] There'd have been some awkward conversations in the elevator if Ralston hadn't been a union man.

◆ ◆ ◆

As hard, and sometimes demeaning, as working as porters must have been, at least Marian and Ralston stayed employed. But Maceo. . . . Well, Maceo seldom figures in Mama's letters, and when he does, she makes it clear she'd "given him up as a hopeless job." When she did hear from him, it was because he needed money. "He claims he has been sick and unable to work for over a year," she told Mattie, "and asked me to send him $15.00. I didn't have it nor would I have sent it if I had."[19] It was the first time she'd heard from him in three years. Years later, someone from Travelers Aid came to Lady Street to ask if she and Papa "wanted Maceo home. We told them not unless he was sick, which he isn't. We also told her he had been sent home two years ago and wouldn't stay. I don't know what the outcome will be but hope we are not forced to take him."[20] Ralston promised that he and his brothers would "look out for" Maceo. Mama wasn't to worry because "[t]here isn't anything serious wrong with him. Too much drinking and carousing that's all."[21]

Likely, Mama wasn't reassured.

The 1920 and 1940 censuses list Maceo as a tailor living in New York, first in Manhattan and then the Bronx, so he must have continued to work, if only intermittently. In 1932, he came to Washington with the Bonus Marchers, seventeen thousand World War I veterans (and some twenty-six thousand family members and supporters) who descended on the city to demand immediate payment of bonuses the government had promised for their service. "Mother put him in the attic," Jo remembered, something in her tone suggesting that—not trusting, or perhaps even liking, her brother—Mattie let him stay only out of a sense of family obligation. Other visiting family members were given the guest bedroom.

Whatever the reason Mattie made Maceo stay in the attic—and perhaps it was only that, three years into the Depression, the guest bedroom had been turned over to a boarder—Maceo felt out of place among the Garrett tribe. Once, in a note to Papa, he lamented that "it seems strange that I am your son just lake [*sic*] all the rest but the family treats me so difference [*sic*] why. Perhaps if you can explain[.]"[22]

I wish I had Papa's reply.

– 15 –

Papa Returns to Allen

After Bishop Chappelle's death in 1925, Papa reconciled with Allen, a reunion that proceeded in fits and starts, as if a core of distrust remained between two estranged lovers. Throughout, Mama resented both school and church. Papa, despite his trials, seems never to have lost faith in either institution, or his reformer's zeal. Even those who disagreed with him—among them the Rev. E. Philip Ellis, William's "foster son" whom Papa had savaged in *The Light* as "rusty" and "pimpy"—had to acknowledge Papa's commitment.

In one column—he wrote regularly for the *Palmetto Leader* in the 1930s—Ellis admitted that "few people have done more to aid struggling boys and girls in South Carolina than Prof. Garrett." Papa, he wrote, had "led bitter fights in the past," which made it difficult to see the principled motivation (and loyalty and love) that lay behind his actions. In that same column, Ellis noted that it had been rumored that Papa was engaged in "a secret fight" against Allen's administration. He dismissed the allegation with this pithy rejoinder: "Who ever heard of Garrett carrying on a secret fight?"[1] If anyone knew it to be true, E. Philip Ellis did.

◆ ◆ ◆

The bishop who replaced Chappelle was William W. Beckett, the former president of Allen whom Papa had hoped to succeed. Mama held out little hope he would do anything for Papa.

"Some folks are talking of demanding Dad's reinstatement," she wrote Mattie. "I don't know, am just 'sawing wood and saying nothing.'"[2] Two weeks later, she was a little more optimistic: "Bishop Beckett has given your Daddy charge of all the [in-state] conferences. That means a little money for him; also his subscription list is growing. But what I want to see is something definite done that will bring in regular salary and stop this hand-to-mouth existence."[3]

Alas, Papa's Beckett-aided rise did not last. The new bishop died on January 1, 1926, just months after being appointed to preside over South Carolina. He'd agreed to give Papa a place at Allen, but his successor, Haitian-born Bishop John Hurst, refused to honor the appointment. Mama was livid:

"[Hurst] dodges behind the "no vacancy" cry. This is a lie. . . .

"Sometimes I am puzzled as to whether there is any justness anywhere. Dad is down and out, with no money, no work, the laughing-stock of the people and church and school for which he has made all but the supreme sacrifice."[4]

Though "it felt like the hardest of all blows," Mama tried to make the best of it, admonishing Mattie not to "worry about my worry." Devastated as she was, she could not afford to despair: "I *must* [emphasis original] work since no one else in the house is, so I am teaching at a country school 16 miles out drive each day. Sometimes the trip is so rough but I grit my teeth and go on. The fifty dollars per month from this will help keep the wolf from the door and something else is bound to turn up when this is out. As long as I can work, the AME church may do its worst. I shall live."[5]

Mama's complaints aside, Papa continued to travel on behalf of the church well into the 1940s. Much was within the state, but he traveled outside it as well, venturing up to Baltimore and down to Florida, west to Little Rock, Denver, and Dallas—journeys that led one wag to dub him "the watch dog of church affairs from Maine to California."[6] "Poor old fellow," Mama told Mattie. "He is about to run his head off trying to keep the A.M.E. Church straight. As soon as he corrals one bunch of renegades another breaks out."[7] Trains were the lifeblood of the country in those days before routine air travel, and Papa's were arduous journeys. Columbia to Jacksonville was more than ten hours; Columbia to Denver likely at least twice that. His trip to Kansas City for the 1928 Republican Convention took two days, via Atlanta, Memphis, and Springfield, Mo. Added to the tedium was the fact that routes below the Mason–Dixon line were uncomfortable and sometimes dangerous for Black men and women.

Relegated to old carriages that were seldom cleaned, they might find that there were too few seats—the colored cars were also used for baggage. After one of her trips north, Mama reported, "We had good seats all the way both going and coming, tho' some folks had to stand while others sat on their luggage."[8] Toilets were filthy. Service could be erratic, especially on smaller lines, so the men (and women) who traveled on behalf of the AME church provided their own entertainment. Sidetracked for hours, they sang hymns and competed to see who could preach the most stirring sermon. Papa, of course, had his copy of the complete works of Shakespeare. Head bowed late at night, he lost himself in the magnificent prose. And, on occasion, perhaps stood, one hand on a seat back in the jolting, swaying car, delighting the others in his party as he declaimed a soliloquy.

Black women bore a double burden. They endured the same discomforts, but they also faced the possibility of sexual violence from white men who drank and smoked in the colored cars.

All the same, train travel was the only option for a man with things to do and so many places to go. And so Papa endured fitful sleep on poorly maintained lines, endured white men's laughter, and their drunken swapping of filthy stories. Given the conditions—his loyalty to church and Allen aside—I wonder if Papa spent so much time on the road just to get away from home. All those journeys suggest the restlessness of a traveling salesman or a rock star.

◆　◆　◆

John Hurst served as bishop in South Carolina for four years until his death on May 6, 1930, at his home in Baltimore. (It was common for bishops to live only part time in their districts or even to commute from their primary residences just for conferences and other meetings.) Mama noted his passing sardonically: "Well," she told Mattie, "South Carolina has killed another bishop of the AME Church."[9]

Immediately after the service, the bishops met and decided to send Reverdy Ransom to South Carolina.[10] Hurst may have been predisposed to dislike Papa because of Papa's activism on behalf of the laymen, but Reverdy shared with Papa a commitment to change. He himself had been "harshly" censured at the 1928 General Conference in Chicago for preaching a rousing sermon on "the abuse of power, including . . . 'burdensome assessments' and . . . dictatorial acts practiced by the leaders."[11] Hurst was among those who had criticized him.

Whatever his reasons, Reverdy convinced Allen's board to offer Papa a job, leaving it to him to choose what he wanted to do. Though he was sixty-five, Papa didn't want "to be confined to classroom work," so he asked to become a "field agent," responsible for traveling the state to keep "in touch with prospective students" and to generate support for the university.[12]

For all that his contemporaries lauded Papa's value to Allen, I've found few accounts of what he said during his travels on behalf of the school. One reported that, after Papa "thrilled the audience as he usually does," he "urged the ministers and laymen to support Allen University, telling them that while it may not be as well equipped in every respect as schools with large endowments or large state schools, it is ours and is all that WE have [emphasis original]."[13] Another account says that he "urged the people to continue their support to the church and school and gave many illustrations of how he struggled against the many odds in his path way." The story said he'd recently returned from Baltimore, Philadelphia, and New York "on a speaking tour in interest of the university."[14]

Reverdy Ransom's presence in South Carolina may help to explain why Papa was chosen as a lay delegate to the 1932 General Conference in Cleveland. It was Papa's first time as an official attendee since 1916. In Cleveland, Papa saw the fulfillment of his efforts toward greater representation for the laymen. They were given places on the all-powerful Episcopal Committee, which decided the number of new bishops, where bishops would be sent, "and which bishops should be retired, suspended, or unfrocked."[15]

◆　◆　◆

Reverdy's tenure may also explain the honorary degree Papa received in 1932, but Papa's one-time student, George A. Singleton, likely helped make it happen. About the time Papa became Allen's field agent, Singleton praised him by placing Papa at "the head of the list" of "the teachers who first toucht [sic] this young life." And, he went on: "More than once has this writer been congratulated by professors in large Eastern and Western universities for his English composition and style. Garrett gets the credit for he was the writer's only teacher of that subject."[16]

That same year, 1930, Singleton argued at least three times that Papa deserved a "testimonial"[17] while he was still alive. Lobbying for the tribute, he suggested that "it would be in order . . . at the same time to present him an automobile"[18] for use in his work as field agent. Nothing seems to have come of the idea. Certainly, Mama would have boasted about it to Mattie if Papa had been given a car!

When Allen awarded Papa an honorary doctor of letters, Singleton was delighted. The degree was, he wrote, well deserved because "Garrett is a maker of men. . . . [and] the last of Allen's most popular teachers."[19]

◆ ◆ ◆

Reverdy Ransom's departure in 1932 marked another downturn in Papa's fortunes. The new bishop, Noah W. Williams, proposed doing away with his job, arguing that clergymen could act as field agents, saving the school Papa's salary of seventy dollars a month. Some members of the board disagreed—they must have felt Papa deserved something for his decades-long devotion to Allen. Williams compromised, changing Papa's job to "custodian of buildings and grounds"[20] and reducing his salary by ten dollars a month.

Did Papa supervise a crew of janitors and groundskeepers, making sure they kept the campus and its buildings in good condition? Or was the title "superintendent" a concession to his ego, because the old man mopped and swept, scrubbed classrooms, dorms, and bathrooms, and emptied the trash? I don't know, though I've found two letters from the late 1930s: one advising Papa that he's in charge of the grounds during the summer and another in which Papa tenders an inventory of the library. But if Papa really became a janitor, he must have felt he had no choice, much like other Black men of his time who settled for jobs beneath their training and abilities. (Women, of course, were not exempt—remember Mama's time in service to the woman in the wheelchair.) As a child in Washington in the 1920s, Jo had a classmate whose father, a Meharry Medical College graduate, couldn't get a loan to open a dental office. Unable to start his own practice or join one, he became a custodian at his daughter's elementary school. The best job he could find, it provided a regular salary and the prospect of a stipend when he could no longer work.

The letter telling Papa he's in charge during the summer addresses him as Mr., not Prof., a change in honorific that symbolizes the humbling turn of events—Bishop Chappelle's posthumous revenge. Papa continued at Allen anyway. What else could he do?

Four years after Bishop Williams changed Papa's title and cut his salary, he convinced the trustees to let Papa go. Williams complained that all Papa did was "to draw his salary and breath," but what really fueled the bishop's ire was Papa's "destructive publication."[21] This must have been *The Light*, though no issues from the 1930s survive.

A month later, the board met again, this time under the leadership of a new bishop, William Decker Johnson. (Their names are the same, but this was not the same man who'd earlier been president of Allen.) After a motion by the Rev. Eugene H. McGill—the son of the Rev. Daniel McGill, who had sued Papa for libel long before—the trustees voted to reinstate Papa. Eugene would be elected president of Allen the following year, so clearly he must have enjoyed some influence. Perhaps it was only that a quarter of a century had passed, but something must have happened for Eugene McGill to support Papa, despite Papa's complicated history with his family.[22]

As usual, Mama was suspicious. "The school and church officials are a bit hypocritical as regards your daddy," she told Mattie. "They do not like him, hardly respect him, yet fear him greatly. The new president told him he wanted him (Dad) to continue to work as before. I wish he would or could refuse to accept but he has accepted it."[23]

Clearly Mama felt that, whether Papa was called superintendent or custodian, the work itself was beneath him.

All the same, Papa's commitment to the AME church and school remained strong. He continued to attend conferences and speak at churches throughout the state. The *Palmetto Leader* reported on scores of his appearances in consecutive issues—once I counted four stories in the same issue. He was elected a lay trustee of Allen in November of 1936 and, in 1938, to the executive board of Allen's Board of Trustees. In 1939, Papa was chosen as a lay delegate for the 1940 General Conference.[24]

These honors didn't mean Papa had decided to keep quiet and go along to get along. When Eugene McGill fell seriously ill—he would die on March 13, 1939—a council of presiding elders made Allen Dean Eldridge Fisher Gregory Dent acting president. Chaos ensued when students struck in protest—perhaps the new acting president was unpopular on campus. He signed his correspondence E. F. G. Dent (and is even identified that way on his tombstone), which may hint at a certain rigidity.[25]

Days into the strike, it was reported that "C.G. Garrett, reputed 'stormy petrel' of the AME Church, was urging Dr. Dent to stick it out as president."[26] Dent was one of Papa's former students, and Papa continued to support him even after Dent's resignation three weeks into his term. He spoke "vociferously" in support of the would-be president and signed a letter that appeared on the front page of the *Palmetto Leader* condemning those who'd opposed Dent.[27] It was all for naught. In June, Papa announced that Dent had been elected president of Kittrell College,[28] where he'd previously served as dean of theology. Also an AME school, Kittrell was under the supervision of Papa's "lifelong friend and former student," Bishop Monroe Davis.[29]

Though Papa lost that battle, his support of Dent didn't hurt him in the church or at Allen.

Early in 1940, he was named one of the "distinguished AME leaders" who attended the 1940 Bishop's Council in Atlanta. In June, the trustees voted to retire him on "full pay less six dollars," Mama told Mattie. "Whereas they were giving him $66, they will now give him $60 the rest of his days. Of course, the bishop [Joseph S. Flipper] is to be thanked for maneuvering it. Now we won't have to be wondering about his re-election or retention each year."

The trustees had finally done "one decent thing." A week later, however, Mama wrote that Allen never had "any money during the summer," so Papa "doesn't know when he will get another check." She continued to worry: "He has had only $15.00 since June, but the trustees and P.E.'s [presiding elders] met yesterday and made their report for Endowment day and he will get some tomorrow we hope."[30]

Now retired—the Columbia City Directory would list him as "emeritus, Allen University"—Papa spoke at a banquet in February 1941 to celebrate Bishop Flipper's eighty-second birthday. It was a long program—there were almost forty speakers. That same year saw another marker of Papa's reconciliation with Allen when he was invited to speak at the laying of the cornerstone of the J. S. Flipper Library, "a stone building worth $75,000." The principal speaker was I. M. A. Myers, once news editor of *The Light* and now a professor of education at Allen. The *Palmetto Leader* reported that "Prof. C.G. Garrett, who is known and respected as one among the strongest laymen of the A.M.E. church . . . gave a vivid history of Allen University, stating that the school started in Cokesburg [*sic*] in 1882, and that in 1886 it was moved to Columbia, S.C., and that he came to Allen, a boy from the country. Prof. Garrett is still an honored member of the faculty."[31]

16

Tap's Almost Success

Many of Mama and Papa's children died before I was born; others, before I was old enough to be curious about the lives of those who'd come before me. Of all their children, though, I'd like most to have known Tap, Mama's "especially favored" son. Like me, he wanted to write. And, like me, he had fleeting brushes with recognition, enough to make him understand how much he craved wider appreciation of his talents.

Early in the beginning of their new life together in New York, Tap and his wife, Cornice, suffered a devasting loss. In July 1919, she gave birth to a girl they named Anna Louise. The infant died seven days later.[1] In time, Tap and Cornice would adopt a son, Alfred, though surely the effects of their loss lingered.

Despite his experience at the Howard School, Tap did not teach in New York. As mentioned earlier, he worked as a Pullman porter, though not for long. He was, as Jo put it, "too elegant to be a porter."[2] He'd also work as a bookkeeper and as a "doorman at the 49th Street Theatre."[3] And he wrote a musical, "Goophered," but opening theater doors was as close as he'd come to a show business career.

News of the musical came in 1926, when the NAACP touted the pending premiere of Tap's "play with music" about "aspects of Negro life in South Carolina . . . [and] the part played by a 'conjure' woman." Tap had written the libretto, or book, and some of the lyrics. The music was by the prominent Black musician and composer Hall Johnson. "Additional lyrics" were from Langston Hughes, who (as the NAACP press release noted) had been awarded first prize for his poem "The Weary Blues" in an *Opportunity* magazine contest the year before.

"This is an attempt to bring before the public a truer picture of Negro rural life than has been seen in the jazz revues," Hall said. "We shall try to represent the real dancing as it is done on the plantation, buck-and-wing, shake-downs, the ancestors of the Charleston which is now so much in vogue. The dancing will be a feature of the production, although like the music and text it will be subordinate to the picture we shall try to draw of Negro life. I am making a big feature too of the choral singing, in which Negro Spirituals and work songs will have a prominent place."[4]

It was the height of the Harlem Renaissance, the flowering of African-American art and literature that began about 1918 and lasted until the mid-1930s. Harlem was in vogue (as historian David Levering Lewis titled his history of the era), and white Americans indulged their craving for Black styles in dance, music, and literature. The all-Black musical *Shuffle Along* opened in 1921 and ran for more than a year and more than five hundred performances, "creating a seemingly insatiable market for similar Harlem musicals."[5] Afterward, the gates opened for Black artists. According to Lewis, Black authors produced twenty-six novels, ten books of poetry, and five Broadway plays between 1925 and 1935.[6] Another chronicler says there were about twenty "Negro revues" on Broadway in the 1920s, when "[t]he black musical set the style for white songwriters and dramatists."[7]

All this explains why Hall Johnson went to such lengths to stress the authenticity of "Goophered." I wonder, though, how much he really knew about plantation life. Although influenced early on by "the mournful sounds of spirituals," Hall was the son of the William Decker Johnson who'd been Allen's president, a graduate of the University of Pennsylvania, fluent in French and German, and so musically inclined he'd taught himself to play the violin at age fifteen.[8] At any rate, the first performance was promised "about May 31st," with Abbie Mitchell (one of "the two finest black actresses of the age"[9]) in the lead role of "conjure woman."

Tap had been secretary of the Columbia branch of the NAACP,[10] working with Green Jackson and others of Papa's contemporaries, which may help explain why the NAACP publicized "Goophered." There was another, more significant, connection, however: Hall (1888–1970) had graduated from Allen in 1908, a year before Tap finished its normal school. He had been Papa's student and Mattie's voice teacher.

A flurry of stories about "Goophered" appeared in African-American newspapers[11] in 1926 and 1927. The *Chicago Defender* headline "Doorman of Theater Becomes Playwright,"[12] deliberately evoked poet Vachel

Lindsay's 1925 "discovery" of Langston Hughes working as a busboy at a Washington, D.C., hotel.[13] Even the *New York Times* ran a brief notice. Like most of the ones in the Black press, it was a version of the NAACP news release, and the *Times* rendered Tap's first name "Caspar."[14] Notices also appeared in *Opportunity: Journal of Negro Life,*[15] which reported that "the libretto by Garrett is to have in it three lyrics by Langston Hughes: 'Mother to Son;' 'The Midnight Blues;' and 'Song for a Banjo.'"[16] That same column also noted that Langston and Zora Neale Hurston were collaborating on an operetta *and* a musical comedy. Nothing came of their efforts, and their friendship would eventually rupture under the stress of another collaboration—Tap might have been well advised not to get his hopes up.

In September, the *Baltimore Afro-American* optimistically reported that the "new musical play by Johnson and Garrett is now in rehearsal at Urban League Hall, New York."[17] A few months later, the *Pittsburgh Courier's* Geraldyn Dismond wrote that "a number of critics, theatrical backers and music lovers" had attended an audition of "Goophered" in New York and that "the songs . . . were marvelously received." Dismond went on, somewhat breathlessly, that "even the book, which always suffers most severely at the hands of producers, is escaping with less than the usual cutting and re-writing. The brokers claim that no amount of money will be spared to perfect it in every detail, and already there is talk of foreign rights." She quoted these lyrics: "When your eyes turn red/And your mouth turns black/Well, you're goophered." Dismond also noted that Johnson had won first prizes for two "numbers" from "Goophered" "in the recent Opportunity contest." Perhaps those lyrics were more compelling.[18]

In his July 31, 1926, application for a William E. Harmon Foundation Award[19]—it was filed a day before the deadline; Hall must have been busy!—Hall noted the music he'd written for his "Negro operetta," adding that the "book is by Casper Garrett and there are three lyrics by Langston Hughes." Undeterred by false modesty, he proclaimed, "Competent judges who have examined this operetta have declared that it will be the most significant thing ever done on the stage by Negro artists. It would have been produced weeks ago but for the fact that it is nearly impossible to find financial backing for Negroes on the stage unless they want to do either a vulgar burlesque on the race or a flashy review with partially undressed women."[20]

Hall included "Goophered" in a list of his achievements when he applied for another Harmon Award (this time in 1930), and in 1934, it was reported that the show would be produced after Labor Day, "the whole piece having to be rewritten and most of the music yet to be completed."[21] It didn't happen. Except for the audition and Urban League Hall rehearsals, "Goophered" never saw the stage.

Tap's draft of the work has disappeared, though traces may survive in Hall's "Fi-yer," a script from 1959. Johnson lists himself as author and composer of the "Negro Music-Drama in Two Acts and Seven Scenes." At the bottom of the title page, however, he offers "grateful acknowledgements to" Hughes for contributing "four song-poems," and to "Casper G. Garret [*sic*], Jr. who helped with the book."[22]

Perhaps Hall was right, and "Goophered" wasn't vulgar enough for Broadway. Or perhaps it was all hype, the willful optimism that drives show-business people to audition in the afternoon after being rejected in the morning. Langston knew Hall (as well as Abbie Mitchell)—Arnold Rampersad, author of the splendid two-volume biography of the poet, recounts several meetings and collaborations (or attempts) between the two in the 1920s—and, in fact, Hall "was busy setting 'Mother to Son' to music"[23] sometime in 1925. Hughes's biographer notes that he always wanted to see his "poetry and other lyrics [set to] music," so "Goophered" may have been just one example of his hankering."[24]

It may also be that the poet's involvement was as limited as the phrases "additional lyrics" and "three lyrics" suggest. Ruth (who found the NAACP press release, and Hall's Harmon Foundation applications) found no signs of "Goophered" in Hughes's papers at Yale. Like Hall, Langston understood that artists make their own luck by embracing opportunities and moving on when they don't pay off. (He also understood "the great American truth that all publicity is good publicity."[25]) His first collection, *The Weary Blues*, was published early in 1926, a direct result of the *Opportunity* award he received the year before for the poem of the same title. Now a published author, he enrolled at Lincoln University that February. When the NAACP issued its 1926 press release, Langston was weeks into his first term, something else that must mean his involvement in the show was peripheral. If he'd believed "Goophered" might provide him with some much-needed cash, mightn't he at least have postponed college?

Langston would go on to become a world-renowned writer, publishing more than forty books of poetry and prose and writing nearly a dozen plays. Hall would enjoy a distinguished career as a composer and arranger on Broadway and in Hollywood. And Tap. . . .

After his encounter with near-fame, Tap went to work as a mail clerk. The job may not have done him in, but it probably didn't help his ambitions. As one *Ebony* magazine writer put it, the post office was a "graveyard of Negro talent,"[26] stifling the aspirations of African-Americans who might have become painters or sculptors, might have written poems, plays, novels, and stories. It provided the security of a living wage, allowed them to buy houses and cars, marry and raise children, and send those children to Lincoln, Howard, Spelman, and Fisk. The cost was their dreams.

When my mother, Ruth, was in graduate school at the University of Chicago, Tap sent her a letter about novels and novelists. He must have known that she, too, lived to read and wanted to write. After discussing Whitman, Wolfe, Faulkner, and Hemingway—Tap found "Hemingway's rotters . . . so attractive that one is tempted to believe it is great fun being one, while Faulkner's people are so low no one would attempt to better them"—he turned to Steinbeck. He liked *Of Mice and Men* better than *The Grapes of Wrath*, adding, "That does not mean I like people who just live as they are, better than people who struggle against insurmountable conditions, but I know an author can win battles of will or see rays of hope through any kind of clouds—clouds he has often blackened himself."

Did Tap mean writers and their characters? Or did he understand that what he'd written could also apply to himself because he'd given up hope of being recognized as a writer? Perhaps, because he ended the paragraph, "Or maybe I am just a disillusioned old cuss."[27]

Ralston, Tap, Maceo, and Marian stayed in New York, but Colon was gone by 1922. He may have taught in Columbia—he received a Richland County teacher's certificate on January 28[28]—but his name doesn't appear in lists of appointments published in the *Columbia Record* about that time. Perhaps Mama convinced him to get certified because she hoped he'd take up the work. After all, it was secure, if not particularly well paying. Perhaps he was teaching in one of Mama's rural schools. If he *was* teaching in a one- or two-teacher country school, the rigors of the work might have convinced him to apply to dental school at Nashville's Meharry Medical College. And one more supposition: Working as a Pullman porter, he'd likely met men who spent summers on the railroad to earn their Meharry tuition. Perhaps they served as examples that he could become the kind of professional Mama and Papa surely wanted him to be.

Colon's wife, Henrietta, also lived on Lady Street. It couldn't have been easy for her. In addition to Mama expecting her to act as unpaid help, she came down with dengue fever, as did her son. She'd go back to Philadelphia, where all too soon, she and Colon would suffer the death of a daughter, Laura Anna, from pneumonia in 1925. The girl was just nine months old.

Colon finished Meharry's dental school two years later.[29] He came home, Mama reported, "just as crazy as ever. He goes to Greenville next week to take the State Board after which he will seek a location. Henrietta and the boy will come down soon. They will go on to wherever Colon is located."[30] In July, the *Palmetto Leader* noted that he'd passed the three-day exam given by the South Carolina Board of Dental Examiners.[31] Three weeks later, Henrietta arrived from Philadelphia to spend "a few days"[32] with Mama and Papa before joining Colon in Dillon, where he'd opened his practice. It was one hundred miles north of Columbia, and seven miles south of the North Carolina border. Soon, the *Leader* would report that Colon had "a growing practice and is well liked generally in Dillon."[33] He even invested in a funeral home.[34]

Colon's status as a dentist meant he and his wife appeared often in the *Leader*'s pages in the 1920s and '30s. The newspaper reported on their trips to Latta—about five miles from Dillon—his on "business,"[35] hers to visit friends. It ran brief items noting when they came to Columbia to see Mama and Papa. Once, brothers Marian and Chris, sister Mills, and niece Jo (Mattie's oldest daughter) came to Dillon for the day, likely because Jo was spending the summer in South Carolina.[36] The editors dutifully noted Henrietta's participation in the Faithful Workers Club,[37] and the occasions both played host to the Idle House Social and Literary Club.[38] When Henrietta made her start as a teacher in a new "school for the first grades,"[39] the paper ran an item, as it did when Colon presented the certificates at a school graduation.[40] Another mark of Colon's status: His name appears as a member of the "honorary state committee" that hosted a "reception and dance" that was held after tenor Roland Hayes—one of the first Black concert singers to be recorded and to perform all over the world—sang at the Columbia Theater in 1931. Whites and Blacks attended Hayes's performance, but only "a limited number of seats . . . [were] reserved for white people."[41]

Meanwhile, three years after he wrote to Mattie asking for permission to visit Ruth, Ira Valentine realized his dreams. He and Ruth were married on February 11, 1924. (Did either think of the symbolism, and possible portent for a happy marriage, if they'd waited three days?) The marriage took place in Cleveland, where Ira worked as a mechanic; perhaps Ruth had fled Columbia to be with her beloved. Even so, Mama dutifully recorded the marriage in her Bible. Perhaps she hoped her wayward daughter would now slow peacefully into marriage and motherhood.

Alas, the marriage didn't last, nor did Ruth find an occupation she could settle into. Perhaps I should write "settle for," because over the next few years, Ruth careered from occupation to occupation, a trajectory that suggests the same restlessness that sent her brothers to New York and Papa from conference to conference on behalf of the church. She just didn't know what she wanted to do.

Most often, she taught. From time to time, she worked at the annual Colored State Fair. She even worked as a maid in Washington.

Mama alternated between optimism and despair.

Back from Cleveland, Ruth was appointed in 1925 to head the "domestic science department" at the new Winnsboro colored school, "a splendidly built brick graded school building. . . . with nine class rooms and an auditorium." The old buildings had been "out of repair and entirely too small and inadequate for the present purposes."[42] Perhaps they were the same ones where Papa had taught—another reason for Ruth to chafe under the confines of family. Mama's pride was tempered by realism: "The Domestic Science room had not been fitted up yet, so she substituted for one of the teachers and handled the first grade this week. Her principal said that if she did as well in her own classes as she did in this, she would give satisfaction. I hope she does as she really needs to work and we feel she will do better if near us. Our plan is for her to go to summer school and do her best to get in the work regularly. It remains for her to succeed."[43]

The next summer, reporting that Ruth wanted to go to Hampton, Mama said, "I'm hoping she makes a success of life after all."[44] Ruth did go to Hampton, apparently on a Richland County scholarship. She continued to teach and, in 1928, went to summer school at State. She opened school for Mama when Mama went to Chicago, and her name appears on a 1929 list of appointees to teach in Columbia's Negro schools.[45] That same year, she went to work in Atlantic City for the summer, but her plans were derailed by illness. By September, Ruth was back in Columbia, and Mama was hopeful that she'd soon be well enough to return to teaching.

As summer approached in 1930, Mama thought Ruth would go to Benedict or South Carolina State for the annual teacher training institute. Instead, she "accepted the position of governess for little Edward Robert Evans, the vivacious seven year old nephew of Dr. M.A. Evans."[46] (Edward was actually one of several children Evans had adopted.) Afterward, she went to Washington. There, she thought about going to Miner—during her stay with Mattie in 1922, Mama had urged her to, so she could "get the finishing touches."[47] When she didn't get in, Mama advised her to apply to Howard University. "I want you to go to school somewhere as you are there,"[48] she told her.

By then, Ruth was twenty-seven, old enough to want to make her own way in the world, even if her choices didn't meet with Mama's approval. Instead of going to Miner or Howard, she got married again. She and her second husband, William B. Butcher—called Jack—were married on October 30, 1935, in Washington. There were four lines left on the Marriages page, but Mama didn't enshrine Jack's name in the family Bible.

Though *he* made it into the Garrett Bible, Ira Valentine appears nowhere in Mama's letters. Jack's name does, though. He and Ruth came back to Columbia and Lady Street but soon moved to York, a small town about seventy-five miles north of Columbia. Mama thought it was a good idea, as it would be cheaper for them to live there. Ruth could work "at nursing, sewing[,] or even at teaching" (though for unexplained reasons—her divorce and remarriage?—Ruth "could never hope to get a school in Columbia district"), and Jack could work "at anything which he can do."[49] Within a few months, they were back on Lady Street.

Things didn't always go well. In their absence, Mama had moved her grandson, George, into what had been their bedroom, so she put Ruth and

Jack in what had been Mills's room. "But," she told Mills, "Jack is so filthy I put him out and made him sleep with George."[50] Ruth was not happy. She must have been even more unhappy with what Mama did next: "I forbade Jack's coming on my premises. He owed Dad some money for long-distance calls and gave impudence when Dad asked him for it. I really wish they'd move but they are too stingy and want to beat their way. Then, too, they both are running with a fast, low crowd and I'm tired of it. Of course, their crowd doesn't come here[,] but I don't care to know about it."[51]

A year after the United States entered World War II, Ruth found work teaching in Kershaw County.[52] "I'm glad she is teaching," Mama said. "And hope she will stay in this time."[53]

She didn't.

◆ ◆ ◆

Concerts and newspaper mentions aside, I have to wonder if Henrietta really was satisfied being the wife of a dentist in a town of just twenty-seven hundred.[54] Even if she had been born in Scuffletown, she'd lived too long in the North to settle comfortably again into small-town life.

A series of brief notices in the *Leader* from 1935 suggest all may not have been well. In April, Colon was "spending some time in Philadelphia visiting his wife and children." He returned the next month having had "a very enjoyable trip." Henrietta and their sons—Casper George III, born in 1929, and Reverdy Ransom, born in 1931—were in Dillon in July. It is interesting, however, that the newspaper referred to them as "Mrs. Henrietta Garrett and her children *of Philadelphia.*" [emphasis added] Two months later, the *Leader* reported that she'd come back from Philadelphia, "accompanied by her two little boys."[55]

In time, Mama would tell Mattie that they'd separated for good: "I think Colon has, at last, got his release from Henrietta. She asked for $150, which he raised and gave her and she signed the papers releasing him. They are to share the children at will."[56] Even so, Colon and Henrietta don't seem to have ever divorced; years later, each was listed as the other's spouse on their respective death certificates.

Colon may have had health problems, although Mama never said what they were. After a visit to Dillon, she reported that he was "much better, physically, than he was at Christmas time but not any better otherwise. He seems doomed and hopeless. Pray for him."[57] Perhaps he was depressed. Perhaps, like Maceo and some of his brothers, he was too fond of drink.

Another of those whispered family stories hints that Colon was forced to leave Dillon after he was accused of "war profiteering." Something must have happened, though, if only his disappointment at not having achieved more. "I hope Colon will get over his bitterness and do something for himself and children," Mills told Mattie. "I can understand his bitterness towards himself, but I can't see how he could let it spread towards anyone else as he has certainly been his worst enemy."[58]

Despite Mama's disapproval—she didn't record it in the family Bible—Marian and Evelyn's marriage lasted 16 years until her death in 1938. Still, it was not without its challenges. After Frank's death, Marian and Evelyn adopted her son George, so perhaps Evelyn was unable to have children. She wanted to work and to go to night school, but she worried about money and Marian's ability to stick to a job. Fourteen years into their marriage, she told Mattie that "in that time he's taken to about 6 different jobs, only to tell me in the end that they are not suited to his type of mind." He was selling insurance and working as a Pullman porter, but Evelyn thought both would be slow that winter. "[O]ne of us must have a job to bring in money to pay the bills with in case the old Pullman job should fall down."[59]

When Evelyn died in 1938, Mama said she hoped "Marian brings or sends George to me. He is such a queer child I fear no one else will treat him properly."[60]

Four years later, Marian married a woman named Olga McCauley. He waited a year to tell Mama. Still, that was better than his first marriage, when he'd left it to Tap to break the news.

"The announcement of Marian's marriage was quite a surprise," Mama told Mattie. "Especially as to the length of time he waited to announce it. But I'm glad he is married, he really needed a wife. The girl sent me a nice Mother's Day card signed 'your new daughter.' I appreciated that very much and wrote her a letter welcoming her into the family. If she is nice to Marian I'll be satisfied."[61] All the same, this new marriage also failed to make it into the family Bible.

Olga may have brought a son to the marriage: In one of his letters, Marian assures Mattie that "Olga and Ronald are just fine." If Ronald were Olga's son, that might explain why things weren't going well with George —now thirteen, perhaps he was having a hard time adjusting to a step-mother *and* stepbrother. George would spend some time at the Wiltwyck School for Boys, an institution for troubled youth in the town of Esopus, N.Y., about 90 miles north of New York City. Marian felt Wiltwyck had "done him a lot of good."[62] Scarcely 12 months later, he'd changed his mind. George's behavior had gotten "so terrible," Marian said, that "for the good of all concerned, I decided to turn him over to the Children's Court to be sent to a training school." Fortunately for George, Ethel (likely the girlfriend or ex-wife of one of the brothers, though I haven't figured out which) offered to take him in. He'd been there a month, but, Marian said, "as I see it, will be there permanently."[63]

Olga and Marian must have parted ways, because he married again, this time to Alma Green, a woman nearly half his age. When Mattie informed Ruth (my mother, not her sister) that "your Uncle Marian and his new wife are expecting a baby this spring," she felt compelled to add "he will be 57 in March and she is in her early thirties."[64] Well shut of parenthood herself, Mattie must have wondered how he'd fare as he entered his sixties.

She needn't have. His daughter, Sue-Lynn, remembers him as a loving, attentive father.[65]

17

Mills

I'd like, as I've said, to have known Tap, but he died when I was just a year old, and I've seen just a few letters from him. By contrast, I have a cache of letters from Mills, beginning in 1918, when she was twelve years old, to 1979, as she neared the end of a teaching career begun more than fifty years before. There's this as well: Although my siblings and I stayed in Philadelphia with Ruth Eidier for a week or two one summer after we'd come from Jamaica, Mills was the only one of the Garrett sons and daughters I really knew. But the real reason she gets more than one chapter is this: Of all Mama and Papa's children, Mills achieved the most, living up to both her parents' expectations.

I'd see her throughout the 1960s and '70s when she came to Jo's home on Illinois Avenue in Washington, D.C.'s Brightwood Park. My mother never learned to drive, and so Jo would relinquish the kitchen to her mother-in-law so she could fetch her younger sister and her sister's four children. Walking out to Jo's Chevy—she always bought Chevrolets, always paid the asking price at Curtis Chevrolet, a mile away on Georgia Avenue from her home—Ruth would exhort us: "Speak French to Aunt Mills. She'll give you money." We were shy children, but once in a while we'd overcome our bashfulness enough to say, "*Bon jour, Tante Mills. Comment allez-vous?*" And Mills, arms folded over her chest on her dining room radiator perch, a folded section of the *Washington Post* or the *Washington Star* between her bottom and the warm curved ribs, would respond, "*Tres bien. Et tu?*" And then go upstairs to the bedroom she had taken over for her stay and come back with a quarter or fifty-cent piece for each of us.

She wasn't tall, but her erect posture and a certain severity of manner gave the impression of height. She wore gray wigs, was thin, and had a slight stutter that must have been like Papa's. Despite her world travels and fluency with languages, she pronounced the word children "chirren," in keeping with her small-city South Carolina roots.

With her sojourn in Haiti, doctorate, Fulbright, and world travels, Mills was the only relative ever held up as an example. And, though Ruth never said so, there was another reason—Mills was the only one of the Garrett siblings who inherited Mama's drive and Papa's love of learning. Men kept interrupting Ruth Eidier's progress toward the security of a career (at least the way Mama saw it), and Mama's sons let alcohol leach their ambitions. But Mills let nothing—including men—impede her. In 1954, nearly thirty years into her teaching career, she became the first of the Garretts and Simonses to earn a doctorate. By then, she was almost fifty.

As with her siblings' choices, Mills's perseverance was rooted in Papa's misfortune. Ten years old when he was forced out at Allen, she was old enough to be aware of the loss of status in the community and the financial struggles that followed. Not surprisingly, she'd prize stability and security—her letters from the 1930s, '40s, and '50s are filled with money worries, and she taught at the same historically Black college and university (HBCU), West Virginia State College—now West Virginia State University—for a quarter of a century. But Mills also had Mama's example of pluck and resilience. Her mother showed her a woman might create her own stability and security and enjoy a career of her own.

It was at Booker T. Washington High (from 1918 to 1948 the only high school for Blacks in Columbia) that Mills became interested in languages, perhaps because her brother, Ralston, had served in France during the war. Languages, she said, always "seemed to come easy to me."[1] She left public school after tenth grade to finish high school at Benedict College, then stayed for her bachelor's degree. Encouraged to take education classes, she balked—she wanted to take French. Eventually, the college allowed her to. Mills did so well that during her junior year she substituted when the French teacher took a leave of absence to care for her sick husband.

She graduated in 1927, the same year Colon finished dental school at Meharry Medical College, and delivered the valedictory address—"The Appreciation of Beauty." The sixty-one Benedict graduates—only thirteen received bachelor's degrees; the rest received "college preparatory" and "Sunday school training teacher's" diplomas—were addressed by the Rev.

R. A. Lapsley of Columbia's First Presbyterian Church. "You must run the race that is set before you," Lapsley admonished them. "Put your whole soul into the race and have a determination and you will not only reach the goal, but you will win."[2]

Mills's first teaching job, at a school in Bessemer City, N.C., would give her a chance to test the truth of those words.

The principal had recruited her with many "fine and exquisite letters" touting the city and "his new school." When Mills got there, however, she found a town of less than four thousand people and "a little country Rosenwald brick building about a mile from the main part of town." (The Julius Rosenwald Foundation, created by the president of Sears, Roebuck, and Company, contributed $4.3 million toward the construction of nearly five thousand Negro schools in the South between 1912 and 1932. African-Americans more than matched his funds, raising $4.7 million.)[3] She was, she told Mattie, "so disappointed . . . that I wanted to catch the next train back home. The only thing that kept me from doing so was the fact that I didn't want to go back home after all the bragging I had done about our new high school building."[4]

Later, Mills would recall that her sojourn in what she called "Hell's Acre" was "almost the undoing of me."[5] Told she'd have classes in Latin and algebra, she spent the summer boning up on those subjects only to find she was to teach French ("to dummies that know no English at all"),[6] reading, spelling, and health. The students "were poor, rural children almost as old as she."[7] When she applied for the job, the principal told her she'd receive a salary of at least ninety-five dollars a month. Once she arrived, he told her it might be as little as seventy-five dollars. Even worse, he was "a despotic, miserly man who required new teachers to live at his house."[8] He fed them poorly—"I don't see anything to eat but rice and grits," Mills told Mattie, adding, "the part of sardine I get depends on when I get to the table. If I get there first I get half of the can. If I am a minute late, I catch the smell."[9] What saved her were parcels from Mama and Mattie and dinner invitations from a former teacher who "knew we hadn't had anything to eat." Mills was grateful for those invitations for another reason—the principal refused to let them go out at night. "He is always afraid a man might speak to us, as if I wasn't grown,"[10] Mills complained. When she and another teacher announced plans to go out one Saturday, he told them school would be open that weekend.

Given how she'd been treated, it isn't surprising that Mills decided to leave at the end of the school year. But when she applied for other jobs, she found the principal had written to warn prospective employers against hiring her. Her former teachers at Benedict wrote on her behalf, but, in the end, she was forced to go to Bettis Academy,[11] a small school in Trenton, S.C., as a last-minute replacement.

Two years later, Mills moved to Bell Street High School in Clinton, S.C., where she taught Latin, French, and English. She also chaired "the declamation group" and refereed and coached girls' basketball—something I found hard to square with the decorous, reserved great-aunt I'd known growing up. "I'm quite sure Allen University will beat us," she admitted, "but they won't have an easy time in so doing. My girls can give the best teams all that they want and a little bit more."[12] She liked her work, but she was paid just sixty dollars a month—white teachers in Clinton received twice that. "[M]ore education," Mills decided, "was the only way to beat the segregated system."[13]

Unable to go full time to earn a master's degree, she took summer courses at Howard University, boarding with Mattie and Alfred on S Street in Washington, D.C. They'd bought the house in 1928. One of her teachers was Mercer Cook (1903–87), an assistant professor at Howard. The son of composer Will Marion Cook and Abbie Mitchell, star of Tap's "Goophered," Mercer was "from the upper crust of the African American community."[14] He'd traveled with his entertainer parents in the United States and in Europe, attended Washington's elite Dunbar High School, and graduated from Amherst College. Afterward, he'd gone on to receive a teacher's diploma from the University of Paris and a master's degree and doctorate from Brown University. Though just three years older than Mills, he became something of a mentor. When he became a professor of French at Atlanta University, he helped her get a scholarship that allowed her to go to school full time there. He'd encourage her throughout her career.

Mills received her master's degree in French from Atlanta University in 1937. That fall, she went to teach at Kittrell College, Kittrell, N.C., where AME Bishop Monroe H. Davis was head of the board of trustees. Monroe

had been Papa's student at Allen, so he must have given Mills a hearty rec-
ommendation. But, though she needed the job, teaching at Kittrell was a
mixed blessing. The school had been closed for three years, a "stormy and
turbulent period of its existence" where bankruptcy proceedings revealed
more than fifty-three thousand dollars in debts, including as much as eight
thousand dollars in unpaid salaries. Somehow, Monroe (who, "close associates" said, "eats, sleeps and lives Kittrell College") managed to reopen the
college. It must have been touch and go—money was still being raised at an
AME convocation in August 1937.[15]

Mills taught French and Spanish. All the while, she dreamed of escaping
to Paris—conditions at Kittrell were nigh unendurable. There was no heat,
and the food almost as bad as what she'd choked down in Bessemer City—
"peas, cornbread, buttermilk . . . cheese toast (a slice, sometimes two)
and tea, or six prunes and tea for supper."[16] Sometimes, they had cabbage
instead of peas and "tough" boiled beef on Sunday.

She didn't receive her first check until mid-October. And, since she
understood she was "working at an AME Church school," she realized,
"I shall probably not receive another check at the time due."[17] She was
right. After the Christmas holidays, Kittrell "started the general routine of
AME schools in not paying its teachers." The trustees said they hoped to
"pay us something by the last of February."[18] In June 1939, the president,
a dean, two teachers, and the matron of women were fired. Two other
teachers would resign to protest the actions of Kittrell's board. The school
year ended with just sixty-three students on the fifteen-building, three-
hundred-acre campus. E. F. G. Dent, ousted as Allen's acting president, was
chosen to lead Kittrell. Though there were fewer than thirty students, Dent
claimed he'd received "many applications," "the outlook was most promising," and "within a very short time, the faculty will be completed with well-
qualified instructors," all with master's degrees.[19]

Whatever changes Dent intended weren't enough to keep Mills. She'd
learned of a government job that would pay "the enormous salary of $115
a month"—only about five dollars a month less than her brother-in-law,
Alfred, brought home after twenty-one years working for the government,
and enough to live on *and* save for her passage to Europe. She took the
civil service exam and was hired as a printer's assistant at the US Bureau of
Engraving in Washington, D.C. In December 1939, she left Kittrell.

Conditions there had been intolerable, but it wasn't the most opportune time to plan a trip to Europe—France and England had declared war on Germany four months before. There was this as well—"enormous salary" aside, working as a printer's assistant turned out to be not all that fulfilling, especially for a woman with varying degrees of fluency in French, Spanish, Latin, and German. Jo's appointment letter for the same job (dated January 30, 1940) specified it was "a mechanical position, the duties of which are to feed power printing presses." As new employees, both women were expected to work from four o'clock in the afternoon to midnight.

Two years after Mills left North Carolina to go to Washington, D.C, the United States entered the war. Many teachers were leaving the profession for higher paying government work. Mills did the opposite, applying to teach high school in Washington—which meant Dunbar, the city's colored academic high school named after African-American poet Paul Laurence Dunbar, or Armstrong, its colored vocational high school, which was named for Gen. Samuel C. Armstrong, who commanded Black troops in the Civil War and founded Hampton Institute. Qualifications deemed satisfactory, she was summoned to take the qualifying Franklin Exam in April 1941 at Cardozo High School. "Boy [as Mama called her youngest son, Christopher] and I had hearty laughs about your description of your examination," Mama wrote her afterward. "Boy says you always say you'll flunk but always come out all right. Let's hope this will be the way this time."[20]

Despite her master's degree in French, Mills lacked a few courses that the District required—in one letter, she mentions that she was supposed to have taken courses in "Educational Psychology" and "Tests and Measurements," as well as one called "Methods of Teaching English." She intended to "read up on"[21] the latter. At any rate, she wound up at Booker T. Washington, a junior high school in Baltimore, perhaps because she didn't have those required courses. It's also possible that she didn't score quite high enough to overcome the fierce competition for a place at Dunbar, which boasted teachers with master's degrees and even some with doctorates. They couldn't find jobs at white colleges and universities—even the ones where they'd earned their degrees—and there was a limited number of jobs at Black institutions. So they taught at segregated schools like Dunbar and made them among the best in the nation.

Mills Garrett, 1942.
Collection of the author.

Mills's new school was woefully overcrowded: Designed to hold about one thousand students, Washington now housed more than two thousand. Worse, because she was new, she "was assigned classes of slow learners who had severe discipline problems."[22] Within weeks, she wrote Mattie that she "felt like resigning and trying to get reinstated at the Bureau, or even going [back] to Kittrell." Students in two of her classes had "made me so angry that I should like to have actually shot about twenty of them." She intended, however, to "have so much work for them that I don't intend for them to have time to cut up."[23] Whatever Mills did, it must have worked. After a year, she was offered tenure, "an unheard of distinction."[24]

A few months later, Mills wrote to thank Washington's acting principal, Elmer A. Henderson. He assured her that she was welcome. "I have confidence in your ability," he wrote, "and at no time has there been any doubt in my mind as to the early possibility of you becoming an excellent teacher.

... I sincerely thank you for your promise to do what you can to make your work constantly show a degree of improvement."[25]

Given Mills's twelve years of teaching and the range of her experience —small country school to small-town high school; eighth grade to college—Elmer's approval seems, well, grudging, but that was in keeping with his character and philosophy of education. He had begun teaching in 1902, four years before Mills was born, when he was just fifteen years old. A believer in "high standards," "discipline and orderliness on the part of both student and teacher," he once offered this blunt advice: "If young teachers want to succeed in the school system, they should love their work, use their brains more than their mouths, and attract attention by a dignified manner and high calibre of work."[26]

Reading between the lines of Elmer's letter to Mills, I wonder if he was warning her not to get too big for her britches now that she had tenure. I wonder, too, if his attitude—and the unruly students—were why Mama pointed out that "it seems that you and Baltimore in general have a hard time getting yourselves adjusted to each other."[27]

Mills got the message, though perhaps not the one Henderson intended. After the end of the Second World War, when her nephew, Al, Mattie and Alfred's oldest son, was beginning his own teaching career, she told Mattie to pass on this advice: "Some people don't like too many suggestions and even good ideas from subordinates. It makes them feel inferior—the worst feeling that any principal, superior, or boss of any kind could ever have."[28]

To be sure, some things were better in Baltimore than they'd been in Bessemer City or at Bettis. Junior high teachers received an average of one hundred eighty dollars a month, three times what Mills had earned in Clinton, although thirty-six dollars less than she would have received in Washington.[29] She was also paid on time. There were other outside-of-work benefits: Her niece, Jo, also taught in Baltimore. Jo and several other unmarried teachers shared an apartment they called Saints Rest and, though Mills took a room in the house of AME Bishop Monroe Davis, she was a frequent visitor. Washington was a brief train ride away. Mills often went "home," as she called the house on S Street, on weekends.

All the same, she wanted more. France was out of reach, but the Haitian government had decided that elementary and secondary school students needed to learn English. Officials asked the United States for help. When the US Office of Education announced it was recruiting English teachers, Mills applied to go to Haiti.

"We certainly hope you can arrange to go," Mama told her. "It will mean so much to you. Travel, French contact, better salary and so many other things I wished for for myself when I was young but they are about to come to you. Maybe then, if you go, you can find a husband. (Smile)"[30]

Mills likely wouldn't have been offended, even if Mama had omitted that pre-emoji parenthetical. Though she was thirty-six and about fifteen years past the average age at which women married then, she was not without a sense of humor about her spinsterhood. At home in Columbia a year after she started teaching in Baltimore, she and a friend stopped at the corner of Pine and Lady Streets "to finish their talk." They must have been good friends—"nearly half an hour" later a soldier approached and tried to join the conversation. The two women ignored him, but. . . .

But let Mills finish the story: "[H]e would have no part of that and tried to get rough. We ran across the street to where T.J. Miles was watering his lawn and he took out [*sic*] behind us, trying to follow us into the yard. However, T.J. sobered him up with the hose and told him that he was about to get a bullet in him. He then wouldn't leave, swearing that he knew us, etc., etc. T.J. soon persuaded him, though, and we came out of the house." Afterward, Mills confessed, her rescuer told her "had he known it was I, he would not [have] interfered as maybe I would have gotten a husband."[31]

Uxorial possibilities aside, there was this that spurred Mama's encouragement—Charity E. Adams, daughter of the Garretts's neighbor, AME minister the Rev. Eugene Avery Adams, had become the first Black woman officer in the Women's Army Corps. By December, Mama reported, Charity had been promoted to captain. (She'd retire as a lieutenant colonel.) But now Mama had something of her own to crow about: "Others are bragging of first one thing then another, but like the Adamses we will be in a class all by ourselves."[32]

The government selected ten teachers—five of them Black. (Only six, and a supervisor, seem to have gone.) Mills was the only woman. There was just one problem—the Baltimore School Board balked at giving her a leave of absence. "I do hope you will be able to make it as it seems to be the one thing you most desire," Mama told Mills. "Perhaps the board will change its point of view after the government people talk with them about it[,] but hope so and keep our fingers crossed."[33] As Mills tried to decide what to do, Mama kept writing to encourage her: "Let's not lose hope and faith, even though it does seem that you can get mixed up with the "pig-headedest" people, if you know what I mean."[34]

Despite appeals from the War Department and the Office of Education, the Baltimore board held firm, citing "an acute shortage of instructors."[35] Mills faced a difficult decision—resign or watch another teacher go to Haiti. "I knew to expect that," she told Mama, "yet, when it came I was really hurt. I could not help but have my usual cry."[36] Not to worry, Mama assured her—crying could be a wonderful release.

What part did Elmer, her principal who'd written that grudging letter, play in all this? Like Papa, he was a staunch AME churchman and had attended several general conferences. He knew, or knew of, Mama as well—in his letter, he asked Mills to "extend my highest regards to your mother and father"—and he must also have known Monroe Davis. Given their connections in that tight little world of the Black middle class, did Elmer support Mills's quest to go to Haiti? The thing is, she was scarcely a year in Baltimore when she applied to go overseas. It wouldn't be surprising if Elmer took it amiss, especially since he'd supported her getting tenure. Like others in his position, he struggled to balance duty to the race with accommodation, another way of saying he hadn't gotten where he was—and in a year he'd become director of colored schools—by acting impulsively. In fact, Elmer himself had turned down at least three chances to leave Baltimore—one to work as a YMCA secretary during World War I, a second to become president of Kittrell, and a third to become principal of a school in New York.[37] He must have thought Mills foolish for abandoning tenure and a guaranteed salary.

And, of course, prudence would have dictated Mills stay in Baltimore. The Haitian excursion was scheduled to last only six months. She'd asked for two hundred dollars a month, but the government offered only one hundred fifty dollars,[38] though she'd also receive free room and board. What decided Mills was the prospect of an adventure.

"Dad says don't worry about afterwards," Mama told her. "Everything will be all right when you come back. The thing now is to go."[39] Later, she repeated the same advice: "If the Board does not release you, then Dad and I both say go anyhow."[40] In the midst of Mills's turmoil, a reporter from

Baltimore's *Afro-American* called, wanting to know if it was true she was one of the teachers selected to go to Haiti. Mills said yes, "but told them I'd tell them whatever I could tell after I had been officially appointed."[41] What she didn't say was that she'd decided to resign. She was going to wait, though, until she received her passport.

Mills got her passport, and Papa took a copy of the picture and a write-up to the *Palmetto Leader*.[42] The story was front-page news, in no small part because the other teachers, including four who were Black, had been given leave. (The *Leader* also reported on the going-away party given by Alfred's Washington Benedict Club.[43])

Papa suggested Mama fly to Miami to see off their "beloved child."[44] Both parents wound up taking the train to Florida—perhaps neither trusted air travel. On her own, separate train journey, Mills reported her "contact with Mr. J. Crow" after she asked directions to the dining car so she could get breakfast. The porter told her to wait, "unless I wanted to be embarrassed as I wouldn't be served." A waiter offered to bring her food, but Mills declined—she wanted to see the dining car. Finally, she was summoned at last call. "Breakfast was fine," she told Mattie, despite this petty indignity: "There was a curtain drawn between me and the others who were breaking their fast. I didn't kick as I know where I am and what good would kicking do?"[45]

Mills's flight left the morning of February 11, 1943. Wartime paranoia meant she had to surrender her camera, film, and binoculars, though they were later returned to her in Haiti. Mama and Papa watched as she "boarded the plane about five minutes before eight. Promptly at eight her plane soared away. Pride in his little girl's achievements kept Dad buoyed up. He was as proud as a peacock and still is."[46]

Six weeks later, the *Atlanta Daily World* reported that the seven teachers had "been stationed in five different cities and will work cooperatively to develop a curriculum and teaching methods."[47] In addition to Mills, the other African-Americans included Arthur F. Carter, John M. Moore, and Forrest O. Wiggins. There were also two white teachers, DeWitt C. Peters and Henry C. Schwartz, and the white project supervisor, James E. Forsythe.

Most had some international experience through work, travel, or study. Forsythe taught at the International School in Geneva from 1931 to 1940 before leaving for Philadelphia's Friends Select School. After he left Haiti, he went to teach at Sidwell Friends where, in a delightful coincidence I wish I'd known then, he taught the English history class I took my first year.[48] Carter had received bachelor's and master's degrees from Howard. Though he'd received a fellowship to "travel and study in Martinique. . . , to supplement his training as a prospective teacher of French," he was working as a clerk at the Federal Security Agency before going to Haiti. At just twenty-five years old, he must have been the youngest member of the group.[49] Moore taught French and German at Virginia Union University in Richmond. He received a master's degree from Columbia University and had studied at the University of Paris.[50] Wiggins had a PhD from the University of Wisconsin. He'd also studied in Paris and received a diploma from the *Alliance Française*. Before coming to Haiti, he'd taught at the North Carolina College for Negroes (North Carolina Central University) and Johnson C. Smith University.[51] Peters had studied painting in France,[52] whereas Schwartz may have attended graduate school at the University of Michigan.[53]

Their first few days were spent at the Hotel Oloffson in the capital, Port-au-Prince. Built as a private mansion by the son of a Haitian president in the late 1800s, the Oloffson had been used as a military hospital when the United States invaded Haiti in 1915. It was turned into a hotel in 1935. Graham Greene would depict it in his 1966 novel, *The Comedians*, as the Hotel Trianon. Mills found the Oloffson congenial. Her balcony looked out "over the entire city," and she spent time "viewing the mountains and the sea" and enjoying the "cool breeze blowing."[54] She was in polyglot company—guests spoke English, French, Spanish, and Creole. She asked the staff to use French so she could practice. She and the other American teachers were invited to meet President Élie Lescot and the minister of foreign affairs and to a reception hosted by the minister of education. She visited classes at a boys' school and taught several herself.

Soon, however, Mills's urban idyll ended with her departure to St.-Marc, a small city on Haiti's west coast about fifty miles north of Port-au-Prince. Derailments might stretch the thirteen-hour train journey to eighteen hours, so she, Forsythe, and three other teachers—Wiggins, Moore, and Schwartz—traveled by bus or car in a "caravan" that included "a truck carrying our luggage." At her first sight of St.-Marc, Mills told

Mattie "I felt I was lost." Only Schwartz said goodbye; he felt sympathetic because he'd been assigned to Gonaïves, about thirty-five miles north, a placement he hadn't wanted. The rest felt they were abandoning her. When James Forsythe returned after taking Schwartz to Gonaïves, Forrest to Cap-Haïtien (a port city on the northern coast), and Moore to Port-de-Paix (another coastal city sixty-five miles—and a five-hour drive today—west of Cap-Haïtien), he told Mills everyone had been "afraid to say goodbye to me when they first left. He was right, because I think it would have brought forth my first boo-hoo!"[55]

– 18 –

Fiftieth Anniversary and
Nearing the End

Mama ruminated on love, marriage, and the difficulties of old age after a visit from two old friends, Hercules Smith and his wife, Sujette. Both were teachers who'd attended Allen's Normal School—Mama and Papa had known them for nearly half a century. The scorns of time must have been on Mama's mind. In two years, on November 26, 1940, she and Papa would celebrate their fiftieth wedding anniversary.

"Suejette [Mama spells it this way in her letters] and Smith were here a few days. . . ." she told Mattie. "They are in very straitened circumstances and are otherwise quite unhappy. Their home was only saved to them by a Federal Home Loan. It is a heavy task to raise $50. per month. They are trying to do so, however. Then Smith's mind is bad. He almost hates Suejette as dearly as he has loved her. But he has the obsession that she has conjured him. It is pitiful. I hope we die before we get to that pitch."

Immediately, however, Mama reverted to the stoic optimism that characterizes most of her letters. She didn't really want to die, at least not until she and Papa had celebrated their anniversary.

"Almost daily the papers tell of some old couple celebrating their golden wedding [anniversary]," she said. "Dad and I are praying and hoping to reach ours. We both feel the aches and pains of old age but are still keeping on, thank God."[1]

◆ ◆ ◆

As the date approached, Mama began to get 2116 Lady Street in order, summoning a slew of workmen to ready the now twenty-year-old house for an influx of visitors. She hired carpenters, electricians, and plumbers to have an extension put on, a bathroom redone or installed (the letters aren't clear), new light fixtures installed, and the kitchen and several other rooms painted. Much of the work must have been done so she could house all or most of her children. White hotels would not have admitted them, and she was probably reluctant to ask friends. Then, too, her youngest son, Christopher (called "Boy" in the letters) was separated from his first wife and had come home to Lady Street. His children—Christopher Jr. and Marian—lived with their mother but came to stay on Lady Street at least part of the time. That may have been another reason Mama wanted the extra room.

Work began on the extension in mid-July. By mid-September, Mama could finally report that "the carpenters, paper hangers, painters, plasterers, brick-layers, plumbers, and all their ilk have gone and left me in peace. There remains only the odds and ends pertaiment [*sic*] to the cleaning to be finished." In November, about three weeks before the celebration, Papa bought "an oil circulator" and had a flue installed. "We are hoping that with the circulator in the front and a good heater in the back that you northerners will keep warm while here," Mama told Mills. A week later, she informed Mills that "the stove man" had installed "two stoves—one at each end of the house." He'd left instructions. Unsure of her ability to follow them, she was counting on Boy, her son Christopher, for "best results."[2]

Apart from the new heating arrangements, Papa was little involved until about six weeks before the celebration, when he "entered into the spirit of it ... and talks about it as much as anyone else." If Mama forgot to tell people on their travels—though she was sixty-eight and he was seventy-five, they continued to visit friends and attend AME conferences throughout the state—Papa would remind her to: "He even invites whole congregations. I am sure Columbia couldn't hold them all if they come."[3]

Papa's congregations aside, Mama wanted a simple celebration. Dinner, on November 26, was to be "a strictly family affair," with a larger reception for friends that same evening or the following day.[4] As the date drew closer, Mama became more and more anxious: "I shall be glad when it is history. Each day I get more nervous over [strikethrough original] from the anticipation and certainly wish some of you were here. No young bride-to-be has ever had more to worry about unless it was her trousseau."

Of all Mama and Papa's children, only ne'er-do-well Maceo and Frances, their adopted daughter, did not come. Maceo was, well . . . it's likely neither Mama nor Papa knew where he was. And had died giving birth ten years earlier. The formal portrait taken in the newly refurbished living room shows Mama and Papa side by side surrounded by their children, grandchildren, and one great-grandchild. Stern and unsmiling, Papa balances the three-tiered anniversary cake on one knee. Mama holds up the other end. Her look is one of forbearance—getting the house ready must have taken all her energy. Their children, Mattie, Ralston, Tap, Colon, Marian, Ruth, Mills, and Christopher, are present, as well as Alfred, Mattie's husband; three of their children, Jo, Phyllis, and Mills McDaniel (Mac); and their grandson, Casper Garrett Simons Jr., the son of Alfred and Mattie's third child, Casper Garrett. Known as Aram, he sits on Mattie's knee. His mother, Vivian, is on the floor in front of him. Also present are Christopher's children, Marian and Chris; and Colon's two sons, Colon Jr. and Reverdy. And there's a woman who may be Ralston's ex-wife, Corrine. The 1930 census says they were divorced, but Mama had announced her intention to invite her—and all her son's ex-wives—because they were "the only ones who married my boys."[5]

Mattie and Mills (who was still three years from going to Haiti), the daughters who were her most frequent correspondents, attended, so Mama did not write about the anniversary party until both had returned home. She'd gone back to teaching though she was "too tired to do much good." Papa had "not recovered his usual strength and spirits. The excitement, the anxiety for the comfort of others[,] and everything in general seems to have left him almost spiritless."[6]

Bearded and balding in that anniversary photograph, Papa bears a passing resemblance to W. E. B. Du Bois. It should have been a happy occasion, but there's something disgruntled about his turned-down mouth—all those invitations to "whole congregations" to the contrary, he must have been ready for the affair to be over and everyone to leave him in peace. I wonder, though, if the celebration wasn't a reminder that, fifty years on, his time had passed. He began in optimism a half-century before, a new husband and newly minted lawyer, so many obstacles overcome, confident he'd conquer those that remained. He would have liked, I think, to have played a larger role on a larger stage, even if only to have been known as the Du Bois of South Carolina in the same way the Rev. Richard Carroll was the state's Booker T. Washington. His best chance had come twenty-four years earlier when he ran for editor of the *A.M.E. Church Review* and

Papa and Mama's 50th anniversary, 1940.

front row: Marian Garrett (daughter of Christopher T. Garrett); Phyllis T. Simons (daughter of Alfred and Mattie Simons); Mills M. Simons, "Mac" (son of Alfred and Mattie Simons); Vivian Craig Simons; Casper George Garrett III (son of Colon H. Garrett); Reverdy Ransom Garrett (son of Colon H. Garrett)

middle row, seated: Corinne Bellamy Garrett (wife of Ralston Garrett); Ralston Garrett; Mama; Papa; Casper Garrett Simons, "Aram" (son of Casper Garrett and Vivian Craig Simons); Mattie Garrett Simons; Alfred E. Simons; Christopher Garrett Jr. (son of Christopher T. Garrett)

back row, standing: Casper Garrett Jr., "Tap"; Naomi M. Garrett, "Mills"; Marian Garrett; Josephine Simons (daughter of Alfred and Mattie Simons); Christopher T. Garrett; Ruth Garrett Butcher; Colon H. Garrett

Allen's presidency. He'd failed in his quest for both. Now, nearing the end of his life, Papa knew he'd gone as far as he could.

Soon after she and Papa celebrated their golden wedding anniversary, Mama accepted a three-week teaching appointment. It didn't pay, but she told Mills "I don't feel I lost anything." A bill to provide pensions for retired Richland County teachers was pending in the State Legislature. If it didn't pass, Mama thought that she'd be able to continue in the fall—this time, presumably with pay.

The bill was approved on May 24, 1941. A few days later, Mama gleefully reported that "I have filled my last blank which puts my application on file: All applications will be passed on in June. Those which are passed on favorably will bring payments of $300.00 per year payable in 12 monthly installments of $25.00." The payments were to start on July 1, and she was counting on the county superintendent, Wade Hampton[7] Cobb, to make sure her application was approved. He was "doing all he can to help me" and had "had the trustees elect me for next year so there could be no question of my being actually at work." The prospect of getting four hundred fifty dollars a month (in today's dollars) made Mama positively giddy: "Just think what that will mean. . . . You can count on me, should my application [be] accepted, to extend my life line beyond the county's greatest expectations. In other words, I mean to really 'get mine.'"[8]

Cobb came through, and the Richland County Retirement Board voted to approve her pension of three hundred dollars a year on June 20, 1941. There were just four recipients that first year. All, colored and white, were grouped together. They were separated afterward, with white teachers sometimes appearing in one column and colored in another. When all retirees appeared in one column, there was a space to separate Black from white. Even if Mama noted it, and was offended, the separation was incidental to what must have mattered more: Colored teachers' pensions were half those of whites.[9]

◆ ◆ ◆

The war that engulfed the world—the second Mama and Papa had seen—marked the convulsive passing of the world they'd known. What replaced it was strange and unfamiliar, with little room for them. Camp Jackson, "a training camp for the National Guard" since the end of World War I, became Fort Jackson, "a permanent training post" that grew to sixty-two thousand acres, three times its original size.[10] (Some of that was land Papa was forced to sell from his farm, much like Alfred's father, the Rev. Isom Wesley Simons, had been forced to sell land when Camp Jackson was established in 1917.) Two months before war was declared, officials reported "a population of 42,000 soldiers and . . . thousands of civilians"[11] at the fort. The number was two-thirds Columbia's 1940 population of 62,396. Over the next five years, some five hundred thousand men—a number that doesn't include "officers, support personnel, or civilians"[12]—would train at Fort Jackson.

"With the exception of Colored soldiers, Columbia looks like war times," Mama wrote Mattie in 1940. "There are more than 1,000 soldiers here but all are white. They keep things lively, tho'. The police, M.P. and civic, have their hands full."[13] A year later, it had gotten worse: "Our town, state, and county are all over run with soldiers. There is scarcely any place for civilians. Maybe it will be over and things become normal again some day.[14]

The influx of soldiers and civilians brought millions into the city's economy, as well as food and housing shortages. Some workers were forced to "hot-bed," sharing the same mattress in shifts. "Butter, tea, sugar, chocolate, red meat, shoes, and gasoline were rationed," and "food prices climbed" despite state price controls. From January 1940 to January 1945, for example, a pound of bacon went from twenty-five cents to thirty-two cents and four ration points, and a pound of ham from fifteen cents to as much as sixty-five cents and twelve ration points. (Everyone, including children, was issued coupon books of ration stamps; each stamp was worth a certain number of points.) Butter went from two pounds for twenty-three cents to nineteen cents a pound; coffee went from fifteen cents a pound to forty-one cents a pound; and a dozen eggs went from thirty-three cents to fifty-two cents.[15]

Worst, though, for respectable women like Mama, were the social changes the war brought. She could hardly have objected when women took over jobs vacated by men who'd enlisted or been drafted, but she was shocked by the loosening morals: "All the women, old and young, white and black, are crazy about the soldiers. There is already the biggest crop of babies ever known here and the crest has not yet been reached."[16]

Mama wasn't telling the half of it. The soldiers' presence sparked an increase in gambling (slot machines and "high-staked dice games"), illegal liquor sales (some bootleggers hired boys to provide "curb service"), and prostitution. One survey (the newspaper doesn't say the source) found "there were more than 150 girls registered" as prostitutes working in houses. More came from out of town, and one working girl guessed "that the prostitute population of Columbia doubles around the first of each month." "[T]ourist camps" asked no questions, as long as couples had cash and parked "behind the cabins so that the South Carolina license plates won't be in evidence to passersby."[17]

This was the climate the time when Mills was accosted by the soldier during a visit home from teaching in Baltimore. Mama warned her "about walking the streets after dark." Thinking herself grown, Mills "paid no attention."[18] After she'd been rescued by a neighbor, arm still "scarred from scratches" where the serviceman had grabbed her, Mills told Jo, "Baby, "your auntie was a scared somebody for the better part of half an hour." From now on, though, she was going to heed Mama's warning: "You can bet I won't do dat no more."[19]

Of course, the Army sought to provide recreational facilities to avoid just those kind of unfortunate encounters, building "one of the first . . . Negro recreation centers on any Army post" in Fort Jackson's "colored area." The center featured "a large assembly room . . . for dancing and other social functions, a 500-volume library and smaller lounge rooms furnished with writing desks and easy chairs."[20] It opened on October 24, 1941, with a "gala dance" attended by two hundred soldiers and fifty young women— Allen students and nurses from Waverly Hospital.[21]

Black Columbians were encouraged to offer the soldiers hospitality. Mama did, of course, inviting "a young corporal" from Mississippi to Christmas dinner. "I 'kidnapped' him and another young soldier and brought them home to dinner on Sunday," she said. "He seems to like being kidnapped."[22] A little later, when she invited more soldiers to dinner, she was "sorry we had no young girls to meet them."[23]

As had happened in the First World War, some Black men got themselves into trouble protesting the war. A Greenville farmer named Will Gaylord was forced from his "home on account of some big talk he'd been doing over race and war situations." Mama didn't know the "particulars,"[24] and the incident doesn't seem to have made the newspapers. None of the Garretts opposed the war, however. At least four of Mama's grandsons—Alfred and Mattie's Al and Bill, Colon and Henrietta's Colon Jr., and Tap and Cornice's adopted son, Alfred—served in the Army. All of Mama's sons registered for the draft, though four—Ralston, Tap, Colon, and Marian—were in their forties and likely to be called up only in the event of invasion or a severe shortage of younger men. Still, Mama thought Tap, who was forty-seven, would have done better to stay in after the first war: "He [could] be a top man now. As it is, if the boys from no. 1 have to go back, he won't be any higher than when he was mustered out."[25] As the war wore on, Tap thought about joining up again, despite his age. "Tap writes he wants to go back into the service," Mama wrote proudly, "only he is afraid he is too soft for action, or that his age may be against him. I am encouraging him to try it. Were it possible, I'd do something myself." In that same letter, she noted that she'd stayed home because of "the gas and tire situation," while Papa went to a conference. She regretted not being able to go. "But," she concluded, "the war must be won, so I'm willing to make any sacrifice necessary."[26]

In the end, the fortitude and stubbornness that had given Mama the strength to provide for her family by going to work when she was nearly fifty would prove her undoing. Sometime during the summer of 1942, she went to see her doctor, Jane Bruce Guignard. (Guignard was white; Mama likely preferred a woman physician and began to see her after the 1935 death of Columbia's pioneering African-American physician, Matilda A. Evans.) After examining Mama, Jane was alarmed enough to order her "to the hospital immediately for an operation." Mama didn't think she "needed that," so she went to another doctor. After x-raying her, he said "I didn't need the operation. Working on the theory that when doctors disagree the patient gets well," Mama went about her life. "I'm feeling fine and believe I'm as well as could be expected,"[27] she reported.

Though Mama never says so in her letters, she had cancer. At about the same time, Mattie was having health problems of her own but putting off seeing anyone. Mama wrote promptly to scold her. That, she said, was "foolish, if true. . . . [T]here are times when professional service is absolutely necessary. I hope you won't jeopardize your health by waiting too long."[28] So Mama knew better, and she should have had more faith in Jane's judgment. Instead, she waited, because she felt the doctors had "tried to rush me."[29]

By early spring of 1943, they were telling her to "have the operation at once 'or else.'" Mama wrote Mattie, asking her Baby to come to Columbia, not because she needed taking care of but because Papa did. "I do not dread it, for I know whatever God intends the outcome to be will be," she wrote. "But your daddy is so helpless without me. I just can't make up my mind to voluntarily leave him alone."[30]

Mama's cancer, Jo once said, "was *her* cancer," and so it wasn't anybody's business but hers. Did Mama tell Papa? I don't know. She must have when the doctors insisted she have the operation, but it wouldn't surprise me if she kept her diagnosis to herself until then.

Certainly Mama didn't tell Mills. Her youngest daughter was applying to go to Haiti, and Mama knew she'd have given up her dream of working and living overseas, perhaps even come home to Columbia to take care of her. And so Mills didn't learn about her mother's illness until March, about three weeks into her sojourn in St.-Marc. Mama wrote her that she was going to the hospital but gave no details, leaving Mills "slightly worried" and "rather anxious." Mama had told her Mattie and Corinne, Ralston's wife, were coming to Columbia, and Mills "knew that this was no time for [S]ister [Mattie] especially to go home unless something was wrong somewhere."[31] (Home, to Mills, was always Columbia.)

About two weeks later, Mattie wrote to tell Mills Mama had come through. She'd brought her two-year-old grandson, Casper Garrett Simons Jr., with her to Columbia—his mother had died the year before—but Mattie had four children still at home. Ruth, my mother, cooked; and Alfred reported that the younger ones, Phyllis and Kemble, "have things under controll. [*sic*]"[32] From time to time, Jo came down from Baltimore. She ironed and cooked, but Alfred complained that while her "dinner was good . . . your bread was missen [*sic*]."[33]

Corinne stayed longer on Lady Street. Tap visited,[34] as did Ralston, though he may only have stopped by during one of his Pullman runs. "The best of all, of course, was finding you so well on the way to recovery and knowing that you are being well cared for,"[35] Tap wrote after he'd returned home to New York. Even Ruth, who Mama had told Mattie couldn't be depended on,[36] helped out: "It was comforting to know that I only had to phone and one of my girls could come to me at once. But of course, I know you girls must do just as all other good wives should and must—follow the men you promise[d] to love and cherish through life. I did just that so I don't complain."[37] After Mattie left, Mama wrote to assure her she was "getting along fairly well so far," adding, "I feel everything will work out all right. *It must.* [emphasis original]"[38]

That June, just weeks after her surgery, Mama learned of Maceo's death. "We took it as we could without fuss or ado," she told Mattie, "though our hearts were and still are burdened heavily."[39]

Perhaps it was just that, like most of his brothers, Maceo liked to drink. He hadn't gone to France in the Great War, so he hadn't been shell-shocked in battle. In the end, though, the "drinking and carousing" Ralston dismissed, caught up with Maceo. He was just forty-six when he died in New York.

"The first break in our group," Mama lamented. "Tho' we didn't know Maceo was ill, yet his death wasn't such a shock since we knew he didn't live a regular life. My wonder is that he didn't suffer violence."[40]

Langston Hughes didn't know Maceo, but he wrote a kind of epitaph for him in "Deceased," his poem about an unfortunate migrant—a drinker like Mama's wayward son—who returned home from Harlem "in a long box."[41]

Protestations aside, the loss weighed heavily on Mama and on Papa. Colon arrived too late and missed the funeral. Mama professed herself glad because "he was in a shameful condition" when he did show. "Dad told him to not come back unless he could come sober."[42] Still, it must have added to her grief.

It used to be easier to establish a family cemetery on property you owned, and so after the service at the Pearson Funeral Home,[43] Maceo was buried on the farm Mama had purchased for Papa. In time, they, too, would be buried there, as would most of their children. The farm remains in the family.

◆　◆　◆

And yet, despite the mortal illness she endured, despite the loss of Maceo and her grief and shame over Colon, Mama still found some comforts.

That Thanksgiving, not "feeling quite well," she stayed home while Papa went to a conference. Most of her friends thought she was away, so she had just two visitors. She was reconciling herself to the possibility of spending her fifty-third anniversary alone when "the dear old man came shuffling in. Couldn't stay away on that great anniversary day. Sometimes I think it's pathetic," she told Mattie, "then again think it grand. Pathetic because of our infirmities; grand because few can reach such a time feeling toward each other as we do. We have much to be thankful for and we are."[44]

Mills in Haiti

After she returned to the States, Mills published an article[1] about her Haitian sojourn. Unfortunately, much of it is the kind of travel writing that must have been popular then, focusing on the exoticism of life in her "dusty, barren hamlet." The days progressed according to predictable rhythms—peasant farmers coming down from the hills to sell rice, corn, fruit, and vegetables; the poor lining up at "the community water pipe across the street" from the Imperial Bar; "*marchandes*"—women street sellers—"in long, loose-fitting blue or multi-colored garments" balancing "huge baskets of fruits, vegetables, oil, and milk" atop their kerchiefed heads; young men in the town square "[on] moonlit nights. . . . casting furtive glances at [amply chaperoned] members of the opposite sex." After sunset, an "appalling quiet" fell over the town.

Threaded throughout are a few more personal observations. People in St.-Marc thought all American women were like the ones they'd seen in the movies (the town had a picture house open Thursday and Saturday)—"For some, the very fact I had come that far from home unchaperoned seemed to cast a dubious light on my reputation." Though soon accepted "as meeting their moral requirements," Mills was advised not to compromise herself by accepting a ride in a man's car, nor was she to let any man—"even a co-worker"—walk her home from school or pay a social visit. (So much for Mama's hoping she'd find a husband.) Things were a little different at the Lycée Sténio Vincent,[2] where she taught. "The faculty and student body seemed delighted to have a women in their school," and Mills found her students eager and willing: "Never have I worked with students who were so appreciative of being able to go to school. . . . For me, working with them was an immense pleasure."

Her time in Haiti made for a more complex experience than Mills let on but propriety, and a desire not to offend her hosts explain her caution in *Opportunity*'s pages. She was more open in her letters, although she didn't always tell all. For one thing, it was war time, and all mail was opened and read by censors. (When the dates of Ruth's and Phyllis's graduations were marked out, Mercer Cook observed that "evidently Howard and Dunbar's graduation dates are military secrets"[3]!) Another reason for her caution was innate reticence—Mills was of a generation (and a line) that held some things were better left unwritten, though they might be said to the right person. All the same, if Mills didn't always satisfy my craving to know everything, she gave a more rounded picture of her stay in her letters to her sister and nieces.

She boarded with the principal of her *lycée* and his wife in a household that also included the principal's mother and sisters. She worked hard, teaching a total of thirteen classes. In addition, she taught English to teachers three days a week and a one-hour evening class twice a week that was open to the public. There were "six-foot-high placards all over town announcing that momentous occasion."[4]

Principal Emile Paultre and his wife, Henriette, were "very kind and solicitous,"[5] but Mills found herself so "blue and lonesome"[6] she wrote long letters home—some of her early ones are six pages long and nearly three thousand words. She missed her family and, despite her years of study, her French wasn't good enough for her to be entirely at ease in conversation. And even if she'd been fully fluent, Haitians spoke Creole, a mixture of African languages, French, and other European tongues, in informal gatherings.

There were other obstacles to comfort as well—the heat and its "enervating effect,"[7] which made her wish for "props to hold my eyelids apart." Particular about her clothes, Mills was thwarted by a laundress who "washed [them] to pieces."[8] Her letters to Mattie and Jo are filled with pleas for them to send her dresses, skirts, blouses, and underwear—and to make them appear worn so as to avoid customs duties. There was no beauty shop. "Not wanting to "insult people when they are oversensitive anyway as to American's [*sic*] opinion of their surroundings,"[9] she didn't ask for her water to be boiled. She tried not to drink it but caught dysentery anyway. Six weeks into her assignment, she told Mattie she had only "three great ambitions": to sleep in a bed with springs; to "eat an American meal without wondering whether the dark spots are flies, gnats, candle flies or just plain good dirt"; and to "spend one whole day without eating peas and rice."[10]

Two or three weeks after she arrived in St.-Marc, Mills was heartened by a visit from an American minister and a Canadian family. "'Twas nice to see some Americans," she told Mattie. Somehow she persevered and, if she never quite got used to the conditions, accepted them and grew fond of Haiti and its people. In late April, she went with fellow American teacher Forrest O. Wiggins to the Citadelle, a fortress begun by the Haitian revolutionary (and the country's only king) Henri Christophe in 1805, and Sans Souci, Henri Christophe's principal residence. It was an arduous journey—nearly thirteen hours by camion, "a truck with hardboard seats"[11] that provided a "bone-racking, liver-shaking"[12] ride. Once at the Citadelle, they rode up a mountain to the fortress "on the backs of some of the most docile, most hungry looking, most worn-out little horses you've ever seen."[13] The return to Port-au-Prince—also by camion—took seventeen hours. Mills told Mattie she ate nothing en route, not trusting the food sold by ragged little urchins at stops along the way.

All the same, she treasured the experience. "*I saw much of rural Haiti,*" she wrote. [emphasis hers] "I wouldn't take the trip again by camion, but I wouldn't take anything for the one I took."

As summer approached, Mills began to worry about the future. If Congress failed to fund the project after September 1, she'd have to return home to look for work. If the project were funded, however, she'd have to spend August in Pétionville, a suburb of Port-au-Prince, preparing for the next year. Mills was disappointed. She'd hoped, despite the difficulty in getting a plane or ship, to be able to come home for a month in August. Although Mama's letters were reassuring, Mills knew that she'd been diagnosed with cancer and, unlike Papa and herself, "has always been a silent sufferer."[14]

James Forsythe left Haiti in July. That same month, Mills returned to Port-au-Prince—she and the other teachers were given twelve-week furloughs, part of which would be unpaid. In October, she received welcome news—Mercer Cook would be the new supervisor of the program.

Mills was supposed to go back to St.-Marc after her summer in Port-au-Prince. Somehow, though, Cook arranged for her to stay in the capital. She was going to teach at a school for girls—the first of its kind in the country, making Mills "somewhat of a trailblazer . . . the first woman to teach in a boy's [*sic*] *lycée* and now the first American to work at the first *lycée* for girls"—and in a teacher-training program. Though she knew the capital would be "better for my mental and physical health," Mills also knew her "students, coworkers, and friends at St.-Marc" would be crushed. And they were. One friend, she told Ruth, "was terribly sick and disappointed because I did not return to St.-Marc." All the same, if the people she knew there "made me feel very bad, almost like a traitor," they couldn't understand what it meant "to an American woman to be subjected to things there, especially when she knows what awaits her, having already experienced, and she has the opportunity of bettering her condition."[15]

In Port-au-Prince, Mills could realize her ambitions for a good bed and American food. Other advantages included fetes and gatherings—receptions and cocktail parties attended by Haitian officials and US Ambassador John Campbell White, art exhibits, a "*soirée musicale*,"[16] and a concert organized by White's wife, Elizabeth, at the Haitian-American Institute, a kind of "International House for the two countries."[17] It may have been at one of these affairs that she met François Duvalier, a physician who would soon head the Haitian Public Health Service. Better known as "Papa Doc," Duvalier would be elected president in 1957. Declaring himself "President for Life," he ruled the country until his death in 1971.

Soon, Mills and the Cooks—Mercer; his wife, Vashti; and their son, also named Mercer—left the Hotel Oloffson for upstairs rooms at the Institute. Mills would have liked to stay at the hotel, but she thought it might be "fun" to keep house. The Institute came with a "yard boy," but they were expected to hire other servants—a cook, a laundress, and three "house boys." (There'd been too much work for one, so they told him to find someone else. Correctly sizing up his North American dupes, he found two.)

After a few months, the Cooks left for a house of their own. Mills remained at the Institute. The "[m]oral requirements" she cited in her *Opportunity* article were less stringent in the capital and so, in addition to official affairs, she went out to nightclubs and dances (called balls), sometimes staying out until five o'clock in the morning. All the same, there limits to where women of good character could go and what they might do:

Two weeks ago tonight I did what we would call at home going slumming. Wiggins and some fellows who are friends of his let me hang on. At first the other fellows were rather shy about taking me and at midnight, when 'twas time to leave the café to go, they all looked at me and asked what should be done with me as "she can't go to those dances." He and I both insisted, and finally they reluctantly consented. We went to several balls before finally coming back in to town to one where we stayed until nearly 4 a.m. At first, the fellows felt I was cramping their style as several of them were accompanied, and finally I decided I'd dance, too, to put them more at ease, according to Wiggins' suggestion. I danced with them and really had a ball. Last Saturday night, Wiggins' last night here, he again asked to be allowed to take me on their jaunt, but this time they were going to a place where I definitely couldn't go, so I had to stay at home. I shall tell you and explain those things to you when I see you. Golly, but I wish you could see one of these native dances. One can readily understand after visiting one why the birth rate among the peasants is so high.[18]

All the same, as Mills concluded, "I can't, of course, let Marco nor any of my other friends here know that I have even seen such things."[19] Marco (a nickname; his real name was Marc) was a Haitian she'd met in St.-Marc. For a while, she thought she was "really falling in love."[20] Scarcely a month later, however, she concluded that "I definitely don't love him. 'Twas infatuation for a moment and I'm glad it's over."[21]

Mills told Jo she was falling in love and Mattie that it had only been infatuation, which says something about her relationships with each woman. Fifteen years older, Mattie had been a surrogate mother and, moreover, Mills' teacher at Allen. That dependent relationship persisted, even after the two women were grown and Mills made her way in the world while Mattie stayed home raising her children. She often asked her older sister's advice in her letters, confessing once, "Really, were it not for her to try to keep my head level, I don't know what I'd do."[22]

By contrast, despite the eleven years separating them, Mills was more Jo's older sister than aunt, and the two shared an intimacy often absent from Mills's letters to her older sister. She signed some of her early letters to her niece "*Le Chat Noir*." As for Jo . . . well, a few months before she married in 1945, she told Mills she'd gotten her own apartment. She must have confided about a visit from her fiancé, George W. Wade, who was studying dentistry in an accelerated wartime program at Howard: Mills responded that she was glad the apartment "gives one the chance of finding out what certain things are like without any inhibitions."[23]

Decades later, when Mills visited one Christmas, the difference in the two women's ages disappeared as they laughed about the time they passed a woman demonstrating makeup in a Baltimore department store. "And for a nice blush," the woman advised, "pinch your cheeks afterwards to bring out the rosiness." To which Mills responded, "Pinch them? I'd have to use a baseball bat."

Attendance at "native dances" aside, Mills's own experience of those "certain things" is missing from her letters, though she had at least one other "heart interest": Manès, a "doctor with a large practice."[24] The two went dancing and on an expedition to a nearby town where they swam in a river. Mills had "a scrumptious time."[25] All the same, she thought it couldn't last: "I am too happy and he is too kind, considerate, and nice. I'm not supposed to know such happiness for long."[26] It was likely more serious on his part than on hers. Near the end of her stay, some members of his family chided her for going home, but Manès "'assured' them that I'd either return or he'd come and get me as he really hadn't yet decided that I could go home." To which, Mills said, "I just laughed, of course."[27]

Whatever Mills said to the good doctor about his presumption is lost, but her letters show that—Mama's hopes aside—she doubted the possibility of a relationship with a Haitian man. "I'm afraid these international set ups just won't turn out right; I fear to trust it,"[28] she told Jo. A few months later, she wrote to Mattie: "It would be nice if I really could fall in love and make a go of it, but I won't find it here. It just would not work."[29]

She might have found evidence for her pessimism in "a very, very amusing incident"[30] one morning when Manès came to drive her to school. (He lived just around the corner.) It was another of those things Mills told Mattie she'd spill when she came home, but whatever took place—likely she saw Manès with another woman—was uncomfortable enough for Mills to decide to time her departure from then on so she didn't see him. All the same, they went to the beach a few days later, and when Mills returned to the States, she kept a picture of Manès on her dresser—much to the consternation of the man she was seeing.

That relationship, with a man named Bill (Mills didn't give his last name, but she seems to have known him from South Carolina), didn't work out either. "Why can't I find someone who'd take even a fleeting moment's interest in me," she wailed. "I am so blue!"[31]

Mills liked men. Certainly they're mentioned often enough in her letters—Marc, Manès, and several anonymous teachers and government officials in St.-Marc she made a point of telling Mattie were single; an anonymous union organizer in New York; Bill; and a man she called "Zeke." He was Elijah Howard Tindel, who worked at the Government Printing Office and lived about ten minutes from Mattie and Alfred on S Street.[32] Though it lasted some time, Mills and Elijah's wasn't an entirely happy relationship. "Tell old . . . Tindel I say he had better treat you right[,]" Charlisena, the estranged wife of Chris, Mills' younger brother, told her, "or else I'll find you another boyfriend . . . and make you quit him altogether."[33] Still, it lasted until Mills left for Haiti. Once there, however, she lamented, "No one loves me, not even Tindel." In her first three months in Haiti—the time she was loneliest—he'd sent only an Easter card signed with his initials. And so, Mills declared, "I couldn't marry that man—I mean unless he asked me to do so."[34]

Mills and Tindel shared frugal tendencies and a commonsense attitude toward money—he had a side business making loans. It wasn't enough, however. Mills complained of "a century of seeing only 'Zeke,' and trying to conform to his standards."[35] Jo mentioned him a time or two, implying he wanted Mills to give up teaching to stay home and raise their family. Mills declined the opportunity.

In her letters, she sounds sometimes as if she'd realized she'd been born without some essential heart's knowledge other women enjoyed. "I've just been lectured to this week," she told Jo, "about inadvertently having driven off two would-be excellent friends (not driven off, but definitely not given encouragement to their intentions). Oddly enough, they are the two people I'd most like to have for special friends. But what can I do? . . . We joke, laugh, and they confide in a mutual good friend that I give no encouragement."[36]

Perhaps Mills looked at Mama and Mattie—a mother who, late in life, had been forced to go to work to feed her family and a sister who had given up dreams of a career to marry and have children—and was torn, hoping before time ran out to find a husband (or have one find her) but already thinking about returning to graduate school once she left Haiti. Decades before the concept of "leaning in," Mills understood she might manage one or the other—husband or doctorate—but not both.

◆ ◆ ◆

At the beginning of 1944, the Haitian program was transferred to the Office of the Coordinator of Inter-American Affairs, an agency run by Nelson Rockefeller formed to promote cooperation in the Americas and combat German influence.[37] Mills had to be fingerprinted (again) and fill out "a million blanks, ... [a]ll the junk I've done a thousand times."[38] Worse, the change in bureaucracies meant checks were delayed.

It was almost too much. Always concerned about money, Mills chided Mattie and her other correspondents for putting too much postage on their letters, told them to find people coming to Haiti to carry parcels so as to avoid customs fees, and to clip off price tags and wrinkle clothing to make it appear used. She had her paychecks deposited to a bank in Washington and kept close track of the bills she had sent to S Street; every month she sent Mattie a check with instructions to pay her insurance premiums, see to her taxes, pay a stipend to support a Laurens cousin's widow and children, make a deposit to her Christmas Club account, and distribute small gifts to her nieces and nephews. (Just to make sure there was no mistake, she often wrote the amounts in figures and then spelled them out in parentheses.) Now, the prospect of weeks without a salary was a reminder that she didn't know what she'd do once she left Haiti. A friend had told her about substitute work in Baltimore. It paid just one hundred ten dollars a month, and, she confessed, "I can't work up much interest in the affair."[39] Still, she thought she might and even look for work in the post office. Jo was somehow managing both, teaching during the day and sorting mail at night.

Mercer Cook had other ideas.

"He wants me to go to Columbia University, of all places but *not* Teachers' College—to the University proper—to work under a former teacher of his. I'll have to ponder that a long time yet. The money has to be forthcoming, etc."[40] (The emphasis that it wasn't Teachers College is Mills's; it wasn't the last time she'd make the point.)

It was all part of Cook's lifelong project to explore (through his own work and that of others) the connections between France and the African diaspora and to establish "the field of black French studies."[41] The first step, with regard to Mills, was to help her get that scholarship that allowed her to go to Atlanta University full time. Now he wanted her to earn a doctorate by doing work on Haitian literature. Mills's declaration that she'd have to "ponder" his proposal—and her comments in letters that followed—suggest a puzzling insecurity quite apart from her legitimate worries about money. She joked about "my poor feeble brain,"[42] a theme that runs through her letters, like Mama's not entirely convincing protestations of modesty when her peers acknowledged her contributions. Writing from Bessemer City sixteen years before, Mills had observed that the principal "wanted one of the smartest who had ever passed through the great halls of Benedict."[43] Instead, he'd gotten her. And she said several times she hoped the censors would let her letters go unexamined, once it was "established that I am not intelligent enough for a spy."[44]

Cook encouraged Mills to apply to the Julius Rosenwald Fund, which provided grants to Black writers, scholars, and artists from 1928 until 1948. She did, though she was shaken when she learned a woman she had studied with at Howard or Atlanta was also applying. The Rosenwald cutoff was age thirty-five, except for "exceptional people." Mills was approaching forty years old. The other woman (unnamed in Mills's letter) was younger and had already begun graduate work on "South American and Haitian lit[erature]" at the University of Michigan. "At first, I felt quite downhearted," Mills told Mattie, "but if I don't succeed this year I shall try again although I shall be even older a year from now." Mills didn't think her rival was "as capable as I am,"[45] so perhaps her insecurities were only a way of spurring herself on.

In late April, Mills received word that she'd received her grant. The timing was good. Soon, she'd receive word that the English program in Haiti was ending. Mercer would stay for a year, and one teacher, a white woman from Oregon named Dorothy Kirby, until September. Work for everyone else would end in July.[46] The Rosenwald Fund awarded Mills eighteen hundred dollars,[47] four hundred dollars less than she'd asked for, but she decided she'd make do. She was in good company—others who received awards that same year included the poet Margaret Walker; Howard University professors E. Franklin Frazier and Rayford Logan; novelist Chester Himes; and lawyer-activist Pauli Murray.[48] (About the same time she received her fellowship, Murray was leading protests outside segregated restaurants in Washington—my mother, Ruth, participated. Decades later, Murray would become the first African-American woman ordained an Episcopal priest.)

"At last I am going to the place I never thought I'd want to go," Mills exulted. There was just one problem—she'd heard nothing from Columbia, perhaps because there'd been a delay in getting transcripts sent from Benedict and Howard. She needn't have worried—Horatio Smith, professor of French and chairman of the French section of the Department of Romance Languages, made it clear "he thought 'my plan' scholarly and would be delighted to work with me."[49]

Mills's joy at receiving the fellowship was overshadowed by Mama's death, "the worst blow I guess I shall ever have to sustain." Weeks later, she was still upset, and trying, she confessed, "not to even think of it because so often when I do it just makes me unfit for anything."[50]

It would turn out that Mama's estate included three houses in Columbia and the farm outside the city. Once three hundred acres, it was now reduced to one hundred seventy-five after the government requisitioned nearly half as part of the expansion of Fort Jackson. Mama had once told Mattie she had "always wanted money and city property,"[51] and she achieved her goal—the property was valued at six thousand fifty dollars when the estate was finally settled in 1949. One house—called "the home place" in the will, it must have been 2116 Lady Street—was left to Mills, with the provision that Papa could live there until his death. The others were left to her children and several grandchildren. Over the next few years, Mills would show that—in addition to Mama's drive and ambition—she'd inherited her (and Anderson Threewitts's) knack for making money. She'd buy out Mama's other heirs, clear one lot, and—much like Mama had done earlier behind 2116 Lady Street—have a two-family rental property constructed.

In her last months in Haiti, Mills was teaching fifteen hours a week and, in addition, had "one hour of club meeting" and helped "with two hours radio a week." It sounded like a light load, she told Jo, "but in the tropics it's impossible. Too, my classes are all at different schools." She was also "taking about five hours a week of French lit" and studying French with the Martinican writer Aimé Césaire. If all that were not enough, she was also doing research on Haitian writers for what would become her dissertation. "I have just begun collecting material," she wrote Jo. "In fact, I have hardly begun. Much of Haitian writing has not been published, as there is such a small reading public and an author loses money ordinarily when he publishes his work. Too, there is no complete *anthologie,* nor history of the lit. Thus I have to read in old newspapers, an old volume of a book here and there and I have such a short time." She had, however, become friends with Phillipe Thoby-Marcelin, author with his brother, Pierre, of the novel *Canapé-Vert,* and Phito, as she called him, had promised to take her "to a friend's place where I'd find a wonderful collection of books that would help me with my research."[52]

As usual in her letters, Mills despaired of getting anything done. Scheduled to leave Haiti in August, she lamented that "I don't see how I shall have my material even halfway completed by then."[53] And, even though she wasn't yet enrolled at Columbia, she proclaimed that "I shall never finish my thesis, I know, but I shall try it anyway."[54]

There's little about race in Mills's letters, but it figures more than in Mama's letters or those of Mattie's that have survived. Around V-E Day (May 8, 1945), which marked the end of the war in Europe, she reported that one of Corinne's brothers had been with "a group of white officers when all of a sudden a bomb landed and . . . [a]ll six white officers were killed immediately." Her sister-in-law's brother was in the hospital but was expected to recover. This, Mills said, "is one time we all should thank Jim Crow, because surely that bomb must've been prejudiced."[55]

Mills didn't always contemplate racism with such acerbic wit, however. Early on, she reported that she'd heard that some people—perhaps members of the Haitian mulatto elite—"want to know why the US Gov't couldn't send all white people here instead of Negroes. Am I boiling!"[56] (Indeed she was—I've deleted six extra exclamation points.) Other organizations did send white Americans—Georgians ("Need I say more?" Mills asked. And, of course, her sister understood she meant the Southerners' innate prejudice.) She didn't think much of the Georgians, or of the "good sprinkling of Texans and Mississippians. . . . people [who] sometimes or very often think that they are in their native states." With considerable understatement, she added, "There is quite a bit of lack of tact, to my way of thinking."[57]

And then there were the Americans she saw "rug-cutting" among "the perfect elite" at Haitian nightclubs: "Other Americans are embarrassed, Haitians are disgusted, usually."[58]

Still, despite the presence of so many white "ugly Americans,"[59] Mills enjoyed experiences in Haiti that would have been difficult for her parents to imagine. When I write that my Sidwell Friends cohort and I were part of the first generation of Blacks and whites to interact under terms of putative equality, I'm discounting her experience, as well as my mother's in an inter-racial co-op at the University of Chicago in the mid-1940s. James Forsythe and two of the original American teachers who came to Haiti were white. Mills mentions James several times in her letters and, when he left, felt comfortable asking him to call Mattie once he arrived in Washington.

She was, however, especially fond of DeWitt C. Peters, who remained in Port-au-Prince when the other teachers scattered to the provinces. "He is white, bachelor, from California," Mills told Jo, "spent several years in France studying painting, and quite nice, though some of the other fellows—Carter & Schwartz, maybe Wiggins—don't like him as much as I do. . . . We used to go for long walks all through the hills of PAP, and then play gin rummy when it was too dark to walk. When I left PAP he gave me a deck of cards for amusement in case St.-Marc was lacking. . . ."[60,61]

Given DeWitt's role in bringing "Haitian art to international attention," one wishes Mills had written more about him. After his stint with the Office of Education program ended, he remained in Haiti. Exploring the country, he "spotted the door of a village bar painted with . . . fanciful colors and motifs." The artist was Hector Hyppolite, a voudon priest whose materials included enamel furniture paint and chicken-feather brushes. Fittingly given what followed, the bar was called *Ici la Renaissance*. Inspired by Hector's work, DeWitt would found *Le Centre d'Art* in Port-au-Prince, "a combination school-gallery-museum." He "supplied materials, guidance, exhibition space and even bought the art himself." He drove around the country in his Jeep, "setting up branch art schools and encouraging those who showed talent to go more deeply into their work." Before his death in 1966, he promoted Haitian art and artists by organizing exhibitions of their work in the United States.[62]

When Forsythe and Henry Schwartz left to return home, their replacements included four women—two white (Dorothy Kirby and Mildred Currie) and two Black (Irene Barksdale and Doris Gaskill). They were "little silly girls," but Mills adored them and the chance to play "older sister."[63] All were assigned to schools in the provinces, and Mills looked forward to seeing them when they returned to Port-au-Prince during the Easter holidays. "I shall spend the time laughing and talking with these four crazy girls," she said, "and I hope that each pair will like the other as much as I like them all. . . ."[64] When they left, she missed "them terribly. It was so refreshing to have them here. It was just as if I had had a week with my nieces—it was hectic and I didn't get a moment's rest, but it was one of the most pleasant weeks I've had in a long time."[65]

In an era when Blacks and whites interacted under strict rules of engagement in virtually all of the United States, there were reasons Mills got on so well with DeWitt and with her "four crazy girls." She'd likely had white instructors at Benedict, which boasted an integrated faculty until its first African-American president, J. J. Starks, let go white teachers in 1930. She also probably had white professors at Howard and Atlanta, though their interactions must have been relatively formal student–teacher relationships. The white teachers who came to Haiti likely hadn't known Black folks at home—Dorothy was from La Grande, a town of seven thousand seven hundred forty-seven in eastern Oregon about sixty miles from the Idaho border. But they were a self-selected group, already predisposed to living and getting along with others. Dorothy had "traveled extensively in Europe and Central America."[66] DeWitt may have spent as much as ten years overseas. James had lived in Europe, and his wife, Anne, was Swiss. Some of the African-American teachers had also had overseas experiences: At least three—Forrest O. Wiggins, John Moore, and Irene Barksdale—had lived in France and, in fact, Irene had "managed to get out . . . a week before it fell."[67]

But even if some of the white teachers had been predisposed to look on their friendship with Mills as part of the exoticism of their Haitian adventure, there were reasons to set aside distinctions inescapable at home. They were all part of the same program, united as strangers in a strange land by the oppressive heat, flies, and the monotony of rice and peas. In the end, they discovered that, for all their differences, they were all Americans. "With all its race riots, etc., etc. prejudice, etc. etc., the USA is a grand country," Mills told Mattie in a 1943 letter. "I didn't realize it until I got here. The funny thing is that our whole group—radicals, leftists, conservatives, rightists, have drawn the same conclusion."[68]

It was an important insight, but not the only one Mills came to.

Her biographer, Ethel O. Davie,[69] concludes that Mills's "Haitian teaching experience was the start of a lifelong interest in helping young people from other countries and was also the awakening of a deep, scholarly interest." That's true, though perhaps Mills didn't see the possibilities immediately. She'd met Phito early on in St.-Marc and presumably other writers as well. But they—and her interest in their work—go unmentioned till Mercer's arrival; it took her mentor's curiosity about Black Francophone literature for her to understand the possibilities for research.

There was more to Mills's Haitian experience, though, than the awakening of scholarly interest. A few weeks after she arrived in Port-au-Prince, someone at a cocktail party asked where she was from. When she told him the United States, he insisted it couldn't be true—Mills must be from Jamaica. Later, after she'd returned home, there were other instances of mistaken identity. Venturing out with the Haitian writer René Piquion, "all N.Y. intelligentsia took me to be of that nationality, too."[70] Her French must have taken on a Haitian tinge, and she may have been wearing a dress or suit she'd had made in Port-au-Prince.

More than that, though, both incidents symbolize a transformation that began soon after Mills landed in Haiti. She'd come to a new appreciation of what it was to be an American, managed at the same time to create an identity that integrated the African-American with the African Diaspora. With that diasporic identity came the purpose that would inform the rest of her professional life.

– 20 –

Mills Returns
to America

Mills entered Columbia University in the fall of 1944, becoming the first Black woman in the French program—a distinction that remains impressive.

New York was "an exciting place for a student of French literature."[1] There were writers in exile who'd fled the Nazis and, once the war ended the following year, many more who flocked to the literary and cultural capital of the nation. Mills's biographer lists several—Camus, Sartre, de Beauvoir—and, in fact, Mills reported going to a reception for Camus at Columbia. But her scholarly interest was in Black writers like 4 and Césaire.

In one letter, she describes accompanying René Piquion about the city after they'd "been visiting by phone every week." (Surely, given Mills's frugality, not long distance to Haiti!) In March 1945—nearly twenty years after Tap's ill-fated "Goophered"—they went to a lecture by Langston Hughes. Langston was "speaking on Neg. writers in Lat. Am," and, noticing René, "presented him to body as Exhibit A of Lat Am. Writer." When Langston had finished, the audience asked René for a "speech or poem." He asked Mills to decline for him. "Finally, after Langston insisted (they are good friends of years' standing, as Langston said Piquion is the only person who has written a biography of him; he has also translated much of Hughes' work into French), he agreed to speak if they allow[ed] him to do so in French and if I should translate it into English. We did and really won acclaim from the whole packed house—white & colored."[2]

Despite Horatio Smith's enthusiasm, Columbia did not accept all of Mills's credits. "Nearly all" of her graduate work at Howard and Atlanta Universities was reclassified "as undergraduate hours"[3] so she could be admitted. It was probably a workaround because Benedict wasn't accredited. The result, though, was that Mills had to resign herself to spending two years at Columbia—she'd hoped to be done in one. In the end, she'd take three years to finish her coursework, and another seven to complete her dissertation.

The reclassification of her credits—and the fact that she was advised not to take one course because "the exam . . . needed at least six months of serious preparation"[4]—must not have helped Mills's confidence. As the end of her first year approached, she told Mattie she intended to confer with Horatio: "It may be that they have already decided that I am not PhD material and he'll suggest that I take a master's from there and call it a day."[5] The next semester, a year into her studies, she told my mother, Ruth, "School is fine, but I'm dumb."[6] Ruth, working her way toward her master's degree at the University of Chicago, likely understood all too well. A semester later, Mills was still wondering if she really deserved a doctorate: "I don't have to have a PhD to live, but I sorta hate having given most of these two years to it, if I'm going to be kicked out."[7]

Perennial self-doubt aside, Mills enjoyed her time at Columbia. There were talks and lectures to attend, some of them connected with her department. She joined the French Graduate Union, which hosted that reception for Camus, and was elected to its executive committee. And there was time just to have fun. She, Tap, and Tap's girlfriend, Jennie Perry, celebrated Jennie's birthday. She and "Sister"—perhaps Mattie, visiting her brothers in New York, though it may also have been Tap's Jennie; Ralston's wife, Corinne; or Marian's girlfriend, Olga—went to the movies and to see Lena Horne at Broadway's Capitol Theatre.

There was also the aforementioned boyfriend, Bill. Mills doesn't give his last name in her letters, but she called him "an old school friend," so they must have known each other in South Carolina. (There was no William in Benedict's class of 1927, but there were several in the classes of '26 and '28.) Whoever he was, there was some history between them. Years before, according to a story Jo confided, Mills had spied a boyfriend making love (in the old-fashioned sense of wooing) to another woman on the train. Perhaps that was Bill. Or perhaps he was the young man to whom she was once engaged but did not marry because she knew she "lacked parental sanction."[8] At any rate, Mills pronounced herself "so happy." When she and

Bill went to visit friends in Brooklyn in early March, he confessed his love while they were dancing:

> He stopped, grabbed me to him and announced, "Surely I'm happy. This girl has known me longer than any of you. She's the only person I've ever loved and ever will. I found her again, don't you see, and I'm going to spend the rest of my life keeping her as happy as she is in this moment." Then he kissed me. It was silly, it seems now; but swell then. Someone said, "Don't kid him, that's the childhood sweetheart of whom he talks so much." Someone else asked, "What happened?"[9]

Mills doesn't tell us how—or whether—either answered. But she must have blurted her excitement to Mattie, because Sister reminded her that she'd once been "hurt rather badly by Bill."[10] (This makes me think he might have been the boyfriend she saw on the train.) Then, too, Bill was married, though he claimed not to be living with his wife. Mills admitted that Mattie was right—"it does not and would not work under the existing conditions, nor can any good come out of it."[11] All the same, they continued to see one another. When Mills left to visit Mattie in Washington and Colon and Ruth in Philadelphia, Bill was distraught: "[H]e broke down and cried & me, too, begged me never to leave him again and I begged him never to allow me to do so again." He wanted to get divorced so that they could be married in a year. Still, tears aside, Mills thought it "[t]oo good to be true and I don't expect it to work out that way."[12] A few months later, little had changed. Mills gave Bill an ultimatum, perhaps that she wouldn't see him until he did something about his divorce. "It was in effect for almost 2 weeks," she said, "and then damn! I was glad to give in as he was to see me again. I am getting nowhere."[13]

She used all the drama and uncertainty, "working like hell so that I'd be too tired to think or even want to see him."[14] And perhaps on some level "friend Bill"[15] (as Mills called him to distinguish him from her nephew, Alfred and Mattie's third son) understood school came first. Her first-semester grades were good, all As and Bs. Nonetheless, Bill chided her and said he'd see to it she stayed home and studied. He needn't have worried. Despite the setting aside of her credits and the difficult classes, Mills persevered. She might not have been as smart as some of her classmates—or so she thought—but none would outwork her.

And so she persisted, even when Rosenwald did not renew her grant, going to work as a bookkeeper at Hawthorne-Lee, a real estate and insurance agency on 125th Street. Her hours were nine o'clock in the morning to one o'clock in the afternoon. Afterward, she had lunch and then went to the university library at two o'clock. Classes done, she arrived home, Tap's apartment on St. Nicholas Avenue, at eight o'clock in the evening. Sometimes she didn't get there until after ten o'clock at night. "Am very tired those late nights," she reported, "but I think I can make it. I have no classes Wednesday nor Saturday and that helps. In the meantime, I am able to see my way financially, at the present anyway."[16] At the beginning of her fourth semester, a friend helped her find an office job "cataloging requests made in French fan mail."[17] She worked from 8:30 to noon. When she was "kicked out of"[18] her job—she doesn't say which one—she used the free time to audit an elementary Latin class.

The next year, Mills received a Columbia fellowship that allowed her to complete her coursework in 1947. She also left Tap's apartment to live in Samuel Johnson Hall, a graduate students' dorm. (Now Wien Hall,[19] it houses undergraduates.) If she had started her dissertation, she hadn't gotten far—that March, she told Mattie she'd been ill and thought she might never "feel physically well again." But, she said, that might turn out to be a blessing, because "if I just die sometime soon, I won't have to write this dissertation." Meanwhile, the end of the school year was approaching and she needed work. She'd asked Jo to send her an application for the D.C. public school's teacher qualifying exam. She had the chance to teach at Benedict, but what she really wanted was to teach at "a larger college where there would be room for advancement." Still, the only offer she had was from Benedict's President John A. Bacoats, and she feared that she might "be glad to consider Kittrell before it's over."[20]

Fortunately, she didn't have to, as she was offered a post at West Virginia State College. One of the original land-grant colleges, it was founded as West Virginia Colored Institute in 1891 and accredited as a four-year college in 1927. In 2004, it became a university. Seven years after she arrived in West Virginia, Mills received her doctorate. Her dissertation, *The Renaissance of Haitian Poetry*, would be issued in 1963 by the book-publishing arm of the magazine "*Présence Africaine*." Decades later, she'd joke that she continued to receive dwindling royalties in francs every few years.

Like Papa, Mills was part of an in-between cohort of Black achievers. Papa was late, coming of age as Reconstruction was ending and opportunities for Black men and women in the larger white world dwindling into nonexistence. Mills was early, finishing her coursework and coming to West Virginia seven years before the 1954 Supreme Court *Brown v. Board of Education* decision that led to the loosening of limits that had constrained black Americans for nearly eighty years.

As she began to think about applying for jobs, Mills dismissed the possibility of teaching at Columbia: "I don't think I'll ever have to worry over accepting or rejecting an instructorship at C.U., I ain't that good. I still remember, as do the authorities, the color of my face."[21] Even leaving aside her tendency toward self-deprecation, Mills was right. Columbia didn't award a Black professor tenure until 1963.[22] Seven years later, the *Columbia Spectator* reported that there'd only been four tenured Black professors in the school's history.[23]

Too early to receive offers from white institutions, Mills likely felt too settled to uproot herself when those schools began to look for Black professors in the 1960s. After she'd retired, she taught at Ohio's Denison University, Rhode Island College, and the University of Charleston and was honored with titles such as university professor and distinguished professor. But even if Denison and other white colleges and universities had pursued her earlier, Mills likely would have declined.

For all her earlier complaints about the failings of Black institutions, she found a measure of security in West Virginia—another lesson to take from Papa's misfortunes. And, just as important, she had a sense of commitment to her students, one rooted in an awareness of duty to the race inculcated long before by Papa and Mama.

– 21 –

Death and Funerals

After her surgery, Mama recovered well enough to travel, with and without Papa. As was their custom, they went to churches and schools within the state, paid weekend visits to friends. Alone, Mama ventured to Atlantic City for a "grand" meeting, the National Convention of her beloved Tents. It was a grueling journey—seven hundred miles and at least fourteen hours on the train—and she considered not going. There was "something very important" she wanted done, however, and she was afraid it would be overlooked if she didn't go. (Alas, she doesn't say what compelled her attendance.) So she stayed home while Papa went to Little Rock and Winston-Salem, "trying to conserve my strength for Atlantic City." After the Convention, she "went on to New York to rest up a bit before starting for home." Once back in South Carolina—it was a seventeen-and-a-half-hour train ride from New York (Mama was lucky; she got a seat though the train was so crowded some passengers had to stand or sit on their suitcases)—she set off for Charleston and a meeting of the Tents' executive board. The financial secretary was leaving the state and, as president of the board, Mama had to attend.[1]

Ruth lectured Mama by letter, admonishing her to "[t]ake it easy." "Mama, you are the child now," she wrote, "so don't be hard-headed. You see, you would tell us to mind, so you must mind now."[2] Mills could do nothing from Haiti, but she was not pleased.

"I do wish that Mama wasn't so headstrong & determined," she told Mattie. "But no one can tell her anything. Do you think that she'll listen to the doctor and stay at home if she gets better and gets up this time? God knows I wish every lodge and the memory of every lodge would just cease and fade away entirely. God forbid that I become that wrapped up in anything."[3]

But Mama was determined to keep on. "Sometimes the going is rough and difficult for us both," she told Mattie, "but we 'stumble on[,]' not meaning to give up till we just can't go any further."[4] All the same, determined as she was, she knew she might get better, but she'd never get well.

Preparing for the end, Mama called undertaker Henry D. Pearson,[5] a man she'd known for years. She made her funeral arrangements, giving him strict instructions that he, and only he, was to prepare her for burial. None of his younger assistants was to touch her. A private person to the end, she also left instructions that she wanted her service to be held at home, with only family attending.

Mama died, aged seventy-three, on February 15, 1944, the day after a federal judge signed a consent decree mandating that the Charleston School Board pay Negro teachers the same as whites. It was almost as if she knew her work was done. In a moving coincidence, a story asking for contributions to fund similar teacher-pay suits throughout South Carolina appeared over her obituary in the *Palmetto Leader.* Just fourteen lines long, that obituary ignores her long career as a school supervisor and teacher, her advocacy in the state's Negro teachers association, and her work with her beloved sororal organizations. Instead, she was described as the "wife of Prof. C. G. Garrett," a mother of eight children, and "a large number of grand- and great-grandchildren."[6]

She deserved more.

The service was held in the house on Lady Street. Only the family attended. Papa asked Jo to play "Lead Kindly Light," a hymn she knew of but had never heard, let alone played. But that wasn't the only problem. The piano (you can see it on the left side of the fiftieth anniversary photograph, behind Tap and Corinne) was old and out of tune. As she bumbled her way through the hymn, Mama's casket at her elbow, Jo imagined her grandmother's chiding her: "'And to think, Baby spent all that money on piano lessons, and this is the best you can do.'" Later, after they'd laid their mother to rest in the family cemetery on the farm outside Columbia, Anna Maria Threewitts's sons gathered on the porch at Lady Street. "Well," one said, "we can smoke now," and all took out cigarettes, They lit them only to put them out almost immediately—"I just can't smoke in her house," one of her boys said sheepishly. "I just can't do it."

After Mama's death, Papa lingered another three years, lurching toward the inevitable.

Mills tried to oversee his care from New York once she returned from Haiti, even though Chris and, perhaps, his wife, Charlisena, were living on Lady Street. Glimpses of their father in letters to Mattie show flashes of the man he'd been amid his slow decline. In one, Mills noted that "Papa, of course, has a house full of girls here whom he was helping."[7] At eighty-one, the man who'd "loved the ladies" was long past amorous adventures—they were boarders come to attend Allen or work in Columbia.

Nearing the end of her coursework, and still feeling occasional uncertainty about deserving a doctorate, Mills agonized over what to do. Benedict's President John A. Bacoats wanted her to teach at his school. She came close to accepting his offer, though she knew she had "no desire to live and work in South Carolina," much less endure another stint at a Negro college (like Benedict) whose president (like Bacoats) was "rather unbusinesslike." Still, she told Mattie, it would "allow me to be at home with Papa so that I can take care of him."[8]

If Chris and Charlisena were taking care of Papa, they weren't doing it to Mills's satisfaction. She managed to get back to Lady Street several times to "clean Dad's closet and room, prepare meals, keep out top dirt, do marketing, etc." On one of those visits, she, Tap, and Papa went to the farm to pick grapes. "Papa enjoyed it immensely," she told Mattie, "and that, after all, is important."[9] Despite encroaching age, Papa managed to get around. In 1946, he went to one last colored fair, though he tried to do too much and had to be taken home by a family friend. The next spring, a few months before his death, he ventured up to Philadelphia. As always, traveling agreed with him—Mills reported that "he seemed so very cheerful."[10]

All the same, no matter where or how fast Papa ran, death pursued, robbing him of his dignity as it stalked him. He suffered "crying spells," lamenting "he had only a few hours to live,"[11] complaining that Mattie, Ralston, and Marian had not come with Tap and Mills. He was in and out of the hospital. Irascible as ever, he threatened Mills if she didn't take him home.[12]

It's not the way I want to remember him.

C. G. Garrett, second from right, and five unidentified men. Collection of the author.

Instead, I think of a photograph of Papa standing on the wooden porch steps of a house in Columbia. I think it was probably taken a year or so before his death. He's with five others, a cohort of grim, fierce-visaged behatted old men in three-piece suits, some girded with watch chains or sporting vest-pocket fountain pens. Though he's leaning on a cane, Papa's face is defiant. And why not? Like the others, he'd survived slavery's aftermath, defied white supremacy, made a way for himself in a world that considered him of little value. Grizzled and gray, he and his cohort of dark old men face a final enemy, one they can neither defeat nor escape.

Even so, they remain unbowed.

Papa died, aged eighty-two, on November 15, 1947. In contrast to Mama's lone obituary, he was remembered in the *Chicago Defender*, the *Baltimore Afro-American*, the *New York Age*, the *Columbia Record*, and *The State*, as well as the *Palmetto Leader*. The *Christian Recorder* lauded him as "among the best known laymen" in the AME church. *The Light*, it said, had been "widely read and nationally recognized for the fearless and the right quality of its editorials."[13]

I have a folder full of telegrams of condolence sent to the house on Lady Street after Papa's death, but copies of his funeral program—if there was one—have not survived. Gone, too, are the remarks at the service made by those who loved and admired him. What did survive is a tribute written by his youngest son, Chris, in a letter to Mattie a month after Papa died:

> We, as his children, took him and his doing and actions mostly for granted. . . . [B]ecause we were with him all the time, we could not see where he had done anything so great. We had been taught that way[,] and the things he did to help people, his church, and school, were the things we thought any person would have, or should have done. But I find that it is only now[,] when people from all over pay tribute to him and the wonderful things that he accomplished, that I can see what a great man he must have been, and how much he had to do with influencing so many people all over the country for good. Whatever may have been his faults, I am convinced that the things he did for good so far overshadowed everything else as to make that part undecernable. [sic][14]

Because his life began at the end of one great event in American history, pleasing symmetry would have had Papa live to see another, the 1954 *Brown v. Board of Education* decision overturning segregation in schools. The changes he dreamed of and fought for were yet to come, however. Still, although he did not live to see Rosa Parks and the Rev. Martin Luther King Jr., he did live to see the Tuskegee Airmen take flight, the NAACP's growing fight against discrimination, the founding of the Congress of Racial Equality, and President Truman's establishment of the National Committee on Civil Rights.

I've tried, and mostly failed, to imagine him. But I like to believe that Papa's writing and his teaching—his entire life's work, in fact—imagine all who would come after.

Including me.

And Their
Children after Them

By the end of World War II in 1945, only Chris remained in Columbia. He worked as a printer, including a stint at the *Palmetto Leader*, after he and Charlisena were married in 1926. In 1930 or so, he caught on with the post office as a substitute letter carrier. He began to work full time in the 1930s. Charlisena may have taught—Richland County records show her with a certificate to teach preschool in 1938. Not surprisingly, because they wed so young, the marriage didn't last. The 1940 census shows them living apart, but they must have reconciled, as the Columbia City Directory shows them at the same address for much of the 1940s. They separated for good late in the decade. Chris married again in the 1950s, this time to a woman named Rochelle Robinson.

By then, the rest of Mama and Papa's children were long gone, settled for decades in Washington, D.C., Philadelphia, New York, and West Virginia.

A year after Maceo's death in 1943, Colon and Henrietta moved to Philadelphia, despite Mama's announcement that he'd secured "his release"[1] from her. Perhaps they were the kind of couple who could live neither with nor without one another. Mama wished them the best, hoping they'd "find work and begin in their middle age to make a go of it."[2] For his part, Colon told Papa that he was "working steadily—trying to straighten up finances all 'round."[3] A year later, he urged Papa "to hasten come see me for the first in my own home, on my own ground."[4] Colon thanked Papa for a loan and promised to repay. He said he was working, though not at what. Four years later, when he died in 1949, Colon's death certificate listed his occupation as janitor. Henrietta died eighteen years later.

Tap died three years after Colon. Mattie died in 1959, three years after the death of her husband, Alfred. Despite the backing and filling during their courtship, when it seemed each feared intimacy as much as being alone, their union had endured nearly forty years. Ralston followed a year later, dying in 1960. Both Chris, the youngest, and Marian died in 1967.

And Ruth, the daughter of whom Mama had despaired. . . .

Despite Mama's hopes, she didn't stick to teaching. Instead, she left Kershaw County to return to Columbia, where she worked at a hospital at Fort Jackson. Wartime work must have paid better, though Mama admitted Ruth was "more of a maid than anything else." All the same, however, Mama conceded that the pay was "pretty fair."[5] Jack also found work at Fort Jackson and volunteered as an air raid warden.

Soon, however, they were on the move again. They went to Philadelphia, about the same time Colon and Henrietta also left South Carolina for the city. The change seemed to agree with them: "I am glad that Ruth seems to be getting along all right in Philadelphia and that she seems happy," Mills told Mattie. "Maybe she [will] become settled there!"[6]

And Ruth did settle down in Philadelphia. At first, she did "days work."[7] Later, she opened a "day nursery."[8] She and Jack would stay married nearly forty years; their marriage lasted longer than those of many of her brothers.

All the same, Ruth hadn't entirely given up her restive ways. In 1973, when she was sixty-nine years old, she met another man and followed him to his retirement community in California. Mama would have shaken her head with rueful exasperation. Jack followed to bring her back, much as Papa had decades before when Ruth was supposed to have run off with the high school principal. According to Jo, he died the same day he arrived in California. Eventually, Ruth came back to Philadelphia, where she lived alone with her collection of owl figurines (made of materials as various as sea shells and macrame), played pinochle (she "was a tough player"[9]), read, and watched baseball on television. She died in 1996, aged ninety-two, leaving Mills the last of Mama and Papa's children.

Mills would stay at West Virginia State as teacher, adviser to foreign students, and chairman of the Department of Modern Foreign Languages for twenty-five years, long enough to see white students begin to enroll after the 1954 *Brown v. Board of Education* decision, a trickle at first, and then a flood. Some Black students complained because they didn't want to go to school with whites. Others felt that the "campus doesn't have the same atmosphere." (To which Mills said, "Thank God!"[10]) Nonetheless, she was able to report three years into integration that white students "are entering into the college life without a hitch." Most were commuters, but a few men tried out for the football team. Some Black college teams objected, but Mills thought they "should be glad that for once they have the opportunity of winning from white folks." One student even "insisted upon living in the dorm to enter more fully into college life."[11]

Throughout her career, Mills traveled, lectured, and studied in Europe, Asia, the Caribbean, Africa, Canada, Mexico, and the Middle East. She received many awards, including a Fulbright that allowed her to study at the Sorbonne, a Ford Foundation Fellowship, and an honorary degree from Denison University in 1979. (Canadian-American writer Clark Blaise also received one from Denison that same year,[12] something I wish I'd known when he was one of my teachers at the Iowa Writers Workshop two years later.) She counted among her acquaintances such luminaries as Leopold Senghor, president of Senegal, and poet Aimé Césaire of Martinique. She knew the novelist René Maran, author of *Batouala*. Even when she retired in 1972, she didn't really quit working—over the next eight years, she'd accept a series of visiting professorships.

Asked, however, what she considered her greatest achievement, Mills might have cited mentoring a host of students from Africa, the Caribbean, Japan, Thailand, Hong Kong, and Taiwan. They arrived lost and lonely in thin shirts and jackets, unprepared for West Virginia winters, daunted by barriers of language and custom. Mills worked tirelessly to feed, house, and clothe them, to make them feel welcome. In March 1966, *Ebony* magazine included a picture of her pouring "holy water in [a] 'Thai National Day' fete."[13] She called the overseas students "her children"; they called her their "West Virginia mother."[14] Later, when she traveled, they opened their homes to her, even writing to friends who hadn't studied at State, bidding them offer Mills their hospitality.

She lived independently to the end, beholden to no man, coming and going as she pleased, setting off for foreign lands without having to ask permission or fret about those she left behind. Jo and the rest of her nieces envied her ambition; I think sometimes they regretted they'd lacked her drive, her will to see things through. Weary of their marriages, sick of attending husbands, children and, in Jo's case, a mother-in-law, they craved her solitude and the selfishness that meant she need not wait on man nor child.

But independence had its price—in Mills's case, a lonely end. For most of the time she taught in West Virginia, she rented an apartment or house. Finally, after some thirty years, she built a cozy little home of her own, filling it with the mementoes and artwork she'd collected on her travels. As she grew older, friends and relatives urged her to give it up for a place where she could get the help she needed, or at least to accept having a care-taker. Mills refused. One day, alone in the house, she fell. She was taken unconscious to the hospital and died there several days later in May 2000. She was almost ninety-six.

Mattie was buried in Washington; Colon and Ruth, in Philadelphia. The rest were brought home to lie beside Mama and Papa in the family cem-etery, deep in the soil of their native Carolina, stands of tall pines towering over their graves, fingers pointing toward the heavens.

– 23 –

They, Too,
Sang America

Papa's life demonstrates an ability to reimagine himself that would have gladdened the hearts of his abolitionist schoolteachers. He was never as well off as, say, Columbia stalwart I. S. Leevy, who died at ninety-one years old having owned a department store, funeral home, real estate company, barber shop, gas station, beauty parlor, and hog farm. And, if all that was not sufficient, he also co-founded and led the Victory Savings Bank.[1] Still, because it was a time when Black families could call themselves middle class on the strength of husbands' steady employment as Pullman porters, mailmen, or government janitors, Papa's position at Allen, his church and political activism, and his newspapers granted the Garretts a place among Columbia's Black elite.

Mama's appointment as supervisor of rural schools came later, but it, too, added to the Garretts' status. But it isn't just that Papa and Mama belonged to what A. B. Caldwell called "the best element of the Negro Race."[2] Their status allowed their children to lead privileged lives. Though bound by racism, the Garrett sons and daughters belonged to a family that enjoyed respect from both Blacks and whites. They were protected from the worst of segregation by a loving, close-knit Afro-Carolinian community, afforded opportunities denied many of their Black contemporaries. Not all went to college or normal school. If they'd wanted to, though, Mama and Papa would have made it happen.

Given their (relatively) privileged backgrounds, the advantages they enjoyed, and the example of their parents, Mama and Papa's children could have been expected to advance even further and to take up the duty to work for the betterment of the race.

Most did not.

Colon became a dentist, and Mills earned a doctorate, but most settled for less, living, well, ordinary lives of little note—Tap's thwarted show-business career aside—especially when compared with what their parents had dared. Perhaps their choices were a consequence of Papa's dismissal from Allen. As the family's hold on respectability became even more precarious, they saw the cost of living for the race and decided to live only for themselves. Perhaps they also saw how dangerous it could be to dream.

It couldn't have been easy being one of Papa's children, especially given his and Mama's accomplishments. Papa's are easier to document, but Mama's are not to be slighted. "Queen Anne," as her children called her, was proud and imperious, strong-willed, energetic, and intelligent—qualities that would have helped her to succeed almost anywhere.

In that letter about Hemingway, Faulkner, and Wolfe that Tap sent my mother in 1942, he praised his niece for her "seeming industriousness," because she was working and going to Howard full time. He was sure, however, that "such industry does not come from the Garrett side. We are known as one-job people, and that only because sleeping out-of-doors is inconvenient and not eating is so very uncomfortable."[3] But neither Papa nor Mama was lazy—Tap's sardonic wit was a preemptive strike against disapproval because of how little he'd achieved.

All the same, if Tap and most of his siblings settled for less in their lives than they might have, not quite measuring up to what Papa and Mama expected, most did well enough to be considered middle class by the standards of the Black community. Two worked for the post office, a government job that provided a steady salary and generous retirement benefits. Two others earned a living wage as Pullman porters and enjoyed the side benefit of traveling the country. Even Ruth went into business for herself with her day care center.

Mama would have liked to see her children do better, but perhaps she concluded that at least they were working. From time to time, she wrote disparagingly—despairingly might be a better word—about Ruth and about her sons. She spared Mills and Mattie, but I wonder if she didn't sometimes allow herself to feel disappointed because Baby, her favorite who'd been Allen's first woman college graduate (and salutatorian of her class), had wanted to become a physician, like family friend Matilda A. Evans. Instead, Mattie married and raised eight children. She'd fallen short even there: Mama had nine of her own and reared ten.

Most of Mama's criticism of Ruth and her sons had to do with their complicated lives, her anxiety about their crumbling marriages (her own lasted more than fifty years), and her disappointment that they didn't send more money home. (To be fair to them, Ruth offered to help financially— "though I haven't done much up to now"—if Mama wanted to stop teaching. And, that same year, 1935, Colon announced that "[y]our sons are to begin this week sending regularly to you not less than five dollars per month as your 'retirement pension.'" He proposed paying his share in "weekly installments,"[4] and enclosed a dollar and fifty cents.)

"I don't know what to think of Cornice," Mama complained, a year or so after Cornice and Tap had settled in New York. "She hasn't written me a line yet. Neither has Tap. None of them write as they should."[5] Two years later, when she had to learn from Tap that Marian had married, she lamented that "my boys have acted so strangely—unnaturally so—until I have about decided to give them up and not care what they do."[6] A few years after that, on the eve of the Great Depression, when Cornice told her she and Tap had separated and that Tap was "drinking heavily," Mama adopted a pose of resignation: "Well, while I hate that things have turned out so badly, I have few regrets. I feel we did all we could for all of you and Tap was especially favored. If he throws away his life and talents, I cannot help it."[7]

In the end, though, Mama was forced to accept that Tap and the rest of her children were beyond her control: "I'm sorry, but not worrying," she sighed. "They have their own lives to live."[8]

Mama read the paper and kept up with gossip, so she must have known, Maceo aside, her children were no worse than the children of some of her contemporaries. In 1915, William Chappelle's younger son, William D. Chappelle Jr., was accused of firing four shots from a pistol on a "public road." (He was in a car with several friends, and they'd probably been drinking.) He was convicted and sentenced to twenty days in jail or a fine of forty dollars. And Seymour Carroll, son of the Rev. Richard Carroll, was tried for arson and acquitted after he was accused "in an attempt to burn the State college for Negroes."[9]

Surely Mama enjoyed moments of *schadenfreude* when she learned of these transgressions, though neither would have lessened her disappointment in her own children. She called them "you northerners," as if they'd forsaken the South, blaming the cities they'd fled to for their fraying lives. "New York has got them both,"[10] she lamented, holding the city responsible for Tap's drinking and the end of his marriage to Cornice. It symbolized all that was new and different in a world Mama was becoming hard-pressed to recognize. But what Mama didn't understand was that for Ralston, Tap, Maceo, and Marian, Harlem was a "race capital," a place where it might actually be "fun to be a Negro."[11] It was *their* city, a "stylish black community,"[12] "the cultural capital of the race."[13] The lives of the Garrett brothers, and all the Black Southerners who'd fled north during the Great Migration, were rooted in a different vision of Blackness—not for nothing did Tap's Harlem contemporaries call themselves New Negroes. That they could do so was largely through the efforts of countless unknown Black leaders, like Papa and Mama. Now—alas!—the world she'd helped create excluded her.

Mama's dismay at a changing world underlies her tart observations about her neighbors and their flaws, foibles, and flailings, their drunkenness, drug abuse, marital turmoil, and financial imprudence. It's displaced worry about her sons' drinking and their precarious marital states, transferred fretting about Ruth and the ne'er-do-wells who flocked to her, unacknowledged anxiety about Mattie, far from home with a husband who had yet to prove himself fit to provide for her Baby. Mama knew the world was a dangerous place, strewn with snares for the unwary. She knew, too, how easily one might slip, how easily one might fall from respectable colored to disreputable nigger. And so, these letters were not just warnings; they were prayers that, by naming the pitfalls, she might sway fate.

Like Papa's, Mama's pride was both personal and racial, the two aspects so entwined it's impossible to untangle whether that pride was the cause, or the result, of their calling to uplift. Chris acknowledged that calling in his tribute to his father, but neither he nor his siblings—with the exception of Mills—carried on with it. They wanted to be themselves, something impossible within the web of family and social ties that had made Columbia such a good place to grow up.

When the son of an acquaintance asked his father for train fare to come back to Columbia, Mama noted what the prodigal should have known all along: "New York is not home."[14] But what she saw as a safe place, her children found confining. Both Ralston and Tap found wives within the African Methodist Episcopal (AME) family. Ralston's was from Florida, two states away, but Tap's was the daughter of the Rev. David A. Christie, the pastor who'd married Alfred and Mattie. (Papa's ally, he was one of the churchmen who spoke out in 1920 against returning Bishop William Chappelle to South Carolina.) Colon's wife, Henrietta, was from Scuffletown, Papa's birthplace. There were other connections as well. Seretha Cannon, the woman Mama accused an AME pastor of seducing, was in Marion's Normal School class at South Carolina State. Christie's second wife, Lottie Sightler, had taught at the Howard School with Tap, and the Sightlers and Simonses were related—for years, Alfred acted as the guardian of a cousin, Alice Sightler. Even away from Columbia, the Garretts found themselves brushing up against the world they'd fled: Colon entered Lincoln University to find six other South Carolinians in his class of forty-three men. Three were from Columbia, and two of those had been his classmates at Allen. Hall Johnson, who wrote the music for Tap's ill-fated "Goophered," had had Papa as a teacher at Allen. And Abbie Mitchell, the singer and actress who was supposed to have starred in "Goophered," was the mother of Mercer Cook, Mills's mentor.

Degrees of separation in the Garretts' world meant that if you didn't know someone, surely you knew someone else who did. Small wonder, then, that Mattie escaped to Washington; Ruth and Colon, to Philadelphia; and Nick, Tap, Maceo, and Marian, to New York, Harlem on their minds. Even if the pastor of Bethel AME—the church Tap joined when he came to New York in 1913—was Benjamin W. Arnett Jr.,[15] son of the bishop who'd led Allen when Papa was a student, and a former teacher at Allen himself, there were fifty thousand other Black Harlemites, almost as many as the entire population of Columbia.

It was, of course, the Great Migration, that momentous shift of Black Americans from Southern farms to Northern cities. The Garretts weren't farmers, of course, but conditions in Columbia had changed since Papa's time, making it more difficult to rise as far and as fast as he had. Then, too, as that poem in *The State* by Wade Hampton Gibbes attested, white men were determined that Black soldiers returning from the Great War resume their subordinate positions under white supremacy.

Only Ralston served overseas and had the heady experience of being treated as an equal by the French. But even if Tap and Maceo remained stateside, each served in the North (albeit in a segregated US Army), and Tap had had the responsibility of commanding men. Their experiences awakened them to possibilities, helping explain why all three settled in New York. Of course, there was discrimination in the big city, but they were free to ride bus or subway without retreating to the rear, free to go to the movies or Broadway shows and sit anywhere they could afford seats, free to register to vote as Ralston did in 1925. It might not have been the full equality their descendants would enjoy, but it was steps closer to the manhood Papa reminded Black men they deserved.

◆ ◆ ◆

After his first wife's death, Marian married twice more, the second time to a woman about half his age. Once divorced, Tap had several girlfriends. The result was that when Mama sat down to decide who should come to her fiftieth anniversary, she wondered whether to invite Barbara and Ethel—the daughter Frank died giving birth to, and the woman (possibly Tap's girlfriend) who adopted her. But she worried that Tap's ex-wife, Cornice, might decide *she* wanted to come, and there were other ex- or estranged wives—Maceo's Jimmie and Chris's Charlesina to consider. By then, however, Mama had mellowed, though she still faulted her sons for not marrying again. "I feel nearer to these first girls," she said, "since they are the only ones who married my boys."[16]

As scandalous as all this might have been in Columbia, however, the Garrett sons' complicated lives meant nothing amidst New York's anonymity.

Sometimes, Mama blamed herself for how her children had turned out. "I know I tried to be a good mother," she told Mattie eight days after Mother's Day—of all days—in 1926, "but sometimes I feel that I made an ignoble failure. But that's because I tried to fashion the lives of my children and to think thoughts for them, not realizing each [was] an independent individual who should think and act himself. However, I have no regrets for what I did, since I acted as I thought and saw [fit]."[17] Later that same year, apparently responding to something Mattie had said, she wrote, "No, it isn't that I think we have the worst children nor the most trouble with them, but just that we were the poorest sort of parents. I don't believe the fault is in the children but in us. We were not fitted for the position of moulding the character and shaping the lives of future citizens. We did the best we could in our weak, ignorant way, but I realize we failed to reach the desired aim."[18]

Mama called Mattie "Baby" well into her adulthood and used the childhood nicknames "Buddie" and "Tap" for Ralston and Casper Jr. long after all three—her oldest children—had left home and established families of their own. She called her youngest, Chris, "Boy" a decade after he'd married and become a father. On some level, each was always a child to her, and what she really wanted was for them, and the rest of her brood, to do what she thought best. But she was being too harsh when she called herself and Papa "the poorest sort of parents."

Nearly all of their children fled the South, seeking better opportunities and freedom from the strictures of segregation. But they also wanted their own lives—no matter what Mama and Papa may have wanted for them—and so, they left home to find those lives in a world far different from the one Mama and Papa had known. It is, perhaps, the most American—no, *human*—of impulses.

Afterword

I've driven down to Columbia six times to research this book. Most of my time's been spent in the Walker Local and Family History Room at the Richland County Library, the State Archives, and the South Caroliniana Library at the University of South Carolina, but I almost always take an hour or two to explore downtown and, sometimes, visit Allen University and Benedict College. It always feels like going back in time. Downtown Columbia reminds me of the Washington, D.C. I knew as a child—many streets have the same three- and four-story buildings with ornate facades, ground-floor stores, and offices above. The people are familiar, too. Courteous and good-natured, they nod and murmur hello, much like the men and women I passed on the sidewalk years ago, when Washington still had a real downtown.

I'm not really going back in time, of course. Like that decades-lost Washington, the Columbia of Mama and Papa's time is mostly gone. Churches like Chappelle Memorial AME and First Nazareth Baptist (pastored by Alfred's father, the Rev. Isom Wesley Simons) remain, but institutions like Good Samaritan Hospital, and the Victory Savings Bank have vanished, as have the Howard and Booker T. Washington schools. All are casualties of the opening of society that eroded the Black community's need to be self-nurturing and self-sustaining. Ironies abound: When Washington High School was torn down, the bricks were used to pave the driveway of the University of South Carolina's Horseshoe, the quadrangle that formed the original campus of the school that was once reserved for whites only.

Papa and Mama's house still stands on Lady Street. Each time I park and get out to walk the neighborhood, I'm disappointed they aren't waiting to greet me. I know, of course, they've been gone more than seventy years, lie resting in the family cemetery on the farm Mama bought for Papa on Screaming Eagle Road outside Columbia. Ralston's buried there, too, as are

Tap; Maceo; Marian; Mills; Chris; Chris's second wife, Rochelle; and their two sons. I've spent years immersing myself in family letters and documents, staring at photographs, scrolling through old newspapers on microfiche and computer screens, enough time to occasionally feel Mama and Papa's world more real than my own. Small wonder, then, that I feel pangs of sadness at finding the city (and community) they'd help make gone and all but forgotten.

It's true even of the Garrett family cemetery, where neighbors laid out a baseball diamond nearby on Papa's land, and some of the headstones are so worn I had to use Photoshop to coax the names and dates visible.

It isn't so much that I would have liked to have lived in that long-gone world. Ignorant of the vagaries of race etiquette, I would have risked injury venturing where I should not, looking when I should have averted my eyes, speaking when prudence dictated quiet. And yet, and yet. . . .

There are times I wish I could walk beside Papa, see what he saw, hear what he heard, know what he knew. I'd like to follow him to the First Calvary Baptist Church, stand near the picket fence watching the photographer go about his work memorializing the Black Columbians who've turned out to welcome Booker T. Washington. I'd like to sit on the train as Washington made his tour of South Carolina, listening to Papa and the other men talk, then come back and watch as Papa wrote up his account of the trip, even help him set type and feed paper while he ran the press. I'd like to have driven to the country with Mama, sat with her in the back of a classroom as she observed teachers, watched her sway a contrary country school board. I'd like to have seen her manage a meeting of Tents, organize a summer teachers training.

◆　◆　◆

Early on in *Black Carolinians: A History of Blacks in South Carolina from 1895 to 1968*, I. A. Newby claims that "black communities in the state were never organized. In fact, they were not communities in the true sense of the word."[1] I'm not sure just what Newby meant, since communities are made up of people who live in the same place and "often have a common cultural and historical heritage." Members of a community share "common characteristics or interests"[2]—just as the Black Columbians of Mama and Papa's world did. Later, Newby advances a proposition that may explain why he believed Black Carolinians didn't enjoy a community. White racism was "the central fact in [their] history," he writes, and race "the criterion used to identify them, define their role, restrict their advancement, thwart their hope, limit their horizons."[3] I don't disagree. Even before the onslaught of the so-called Redemption that ended Reconstruction, real freedom was only a flickering promise for Afro-Carolinians. Like African-Americans throughout the nation, they lacked basic civil rights and political and economic power, were forced to endure in a culture and system of government that enshrined in law and custom the principle of separate and unequal.

Many—particularly those in rural areas who dared to accumulate wealth and property or refused to bow to white supremacy—faced the threat of violence. But even if colored Columbians were relatively immune from the risk of reprisal, they lived under a system of written and unwritten rules. Laws defined who was Black and who was not; mandated separate schools; directed Black millworkers to separate entrances, exits, and pay windows; stipulated where black men and women might sit on buses and streetcars; prevented them from marrying whites or adopting white children; barred black doctors, nurses, and lawyers from white professional organizations. Until 1942, when the Carver Theater opened, African-American Columbians went to the movies or the theater at special times or sat in separate sections. They could shop at the S. S. Kress five-and-dime and Tapp's Department Store (and, indeed, Tapp's sought their business by advertising in the *Palmetto Leader*) but not eat at either lunch counter.[4]

It was a system of daily indignities that denied black humanity. Colored Columbians might go to a white doctor for treatment, but they used separate entrances and sat in separate waiting rooms. White specialists operated on African-American patients at Good Samaritan Hospital, established by a Black doctor because white hospitals would not admit Blacks. And, while some might be liberal enough to refrain from calling Black men "Uncle" and Black women "Aunty," white men and women refused them the honorifics "Mr." and "Mrs." they insisted on among themselves. This wasn't absolute—remember how, after Papa struck Bishop Chappelle, the judge said he was going to "treat them as he would prominent white men that happened to be connected with such disorders"[5]? Still, on those occasions when whites extended simple courtesies, they soon revealed how much they were bound by the customs of their time. In her affidavit supporting Mama's claim after she broke her ankle on Main Street, Mrs. Dora Dare Baker calls Mama "Annie M. Garrett" once and "Mrs. Annie M. Garrett" a second time. Correcting her initial failure to use the honorific, she accords Mama dignity; it's another act of human kindness in keeping with her stopping to help and to make sure an ambulance was called. All the same, no one who knew Anna Maria Threewitts Garrett would have called her "Annie." And there's this as well: Dora felt compelled to note something she mightn't have felt necessary had Mama been white—Mama, she said, had "seemed to be a very respectable woman."

All the same, the system that reinforced white supremacy and denied Black humanity wasn't the whole story. Had it been, Benedict College and Allen University wouldn't have graduated scores of students each year, and Black Columbia would not have boasted professors and businessmen, carpenters, contractors, and ironworkers, preachers and undertakers, tailors, dressmakers, mailmen, dentists, doctors, and bakers. Relatively independent of white control because of their work, they formed a kind of colored aristocracy, sustaining (and sustained by) "autonomous sanctuaries"[6]—a nexus of churches, schools and colleges, fraternal and sororal groups, secret orders, and charitable and civic organizations.

That nexus, and their own integrity, helped insulate Mama, Papa, and their cohort from white thoughtlessness and misbehavior. True, life was easier in Columbia than it would have been in some smaller, more isolated town. Anywhere they lived, however, Papa and Mama would have been protected by inner resources born of breeding, class, religious faith, and an unshakeable sense of their own worth. Now forgotten Black leaders of their time, they understood something we've discarded as no longer useful: That they had no choice but to make up their own lives, invent their own world.

They were Garretts and Simonses, Perrins, Sightlers, Saxons, Nances, Palmers, and Chappelles. Some were Columbia born and bred. Others flocked to the capital city from throughout South Carolina, coming to study at Benedict or Allen from places like Marion, Georgetown, Due West, Monck's Corner, Barnwell, Ninety Six, Aiken, Anderson, Spartanburg, and Rock Hill. Afterward, many returned home to teach or preach. Others stayed to make new lives in Columbia. They were joined by marriage and by employment in the colored schools, meetings of the Parent–Teachers

Association of Old Howard School and the Richland County Teachers Association, connected by church membership and participation in secret organizations such as the Masons, the Heroines of Jericho, the Order of Good Samaritans, and the Daughters of Samaria. Some went to the Columbia Theatre for plays and comic operas, suffering the indignity of the colored balcony for the sake of art. They read popular books of the day, gathering in each other's homes for discussions, lending each other volumes they'd finished. They went to football games at Benedict and at Allen, motored to baseball games at high schools throughout the state. They subscribed to newspapers like *The Light*, the *Southern Indicator*, and the *Christian Recorder* and magazines like the *A.M.E. Church Review* and *The Crisis*. They played croquet.[7]

The nurturing world they and their friends created for themselves is one reason the horrors and indignities that surrounded them appear so seldom in Mama and Papa's letters. It's almost as if white people (the source of those horrors) were a fact of life, no more to be blamed or resented when their foolishness turned lethal than floods or storms. Good Christians, Black Columbians forgave even when they did not forget. White people were relations, errant but relations nonetheless. The appearance, over and over again, of the same surnames in both communities attests to that. Nathan Barksdale, the US senator Papa met with in 1922? He was from Laurens, as was Papa's cousin, Lucy, a Mills who'd married a Black Barksdale, and a member of Spelman College's first graduating class. And Papa's daughter, Mills, wrote briefly of a visit to Laurens, where Papa's "white kinfolks," gave him "2 bushels of the biggest Elberta's I've ever seen."[8] She doesn't tell us their names, but surely, Papa, Mama, and their cohort must have thought that one day these blood relations would acknowledge their connection and come to their senses.

Of all the men and women I write about here, I identify most with Papa. That's not surprising, given the parallels in our lives. My twentieth-century equivalent of Papa's Northern missionaries and New England schoolmarms were the white liberals (and their Black cohort) who campaigned to integrate Washington's private schools. They were the reason I went to Sidwell Friends. I didn't go to law school, but, like Papa, I became a writer and, like him, used my pen to attack those I thought foolish and wrong. But given how little I can know about him, do I see Papa as he really was? Or only my own distorted reflection? I ask myself the same questions about my parents, Ruth and Roy, and others (like my uncles Al and Bill) as I pore over their lives, trying to understand those who came before me. Sometimes I think I see patterns—sorrow, abandonment, and grief—leaping from generation to generation like shared DNA. Are they real? Or has the past simply become a mirror, all my research, all my attempts to puzzle out, merely confirming what I already knew?

I'm never quite sure. And, in the end, find myself grateful for other writers' affirmations that it's impossible to know the truth. Just trying to tell the story means telling a lie.

Still, superficial though they may be, similarities are a way to try to understand Papa, even though I know no matter how much I ponder his life, it's impossible to truly understand him. For one thing, though I've been called "nigger" (though only twice to my face by white people), nothing I've had to endure can compare with the presumption of inferiority Papa endured. In his fierceness and his rectitude, he's like Isom Wesley, my other American great-grandfather, "a daguerreotype from the last century, one of those stern, severe faces that their descendants can feel weighing them across the chasm of years, judging them small, insignificant, unworthy people."[9] Without his letters and his journals, with only fragments of his "Reminiscences"—like photographs, they represent only instants of a life—I'm left with my own imaginings.

Papa's lost "Reminiscences" might have provided more about his early years and his career, though the neo-Victorian prose quoted in that sesquicentennial history of Columbia is stilted and impersonal, designed for public consumption. From time to time, however, a hint of something personal shines through. It's just enough to crave more.

Here is Papa writing about the enslaved in the years leading up to the Civil War: "The slaves knew from the strained look on the faces of the masters and by their nervous actions that something serious was about to happen. What it was he [*sic*] could not tell. If, sometimes by eavesdropping, a maid or carriage man or butler was lucky enough to catch a word or so of a whispered conversation, it was immediately broadcast with numerous additions by means of the grapevine telephone."

Surely Papa, passing on what he'd been told, was thinking of Samuel Garrett, his own hero-father "marked for slaughter" because he dared read news of the war to slaves on the plantation.

Papa was both blessed and disadvantaged by being born after the end of the Civil War. He escaped the privations and humiliations of slavery, had advantages and opportunities his parents could have only dreamed of. By the time he finished at Allen and was admitted to practice law, however, Reconstruction's flickering promise had guttered out.

He made the best of his opportunities (as did Mama), but Papa might have done better if he'd passed up the law, taken a degree in theology, and been ordained in the AME church—like teaching, preaching was one of the few professions open to African-Americans of Papa's time. But Papa would have chafed under episcopal authority and, given his apparent deafness to social niceties, would have been temperamentally unsuited to the pulpit.

In the end, like Mama and the Afro-Columbians whom both called friends, Papa did what he could with what he had and didn't waste time letting what he could not do deter him from what he could. There are no streets named after them, and, apart from the cornerstone of that Rosenwald schoolhouse Mama oversaw the construction of in 1925, no buildings bear their names. They published no books, held no political office, explored no uncharted lands. In the end, though, they did something far more difficult, something that required far more courage: They remained Americans. It's easy, you see, to love America if you're white and reasonably well off; much harder if you're Black and aware of the unrequited love generations of your ancestors showed their country in struggle and sacrifice. Mama and Papa may have wavered, but they never faltered.

In the end, they were far more faithful than the nation they loved deserved.

ACKNOWLEDGMENTS

I began this book late in Barack Obama's first term as president. After setting it aside to research a biography of Papa's nemesis, AME Bishop William David Chappelle, I returned to it about the time Donald Trump was elected. Trump's election symbolized a whiplash paradox; in eight short years, we'd gone from intellectual to buffoon, meticulous ego to meretricious id. A similar paradox lay at the heart of America. On the one hand, we were (or wanted to think ourselves) a country of decent, hardworking plain folk, residents of a shining city on a hill. On the other hand, these same good folk hunted the Plains Indians to near extinction, with all the gleeful malice of teenagers swerving to crush a squirrel in the road. How to hold these two aspects, the decent and the despicable, without going mad? I had to, in order to lay claim to my psychic citizenship.

As important as it was to write this book for myself, it was equally as important to write it for my son, Andrew; for his cousins, Nia, Corinne, and Elena; and for Nia's children, Ari and Ilan. I want them to know what I didn't until it was almost too late. *The Garretts of Columbia* is their book.

It's also Jo's. Near the end of her life, as her own story drew near its close, the oldest of my mother's siblings spent hours telling tales. Looking out the window of her sixth-floor apartment as she reminisced, my aunt would sometimes interrupt herself to ask why I was interested in "all this junk." And sometimes, after some long-secret revelation, admonish me: "Now don't write that down!" (I'd wait until I was in my car—then scribble furiously before I forgot.) But Jo never tired of remembering her childhood visits to South Carolina as a child, the one hundred block of S Street as it was when she and her family moved there in 1928, her years at Dunbar and Miner Teachers College.

Most of all, though, *The Garretts of Columbia* (and the book about Alfred, Mattie, and their children I hope to live long enough to finish) is my mother Ruth's book, even if I've included things she would have discreetly omitted. A longtime manuscript librarian at the Library of Congress, Ruth understood the value of the thousands of family letters, journals, photographs, school notebooks, handbills, and records of Washington, D.C.'s South Carolina Club and branch of the Benedict College Alumni Association she discovered in the 1980s in the attic of the family home in Washington, D.C. Covering more than one hundred years of the Simonses and the Garretts in South Carolina and in Washington, D.C., the Simons Family Papers are now in the Library of Congress.

She labored to fill in the gaps, so much so that, time and again, congratulating myself as I uncovered some gem in an archive, at a library, or on the Internet, I went back to the stacks of photocopies and note cards Ruth had amassed and found she'd uncovered the same material decades before. It happened so often that I believed one day I might come across a note in her familiar handwriting. *If you've found this,* she'd whisper across the decades, *it must mean you're writing the book I always hoped you would.*

In the end, this is Ruth's book, her song because she could not sing it.

That said, I couldn't have written *The Garretts of Columbia* without the love, support, and encouragement of my wife and son. Liz listened as I talked through sections, made comments and suggestions that were always incisive and helpful. Andrew showed an insatiable curiosity about the men and women who people its pages, often repeating to his teachers and schoolmates stories I told him. Twice when he was younger, I was invited to talk to his elementary school classes, because the stories he repeated had piqued his teachers' interest. One winter during the pandemic, on a leave of absence from Bowdoin College, he transcribed several hundred letters.

Had I known how long it would take to finish, I might not have started, and so I am grateful for the help, advice, and encouragement from many professional researchers and historians. Errors of fact or interpretation are mine, and mine alone, but I have been gratified (and pleasantly surprised) by how receptive all were to my questions, even when they involved revisiting work they'd completed decades before.

I am particularly indebted to Debra C. Bloom, former manager of the Richland County Public Library's Walker Local and Family History Room. No matter the request for arcane information—such as the location of the Columbia train station in 1885—Debi always came through. Conversations with Bobby Donaldson, associate professor of history and director of the Center for Civil Rights History and Research at the University of South Carolina, pointed me to avenues I had not considered. Margaret Dunlap, now manager of the Walker Local and Family History Room, generously answered last-minute queries. Karl Evanzz, a former *Washington Post* colleague who became an independent writer and researcher, unearthed several documents concerning Dublin Hunter, including information about the Lewerses. Lacey K. Ford Jr., professor of history, vice provost, and dean of Graduate Studies at the University of South Carolina; and Janet Hudson, then an associate professor of history, Extended University, University of South Carolina, helped me understand more about race in South Carolina and race relations in Columbia. David Levering Lewis and Arnold Rampersad offered examples and encouragement. My cousin, LaBrenda Garrett-Nelson, the family genealogist, graciously shared her research. Thanks are also due to Vennie Deas Moore, South Carolina genealogist, writer, and photographer; Henry Fulmer, former director of the South Caroliniana Library at the University of South Carolina; Allen Stokes Jr., another former director of the Caroliniana Library; the staff of the Library (especially Beth Bilderback and Todd Hoppock), the South Carolina State Archives, and the Greenville Public Library. Special thanks to Bill Higgins, a volunteer at the Walker Local and Family History Room, who helped track down the poem by Mayor Gibbes that prompted Mama's letter to *The State*.

I must also thank Selicia Allen, Special Collections Librarian/University archivist, Virginia Union University; Canter Brown Jr., professor of history, Fort Valley State University; Randall Burkett, former curator of African-American collections at the Emory University libraries; Avery L. Daniels, of the South Carolina State Historical Collection & Archives at South Carolina State University; Dennis Dickerson, AME church historiographer and professor of history, Vanderbilt University; Janice Gilyard, for a copy of George Singleton's autobiography; Michele Herman, who read the manuscript and made extensive comments; Ramon Jackson, then a doctoral candidate at the University of South Carolina, for information about Allen University; Jesse Kass of the University of South Carolina, whose blog "Blind Man with a Math Degree," provided valuable information about Forrest O. Wiggins; Patrick Kerwin, of the Manuscript Division Reading Room, Library of Congress; historian Les Melnyk; Jacquelyn C.

Miller, associate director for faculty professional development, Seattle University; William Montgomery, emeritus professor of history, Austin Community College; Gary B. Nash, professor of history at the University of California, Los Angeles; Linda M. Perkins, associate university professor at Claremont Graduate University; Christopher J. Anderson, Cassie Brand, Kwang Yu Lee, Brian Shelter, and Zannah Buck of Drew University's Methodist Library; Kathy Shoemaker of the Stuart A. Rose Manuscript, Archives, & Rare Book Library, Emory University; my Sidwell Friends classmate, Hugh Talman, for advice and help with photographs; and the staff of The Virginia Center for the Creative Arts (VCCA), in particular, Beatrice Booker, who made my stay there in February and March of 2019, such a pleasure. Conversations at VCCA with Lynn Rainville and Kathryn Levy helped shape my thinking about parts of this book. Writer friends, among them Deborah Clearman, Calvin Forbes, Elizabeth Hand, E. Ethelbert Miller, Opal Moore, Rick Peabody, Leslie Pietrzyk, Eileen Pollack, and Kim Roberts, helped me stay the course. The late Bharati Mukherjhee, my teacher at Iowa, was generous with her encouragement. Without her belief in me, I might have quit writing long ago.

Last, I must acknowledge my debt to Michael P. Johnson and James L. Roark. I have never met them, but their books, *Black Masters* and *No Chariot Let Down*, were early inspirations in my search for The African.

CAST OF CHARACTERS

The Garretts

MARTHA (HYDE) GARRETT KENNEDY, ca. 1836–?, mother of Casper George Garrett

CASPER GEORGE GARRETT, 1865–1947, "Papa," lawyer, editor, Allen University professor, AME church gadfly

ANNA MARIA GARRETT, 1871–1944, "Mama," teacher and supervisor of Richland County rural colored schools

The Threewittses

ANDERSON THREEWITTS, 1830–92, Mama's father

PHILLIS THREEWITTS, 1836–93, Mama's mother

Mama and Papa's Children

MARTHA PHYLLIS GARRETT (1891–1959), also known, but only to Mama, as "Baby"

RALSTON PROUDFIT GARRETT (1893–1960), also known as "Nick" or "Buddie"

CASPER GEORGE GARRETT JR. (1895–1952), also known as "Tap"

FLEMING MACEO GARRETT (1897–1943), known as Maceo

COLON HUNTER GARRETT (1899–1949)

MARIAN THREEWITTS GARRETT (1901–67)

RUTH EIDIER GARRETT (1904–96)

NAOMI MILLS GARRETT (1906–2000), known as Mills

CHRISTOPHER THREEWITTS GARRETT (1909–67), also known as "Boy"

ELIZA FRANCES PEACHER GARRETT (1912–13); Ralston's out-of-wedlock daughter; she was also known as "Frank"

Prominent Columbians and Others Mentioned in the Book

WILLIAM W. BECKETT, 1859–1926, South Carolinian who attended Clark University and Gammon Seminary. President of Allen 1912–16, he was elected bishop in 1916 and assigned to South Africa.

ANNA LOVE BOYD, 1857–1957, remembered as "Mother Boyd," she started the school named after her in 1917. Located in Columbia's State Park neighborhood, it was one of the first primary schools for African-American students.

RICHARD CARROLL, 1859–1929, was born in slavery. He attended Benedict College and Shaw University. An accommodationist, he espoused "a conservative and pragmatic posture on . . . race relations, segregation, and white supremacy."[1] He served as an Army chaplain in the Spanish-American War and, according to his obituary, declined Woodrow Wilson's offer to represent the United States in Liberia.

WILLIAM DAVID CHAPPELLE, 1857–1925, Papa's ally and later antagonist, twice president of Allen University and AME church bishop.

ARTHUR J. COLLINS, 1890–1977, studied at Claflin College and Howard University's dental school. He practiced dentistry in Columbia for more than sixty years and was active in the city's civil life; in particular, the Colored State Fair.

ABRIEA "ABBIE" MITCHELL COOK, 1884–1960. Born in New York, she was of mixed race and was discovered singing on a fire escape by composer Will Marion Cook. They later married. She appeared in musical productions in the United States and in England.

WILLIAM DEMOSTHENES CRUM, 1859–1912, attended Charleston's Avery Normal Institute and the University of South Carolina before receiving a medical degree from Howard University. After he resigned as customs collector for the Port of Charleston, President Taft appointed him minister to Liberia.

MONROE HORTENSIUS DAVIS, ca. 1886–1953, was born in Marion, SC. He attended Allen before receiving degrees from Drew University and Howard University. He became the AME church's fifty-third bishop in 1928. According to one obituary, he was suspended after "he became involved in church administration difficulties," but later reinstated.[2]

JAMES DEAN, 1858–1914, a graduate of the Howard University Law School. Remembered as Florida's first Black judge, he was removed from office after it was alleged that he had issued a marriage license to an interracial couple.

E. F. G. (ELDRIDGE FISHER GREGORY) DENT, 1889–1962, was from Lexington County, SC. He studied at Allen and at Boston University. He became president of Kittrell College in North Carolina before returning to Allen as a dean.

GERALDYN DISMOND, 1894–1984, also known as Geraldyn Major and Gerri Major was born Geraldyn Hodges in Chicago. She graduated from the University of Chicago and taught for several years before becoming a Red Cross nurse during World War I. Active in many organizations, she owned her own public relations agency and wrote for several newspapers, including the *Pittsburgh Courier*, the *Chicago Bee*, the *Baltimore Afro-American*, the *New York Age*, and the *New York Amsterdam News*.

EDWARD PHILIP ELLIS, 1876–1954, was an AME pastor and columnist for the *Palmetto Leader*.

JOSEPH S. FLIPPER, 1859–1944, attended Atlanta University and was president of Morris Brown from 1904 until 1908, when he was elected bishop. He was president of Allen 1936–44, and built the Flipper Library, which *The State* (October 9, 1941) reported cost $35,000 when it was erected.

JOHN H. GOODWIN, 1872–1928, graduated from Benedict College in 1892 and received his medical degree in 1908 from Leonard College. An active Republican, he was an at-large delegate to the 1928 Republican Convention, but ill health prevented him from attending.

JANE BRUCE GUIGNARD, 1876–1963, graduated from the Women's Medical College of Philadelphia in 1904 and began practicing in Columbia in 1905. She was active for nearly sixty years.

JOHN HURST, 1863–1940, was the thirty-sixth bishop of the AME church. Born in Haiti, he attended Wilberforce University and was elected bishop in 1912.

GREEN JACKSON, c. 1860–1934, was educated at Claflin College, South Carolina State, and Allen University. He was active in the Columbia branch of the NAACP and in efforts to register Black voters. An Allen University graduate, he was admitted to the South Carolina bar in 1898, eight years after Papa. In the early 1920s, he became Allen's treasurer. He was also secretary of the colored fair and a delegate to two AME General Conferences.

CORNELL ALVIN JOHNSON, 1882–1970, was born in Greenville, SC, and came to Columbia when young. He attended Biddle University, now Johnson C. Smith University, in Charlotte, NC. He became principal of the Booker T. Washington School in 1914 and principal of the Howard School in 1916.

WILLIAM DECKER JOHNSON, 1842–1909, was a graduate of Lincoln University. Born in Calvert County, Maryland, he was ordained in 1867 and was the AME church's commissioner of education. He was president of Allen University from 1904 to 1908.

I. S. (ISAAC SAMUEL) LEEVY, 1876–1968, was from Antioch, SC, and attended Hampton Institute. Active in Columbia's civic affairs, he supported education by founding three schools in the city. He helped found the Columbia branch of the NAACP in 1917 and made several unsuccessful runs for Congress between 1916 and 1954.

EUGENE H. MCGILL, 1887–1939, son of Papa's one-time antagonist, the Rev. Daniel M. McGill, he graduated from Allen at age sixteen and received a theological degree four years later. He pastored churches in South Carolina and taught theology at Kittrell College.

THOMAS EZEKIEL MILLER, 1849–1938, attended schools for free Blacks in Charleston before moving north after the Civil War. He graduated from Lincoln University. After returning to South Carolina, he read law and was admitted to the bar. He served in the State House of Representatives and Senate and became the first president of the Colored Normal Industrial Agricultural and Mechanical College of South Carolina, now South Carolina State University.

JOSEPH WHITE MORRIS, 1850–1913, was purchased from slavery by his father, a wheelwright, and raised as if free. He graduated from Howard University in 1875 and studied law at the University of South Carolina during Reconstruction. Like Papa, Morris practiced law briefly before becoming principal of Payne Institute. He served twice as president of Allen—1885 to 1894 and 1895 to 1897. Morris was vice president of Allen in 1913.

ISAIAH MALACHI ALEXANDER MYERS, 1880–1960, studied at Allen and taught in Orangeburg and Richland counties, as well as in Allen's Normal Department. He acted as an agent for the Colored Teachers Agency and as executive secretary of the South Carolina State Teachers Association before becoming principal of Columbia's Booker T. Washington School. He was city editor of the *Southern Sun* and news editor of *The Light* and freelanced for *The State*. Like Papa, he was one of those energetic, civic-minded Columbians whose deeds deserve to be remembered.

BUTLER W. NANCE, 1870–1923, was from Newberry, SC. He lived in Columbia for more than twenty years, where he practiced law, and was vice principal of the Howard School.

REVERDY RANSOM, 1861–1959, was born free in Ohio and attended Wilberforce University. Like Papa, he did not know his father and was encouraged to excel early on by his mother. He was elected bishop at the 1924 AME General Conference.

GEORGE A. SINGLETON, 1894–1970, was born in Conway, SC. He was educated at Allen, Boston University, and the University of Chicago. During World War I, he served as a chaplain in the Army. He was editor of the *A.M.E. Church Review* and the *Christian Recorder*. In addition to teaching at Allen, he pastored churches in South Carolina, Kentucky, Illinois, and Iowa.

DAVID R. STARKS, c. 1878–1957, was born in Winnsboro but lived in Columbia for sixty years. An officer of the Victory Savings Bank and the state colored fair, he also sold insurance and worked as a "merchant tailor."

NOAH W. WILLIAMS, 1876–1954, AME bishop who headed Allen's Board of Trustees from 1932 to 1936. He was born in Springfield, IL, and licensed as a local preacher at nineteen years old. He served as an assistant to the chaplain during the Spanish Civil War and as a chaplain in World War I. He stepped down as bishop in 1948.

TURNER HENDERSON WISEMAN, 1881–1939, the pastor whom Mama disparaged for his alleged dalliance with a female parishioner, was born in Jefferson City, MO, and studied at Kittrell College. He volunteered to serve in the Army during the Spanish-American War and joined the AME church in California.

RICHARD R. WRIGHT, 1878–1967, was born in Cuthbert, GA, and educated at George State College and the University of Pennsylvania, where he received a doctorate in 1911. He was the longtime editor of the *Christian Recorder* and was elected the fifty-seventh bishop of the AME church in 1936.

NOTES

Confessions of a Weary Integrationist

1. Names occur and reoccur in my family, as if parents were too poor—or too proud!—to give new ones to their children. Mattie was named Martha Phyllis after her grandmothers, Martha Garrett Kennedy and Phillis Peacher Threewitts. She named her daughter Jo after her grandmother, Minnie Josephine Simons, and her daughter Phyllis after her great-grandmother, Phillis Peacher Threewitts. My sisters Phyllis and Jo were named after Ruth's; and my brother, William, after Ruth's favorite brother. And that brother, Bill, was named for his uncle who worked for the YMCA in Africa during World War I and, decades later, died a missionary in Nigeria.

2. James Zug, "The Color of Our Skin: Quakerism and Integration at Sidwell Friends School," *Quaker History*, 98, no. 1 (Spring 2009), 43.

1 — The African

1. Garrett's account of his great-grandfather appears in A. B. (Arthur Bunyan) Caldwell, ed., *History of the American Negro: South Carolina Edition* (Atlanta: A. B. Caldwell Publishing Company, 1919), 316. See pages 28, 288, 738, for the claims regarding ancestry.

2. Caldwell, *History*, 28, 288, 738.

3. Caldwell, *History*, "Preface."

4. The subjective description of Hunter's color, provided by James Hunter or some other white person, may support Papa's claim that his ancestor came directly from Africa.

5. "Bought Himself Twice: Remarkable Negro, Who was Sold Twice, but Finally Became Free," *New York Daily Tribune*, June 16, 1902, 2.

6. *History of Wages in the United States from Colonial Times to 1928*, Bulletin of the United States Bureau of Labor Statistics No. 604 (Washington, DC: Government Printing Office, 1934), 56.

7. See "An Act to Restrain the Emancipation of Slaves, and to Prevent Free Persons of Color from Entering into this State; and for Other Purposes," in, *The Statutes at Large of South Carolina, Vol. 7, Containing the Acts Relating to Charleston, Courts, Slaves, and Rivers,* ed. David J. McCord (Columbia, SC: A. S. Johnston, 1840), 459–60.

8. Lacy Ford, "Reconfiguring the Old South: 'Solving' the Problem of Slavery, 1787–1838," *Journal of American History*, 95, no. 1 (June 2008), 95, 110.

9. Frederick Douglass, *My Bondage and My Freedom* (New York: Miller, Orton & Mulligan, 1855), 196.

10. Loren Schweninger and Marguerite Ross Howell, eds., *Race, Slavery, and Free Blacks: Series II, Petitions to Southern County Courts, 1775–1867: Part D: North Carolina (1775–1867) and South Carolina*

(1784–1867) (Bethesda, MD: LexisNexis, 2005), 222.

11. Schweninger and Howell, *Race, Slavery, and Free Blacks*, 222.

12. M. [Maximillian] LaBorde, *History of the South Carolina College from the Incorporation Dec. 19, 1801, to Dec. 19, 1865, Including Sketches of its Presidents and Professors, With an Appendix* (Charleston, SC: Walker, Evans & Cogswell, 1874), 531; David Zimmerman, Laura Zimmerman, and Anne Sheppard, "Our History." www .firstpreslaurens.org/our _history (revised April 1993 and April 2007); Margaret Peckham Motes, *Blacks Found in the Deeds of Laurens & Newberry Counties, S.C.: 1785–1827, Listed in Deeds of Gifts, Deeds of Sale, Mortgages, Born Free and Freed, Abstracted from Laurens County, SC Deed Books A-L and Newberry County, SC Deed Books A-G*, (Baltimore: Clearfield, 2002), 94; and George Howe, *History of the Presbyterian Church in South Carolina*, Vol. II (Columbia, SC: W. J. Duffie, 1883), 728.

13. See Motes, *Blacks Found*; and Howe, *History*.

14. Laurens District, Deed Book L, 46.

15. Laurens County Deed Book, 66 11-1822.

16. If Sall was about two years old in 1793, she would have been about twenty-two when Amy was born.

17. Sall and Sophia were sold together for four hundred seventy-nine dollars. Suzette was sold for one hundred eighty-one dollars.

18. Michael P. Johnson, and James L. Roark, *Black Masters: A Free Family of Color in the Old South* (New York: Norton, 1984), 23.

19. Motes, *Blacks Found*, 99. Lewers also became guardian of at least one other free man of color (p. 100).

20. McCord, 461–62.

21. I've borrowed part of a quote from Ralph Ellison's "Invisible Man." The full quote is "Live with your head in the lion's mouth." It appears on pp. 15–16 of the 1994 Random House Modern Library edition.

22. Johnson and Roark, 43.

23. McCord, 461.

24. Caldwell, *History*, 316

25. "Sale Bill of the Estate of Charles Simmons deceased," photocopy in the possession of the author. The sale took place on the twenty-seventh day of a month that is, unfortunately, illegible.

26. "Bought Himself Twice: Remarkable Negro, Who Was Sold Twice, But Finally Became Free," *New York Daily Tribune*, June 16, 1902, 3.

27. Richard's story is taken from several contemporary sources. These include: "Bought Himself Twice: Remarkable Negro, Who Was Sold Twice, But Finally Became Free," *New York Daily Tribune*, June 16, 1902, 3; "Dick Hunter Dead: One of the Best Known Negroes in the County," *Laurens County Advertiser*, June 4, 1902, 4; and "Dick Nugent, an Old Time Negro, Paid Twice for His Freedom," *The State*, June 15, 1902, 3.

28. "Novelists: Ovid in Ossining," *Time*, March 27, 1964, 67.

Transcription

1. Transcribed by David Nicholson and Elizabeth MacGregor from a copy of the original.

2 — Mr. Washington Comes to Columbia

1. Account of Washington's visit to South Carolina taken from various sources, including *The State*, Columbia, SC, March 15, 1909 (pp. 2, 7), and March 16, 1909 (pp. 2, 8); *Indianapolis Freeman*, Feb. 20, March 27, and April 3, 1909; and David H. Jackson Jr., "Booker T. Washington in South Carolina, March 1909," *South Carolina Historical*

Magazine, 113, no. 3 (July 2012), 192–220; as well as Richard Carroll's flyer advertising the tour, Booker T. Washington Papers, Library of Congress.

2. "Negro Educator is Here Today: Dr. Booker T. Washington to Tour This State," *The State*, March 15, 1909, p. 7.

3. Jackson, 197, 198.

4. Both the anonymous letter and advertisement appear in *The State*, March 15, 1909, p. 2.

3 — Finding Papa

1. John F. Marszalek, "The Black Leader in 1919—South Carolina as a Case Study," *Phylon* 36, no. 3, 249–59.

2. Naomi Mills Garrett (NMG) to Ruth Esther Simons Nicholson (RESN), Sept. 21, 1975.

3. The word *conference* has two meanings in the AME church. First, it indicates geographical boundaries for a group of congregations. Conferences are also meetings on church business. These include quarterly, district, and annual conferences, as well as the General Conference, a national meeting held every four years. Papa spoke at local annual, district, and quarterly conferences but was also elected a lay delegate to the General Conference.

4. "Casper Geo Answers Final," by George A. Singleton.

5. "Florence, S.C., District," *Christian Recorder*, May 8, 1913, 8.

6. "Garrett Rites Largely Attended: Allen's Auditorium Crowded," *Palmetto Leader*, Nov. 22, 1947, 1.

4 — "Tell Them We Are Rising"

1. Pronounced Mah-RYE-uh.

2. Caldwell, *History*, 316.

3. There's that surname again.

4. *Christian Recorder*, July 15, 1886.

5. The 1880 census says Martha was forty-four, so she must have been born about 1836.

6. Richard R. Wright Jr., ed., *Centennial Encyclopedia of the African Methodist Episcopal Church* (Philadelphia: Book Concern of the AME Church, 1916), 94.

7. Ethel O. Davie, "Naomi M. Garrett, 1906–," in *Missing Chapters II: West Virginia Women in History*, edited by Frances S. Hensley (Charleston: West Virginia Women's Commission, 1986), 73.

8. *Goodspeed's History of Tennessee* (Nashville, TN: Goodspeed Publishing Company, 1886–87), 875. www.tngenweb.org/records/shelby/history/goodspeed/history7.html.

9. March 8, 1865, Furman Papers, Furman University Library, Greenville, SC.

10. Claude Henry Neuffer, ed., *Names in South Carolina* (Spartanburg, SC: The Reprint Company, 1983), 102. Unfortunately, Neuffer doesn't tell us the derivation of Scuffletown.

11. Martha says so in an April 17, 1901, letter to the editor of the *State*.

12. Wright, *Centennial*, 94–95.

13. Wright, *Centennial*, 94.

14. Caldwell, *History*, 318.

15. Wright, *Centennial*, 94; Caldwell, *History*, 318.

16. "Annual Report of the County Treasurer Of Laurens Co., S.C.," *Laurens County Advertiser*, Feb. 17, 1886, 2; "Annual Report of the School Commissioner of Laurens County S.C. of Claims Approved by him during the year 1885," L30158, South Carolina State Archives.

17. *Southern Sun*, Feb. 25, 1906, 1.

18. Interview, Naomi Mills Garrett, Jan. 1, 1984.

19. Lynn Sims Salsi, *Columbia: History of a Southern Capital* (Charleston, SC: Arcadia, 2003), 101.

20. Helen Kohn Hennig, ed., *Columbia: Capital City of South Carolina, 1786–1936*

(Columbia: Columbia Sesqui-centennial Commission, 1936), 325, 358–59, 363.

21. The Rev. David H. Johnson, "Allen University," *Christian Recorder*, June 23, 1887, 4.

22. Ibid.

23. Joe M. Richardson, *Christian Reconstruction: The American Missionary Association and Southern Blacks, 1861–1890* (Athens: University of Georgia Press, 1986), 20.

24. *Catalogue of Allen University Columbia, S.C., 1890 and 1891*, 28–39.

25. Caldwell, *History*, "Preface"; "Casper George Garrett," 318.

26. George A. Singleton, "Pointed Points," *Palmetto Leader*, Nov. 19, 1927, 4.

27. "Negro Merchants Holding Thereon, Where the Negro for Bank President—Farmers In Good Condition—Old School Boys Reunion," *Southern Sun*, Feb. 25, 1906, 1. According to Allen's 1908–10 catalog, Sandy Simmons, Doctor Cook, and L. A. Hawkins were members of Papa's class of 1890. Daniel A. Perrin was a member of the class of 1889. Perrin and Simmons became AME pastors, and Cook taught in Laurens. Hawkins was probably Lazarus A. Hawkins, who was principal of a school in LaGrange, GA, according to the 1911–12 Allen catalog (p. 61). He's listed in the 1922 Columbia city directory as being in real estate. Although there is no one surnamed Smith in either class, there is a Hercules Smith in the class of 1891 listed in the 1911–12 catalog. His occupation was listed as mechanic. However, he's listed as a teacher—and census enumerator—in the 1900 census. Smith is identified as a pastor living in Salisbury, NC, in the 1923–24 Allen catalog. He and his wife, Sujette, were friends of the Garretts. Morris taught Papa at Allen, and Papa held him in particular esteem—one of his biographies notes that "he sat at the feet of Prof. J. W. Morris."

Morris practiced law briefly and was twice president of Allen. I found no French Bend, but perhaps Papa meant the French Broad River, which runs from Tennessee to North Carolina.

28. Johnson, "Allen University."

29. "Local," *Laurens Advertiser*, Feb. 8, 1888, 3.

30. Information about Proudfit also from Frank Willing Leach, "Old Philadelphia Families," *North American*, Philadelphia, July 7, 1912. http://archiver.rootsweb.ancertry.com/th/read/philly-roots/200308/1061232877

31. Gary B. Nash, *Forging Freedom: The Formation of Philadelphia's Black Community, 1720–1840* (Cambridge, MA: Harvard University Press, 1988), 113–16.

32. "Commencement Day" and "Honors," *Christian Recorder*, June 12, 1890, 5. Papa's diplomas and South Carolina Supreme Court certificate, which entitled him to appear in any state court, are in the possession of his granddaughter, Phyllis Threewitts Simons Ferguson.

Law Department tuition, according to the 1890–91 Allen catalog, was thirty-five dollars a term, payable in advance unless the Board of Trustees gave permission for monthly payments. Meals and room rent totaled $3.50 per month for students who lived on campus. Off-campus accommodations could be had for as little as three dollars a month. During their junior years, students in Allen's Law Department took courses on the US and state constitutions and studied Blackstone's Commentaries. During senior year, they took courses in equity, pleading, and criminal law, as well as classes on the South Carolina Code of Procedure and General Statutes. Because many courts—including the South Carolina Supreme Court—were in session in the city, students were encouraged to attend them.

33. Peacher from *African American Religious Leaders*, by Jim Haskins and Kathleen Benson, (San Francisco: Jossey-Bass, 2008), 59, 61; Alonzo Johnson and Paul T. Jersild, eds., *Ain't Going to Lay My 'Ligion Down: African American Religion in the South*, (Columbia: University of South Carolina Press, 1996), 102; and from Stephen Ward Angell, *Bishop Henry McNeal Turner and African-American Religion in the South* (Knoxville: University of Tennessee Press, 1992), 24–25.

34. Peacher to the Rev. William McClain of the American Colonization Society, Nov. 11, 1856, (photocopy in the possession of the author).

35. "Life and Works of Henry McNeil [sic] Turner: The Bishop's Four Wives," typescript, Moorland-Spingarn Research Center, Howard University, Box 1, folder 14. Angell says Joseph hired a teacher so his daughter, Eliza, could learn to read, but not write (p. 9).

36. The June 1859 issue of *The African Repository*, the journal of the American Colonization Society, contains a letter from Peacher dated Feb. 15, 1859.

37. Twenty-First Annual Report of the *Board of Managers of the Massachusetts Colonization Society*. Presented at the Annual Meeting, Boston, May 28, 1862, 20–21.

38. "List of Exhibits," *Fairfield News and Herald*, Jan. 24, 1894, 2.

39. "Local Intelligence," *News and Herald* (Winnsboro, SC), Aug. 5, 1891, 3; "Colored Graded School," *News and Herald*, May 2, 1894, p. 3, says it was his third "scholastic year."

40. "Twenty-Sixth Annual Report of the State Superintendent of Education of the State of South Carolina," in *Reports and Resolutions of the General Assembly of the State of South Carolina at the Regular Session Commencing November 27th, 1894*, 2

(Charles A Calvo Jr., State Printer), Columbia, SC, 1894, 93.

41. Dated Oct. 28, 1893, Mama's certificate is in the author's possession; "Annual Report of Country Treasurer," *News and Herald*, May 18, 1895, 2.

42. Caldwell, *History*, 318; *AME Centennial Encyclopaedia*, 94; "Twenty-Sixth Annual Report of the State Superintendent of Education of the State of South Carolina," 93, 84.

43. "Colored Teachers' Meeting," *News and Herald*, Sept. 13, 1894, 3; "Colored County Fair," *News and Herald*, Oct. 3, 1894, 3.

44. "Colored Graded School," *News and Herald*, May 2, 1894, 3.

45. The four-page sketch appeared in *Dialogues No. 27*, from Beadle and Adams, which appeared December 18, 1880. (Founders Erastus F. and Irwin P. Beadle were the originators of the dime novel.) The *Dialogues* were a series of collections of "colloquies, farces, exhibition pieces, parlor dramas and school scenes, all arranged for easy production on any stage or platform." Odious title, crude dialogue, and stereotypical African-American character aside, the sketch is quite funny. Throughout, the Black man proves himself more intelligent than the white (who is actually the ungrateful one) and, in the end, outwits him.

46. "Apparently a Small Matter," *News and Herald*, May 2, 1894, 3.

47. "Playing at Politics," *Weekly Union Times*, Sept. 26, 1890, 1; "They Want Haskell," *Manning Times*.

48. "Murray's Speech," *News and Herald*, March 26, 1895, 2.

49. "Changes in the Colored Schools," *News and Herald*, June 20, 1895, 3.

50. "Allen's Commencement," *The State*, May 26, 1895, 5. Papa's election to the faculty was reported in "Elections at Allen," *The State*, June 7, 1895, 4.

51. "Annual Report of Country Trea-surer," *News and Herald*, May 18, 1895, 2.

52. Elizabeth Proudfit (EP) to Casper G. Garrett (CGG), Feb. 22, 1894.

5 — Papa Returns to Columbia

1. *The Columbia City Directory, 1895*, The State Co., Columbia, 1895, 8–13. See also "The Columbia Movement," in James L. Felder, *Civil Rights in South Carolina: From Peaceful Protests to Groundbreaking Rulings* (Charleston, SC: The History Press, 2012), 72. Though he writes about a later period, Felder notes that Black Columbians "felt insulated from the prejudices of the white community because of the economic and educational institutions in their own neighborhoods."

2. *The Columbia City Directory, 1895*, C. M. Douglas, Columbia, 1895, front mat-ter; 8, 20–43.

3. "Get the Habit," *Southern Indicator*, Columbia, August 12, 1922, 11.

4. "General Notes," *Christian Recorder*, June 12, 1890, 5.

5. George Brown Tindall, *South Carolina Negroes, 1877–1900* (Columbia: University of South Carolina Press, 1952), 239. Different sources cite different figures for the number of murders. For example, "Lynching in America: Confronting the Legacy of Racial Terror," second ed. (Mont-gomery, AL: Equal Justice Initiative, 2015) says, one hundred eighty-four (p. 16); the *South Carolina Encyclopedia* (https://www.scencyclopedia. org/sce/entries /lynching/) says one hundred fifty-six lynchings occurred in the state. Terence Finnegan, in *A Deed So Accursed: Lynch-ing in Mississippi and South Carolina, 1881–1940* (Charlottesville: University of Virginia Press, 2013), footnote 14, 193, cites two hundred thirteen deaths in South Carolina and seven hundred five in Mississippi.

6. "Regulations for the Fair," *The State*, Oct. 18, 1906, 4.

7. "Columbia, S.C.," *New York Age*, Feb. 3, 1916, 5

8. "Allen University Thriving School: Has Had Nearly Seven Hundred Students During the Year Now Closing," *The State*, May 27, 1915, 5.

9. Underwood and Burke, eds., *At Freedom's Door*, 119. Papa's name appears in a 1911 South Carolina Supreme Court ruling, but he was acting as agent for a man selling quilt-making equipment. He, and no one else, is identified as "colored," so the other men in the case likely were white. [Russell v. Tillman, *Reports of Cases Heard and Determined by the Supreme Court of South Carolina: Volume LXXXIX Contain-ing Cases of April Term, 1911*, C. M. Efird, State Reporter, R. L. Bryan, Columbia, 1919, 257–60.]

10. "General Church News," *Christian Recorder*, Oct. 7, 1897, npn.

11. "Garrett Rites," 1.

12. Richard R. Wright Jr., *Encyclopaedia of the African Methodist Episcopal Church*, Second ed. (Philadelphia: AME Church, 1947), 485; "Northeast South Carolina Conference," *The Christian Recorder*, Jan. 11, 1900, npn; Canter Brown Jr., *Florida Black Public Officials, 1867–1924* (Tusca-loosa: University of Alabama Press, 1998), 84; Canter Brown Jr. and Larry E. Rivers, "The Pioneer African American Jurist Who Almost Became a Bishop: Florida's Judge James Dean, 1858–1914," *Florida Historical Quarterly*, 87, no. 1 (Summer 2008), 16–49.

13. See also Wright, *Encyclopaedia* (1947), 328, 370, 388.

14. "But It Really is So," *Christian Recorder*, May 10, 1900, 1, 6.

15. *Journal of the Twenty-first Quadren-nial Session of the General Conference of the A.M.E. Church, Held in the Auditorium,*

Columbus, Ohio, May 7th to May 25, 1900, (Philadelphia: AME Book Concern), 46.

16. Janet G. Hudson, *Entangled by White Supremacy: Reform in World War I-era South Carolina* (Lexington: University Press of Kentucky, 2009), 35. I am grateful to Hudson for many conversations and e-mail exchanges regarding Columbia and South Carolina in the early 1900s.

17. Information about William D. Chappelle taken from Caldwell, *History*, and from D. W. Culp, ed., *Twentieth Century Negro Literature or a Cyclopedia on the Vital Topics Relating to the American Negro by 100 of America's Greatest Negroes* (Atlanta: J. L. Nichols & Company, 1902), 63.

18. Wright, *Encyclopaedia* (1947), 376.

19. The thirteenth bishop of the AME church, Dickerson was born in Woodbury, NJ, in 1844 and died in 1884. He had been assigned to South Carolina and Georgia in 1880. According to Papa, Dickerson led the effort to move Payne Institute to Columbia and rename it Allen University. "Let the school catch up with the name," he's supposed to have said. [C. G. Garrett, "Reminiscences," MS, quoted in Hennig, 310.]

20. Caldwell, *History*, 18.

21. J. C. White, "Bishop William Chappelle Passes at His Home in Columbia, *Palmetto Leader*, 1; Culp, *Twentieth-Century*, 62b.

22. Johnson, "Allen University."

23. The Garrett family Bible shows that William christened Mattie in "the [or perhaps Ma] Threewitts house." After William returned to Columbia from Nashville in 1908, city directories show him living at 1208 Harden Street. Garrett lived at 2210 Lady Street, a little more than two blocks away.

24. "The Colored Fair Association," *Newberry Herald and News*, Aug. 6, 1891, 3; "Newberry News Notes," *The State*, Aug. 7, 1891, 4.

25. "No More Fake Fairs," *The State*, Nov. 27, 1896, 4.

26. "No More," 4; "That Colored Fair: Some Echoes of the Dismal Failure of Hampton," *The State*, Nov. 27, 1896, 5.

27. "No More," 4; "Colored State Fair: A Stock Company formed and Charter Asked For," *The State*, Feb. 3, 1897, 5; "The Colored Fair: Earnest Effort of Negroes to Help Themselves," *The State*, Feb. 23, 1897, 2.

28. *The State*, Nov. 13, 1897, 2; Dec. 10, 1897, 44; Nov. 19, 1899, 6; Oct. 30, 1897, 1; Dec. 1, 1899, 3; "Negro Societies Air Their Troubles: Several Wrangling Over Property, Appeal to Courts," *The State*, Sept. 10, 1903, 9.

29. "Hampton Loses Out," *The State*, July 1, 1904, 8.

30. For more on early fairs, see "Colored Fair Reorganized: An Entire Change of Officers and Directors," *The State*, Jan. 28, 1892, 8, and "A Fight for Fair Fame: The Rival Colored Fair Associations," *The State*, Aug. 6, 1892, 8; the Eugene Avery Adams papers in the University of South Carolina Caroliniana Library, which contains a card announcing "a special appeal" for the "Fourth Annual State Fair of the Colored State Fair Association Dec. 12th to 17th, 1892"; and Rodger E. Stroup, "The Colored State Fair: 1890–1969," in *Meet Me at the Rocket: A History of the South Carolina State Fair* (Columbia: University of South Carolina Press), 2019.

31. "Football Contest to Draw Crowd to Negro Fair," *The State*, Oct. 26, 1944, 2. Also see: *Meet Me at the Rocket,* chapter 5; "Negro State Fair at Height Today: Thursday Big Day of Whole Week," *The State*, Nov. 1, 1928; "Meet Your Friends at the Colored State Fair," *Palmetto Leader*, Oct. 25, 1930. 1; "State Fair Closes Best Exhibition in Its History," *Palmetto Leader*, Nov. 7, 1931, 1.

32. "The 1939 State Fair," *Palmetto Leader*, 2. Jim Haney, "Palmetto State Fair Ends After 70 Years," *Columbia Record*, Dec. 1, 1971, 1, 8; "Collins to Retire; Palmetto Fair No More," *The State*, Dec. 2, 1971, 2B.

33. Haney, "Palmetto State Fair Ends."

34. "Charter Granted," *The State*, June 10, 1894, 8.

35. Caldwell, *History*, 319.

36. William J. Harris, *Deep Souths: Delta, Piedmont, and Sea Island Society in the Age of Segregation* (Baltimore: Johns Hopkins University Press, 2001), 211; John M. Matthews, "Black Newspapermen and the Black Community in Georgia, 1890–1930," *Georgia Historical Quarterly* 68, no. 3 (Fall 1984), 357; Bobby J. Donaldson, "Standing on a Volcano: The Leadership of William Jefferson White," in *Paternalism in a Southern City: Race, Religion, and Gender in Augusta, Georgia*, edited by Edward J. Cashin and Glenn T. Eskew (Athens: University of Georgia Press, 2001), 161–6. I am indebted to Bobby Donaldson for insights offered in conversation on several visits to Columbia.

37. William H. Ferris, *The African Abroad or His Evolution in Western Civilization, Tracing His Development Under Caucasian Milieu, Vol. II* (New Haven, CT: Tuttle, Morehouse & Taylor, 1913), 906. Ferris quotes Papa in a chapter titled "The Negro as Leader, Continued—A Critical Examination of the Scientific Validity and Historical Truth of Dr. Washington's Optimism." Although he doesn't give an edition, the *Sun* was published in 1902–09.

38. "They Want Haskell: The Colored Convention Endorses Judge Haskell," *Manning Times*, Oct. 22, 1890, 1.

39. "A Ghastly Assemblage: The Rattling of Bones by the G.O.P. Skeletons," *The State*, Sept. 30, 1892, 1, 8.

40. "A Communication," *The State*, April 6, 1896, 6.

41. "Republicans Row at State Convention: Capt. J.G. Capers Knocks Negro from the Platform," *The State*, April 29, 1908, 1, 2; "Capers Carries State for Taft: Knocks Man off Rostrum When He Refuses to Keep Quiet," *Washington Times*, April 29, 1908, 11.

42. "Factions Divide Republican Party: Two Sets of Delegates Chosen Here Yesterday," *The State*, Feb. 6, 1920, 9; "Re-elect Tolbert Head of Party: Again Made Chairman of Republican Organization," *The State*, Sept. 24, 1926, 2.

43. Caldwell, *History*, 319.

44. "Galvanizing the 'G.O.P.,'" *The State*, Jan. 8, 1892, 8.

45. "National Jubilee in Celebration of the Fiftieth Anniversary of the Emancipation Proclamation," Daniel Murray Papers, Washington, DC, Library of Congress.

46. Used by whites as a derogatory term, it was a common male name of African origin, believed to derive from the Akan name Kofi, or "born on Friday."

47. Hudson, 201; "A Ghastly Assemblage," *The State*; "'Lily Whites:' Melton-Drayton Republicans in Convention," *The State*, April 15, 1896, 1, 2.

48. Anna Maria Threewitts Garrett (AMTG) to Mattie Phyllis Garrett Simons (MPGS), n.d.

49. "Delegates Leave for Convention: Republicans Leave Saturday for Kansas City," *The State*, June 8, 1928, 12; "S.C. Republicans Leave Saturday for Kansas City: Approximately Forty South Carolinians to Attend Convention," *Columbia Record*, June 3, 1928, 9.

6 — *The Light*

1. "Trouble at Allen: Some of the Professors have Ceased Teaching—Financial Differences," *The State*, January 12, 1893, 2.

2. *Catalogue of Allen University 1911 and 1912* (Columbia, SC: Allen University, 1912).

3. George A. Singleton, "Pointed Points," *Palmetto Leader*, Aug. 1, 1931, 4.

4. Just as I don't know the source of Maceo's first name, I don't know why Papa and Mama gave Colon a first name that would lead to teasing by anatomically minded classmates. Ruth's middle name may have come from D. W. Eidier, an African-American of some consequence who abandoned Columbia for Washington, DC, at the end of Reconstruction.

5. Plaintiffs in these cases—numbers 8311, 8667, and 8910—included the Carolina National Bank, National Loan and Exchange, and the Bank of Columbia.

6. Hudson, 27; "Green Jackson Funeral Sunday," *The State*, June 9, 1934, 5.

7. John Hammond Moore's *South Carolina Newspapers* (Columbia: University of South Carolina Press, 1988); MPGS to Alfred Edgar Simons (AES), Jan. 21, 1918. Martin may have been Arthur J. Martin, a teacher listed in the 1916 City Directory. "I.M.A. Myers, Ex-Allen Dean Dies in NY," *The State*, June 19, 1960, 2-E.

8. *The Light*, May 27, 1920.

9. Likely, Benjamin A. Blocker, listed as a tailor in the Columbia City Directory and US censuses.

10. *The Light*, Jan. 3, 1918, 2.

11. *Palmetto Leader*, June 13, 1925.

12. "Columbia, S.C.," *New York Age*, April 7, 1928, 9.

13. "'Ignorant Dr. Mance,'" *Palmetto Leader*, March 31, 1928, 4.

14. William P. Poole, "Letter to the Editor," April 17, 1926, 7.

15. AMTG to MPGS, May 1923.

16. "Garrett Rites," 1.

17. *The Southern Sun*, February 25, 1906, 2.

18. "The Negro's Last Crum," *The Bee* [Washington, DC], March 27, 1909, 4. The words "From Columbia South Carolina Light" appear beneath the headline.

19. Craig Thompson Friend, ed., "From Southern Manhood to Southern Masculinity: An Introduction," in *Southern Masculinity: Perspectives on Manhood in the South Since Reconstruction* (Athens: University of Georgia, 2009), x.

20. "Negro Editor is Attacked by Two: C.G. Garrett, Publisher of *The Light*, is Beaten With Stick," *Columbia Record*, Sept. 2, 1921, 3; AMTG to MPGS, Sept. 9, 1921; "Negro Editor is Attacked Again: C.G. Garrett Struck With Stick and Has Preacher Arrested," *Columbia Record*, Oct. 20, 1921, 10.

21. "Negro Preacher Run Out: Said 'White People are Curs' and Other Bad Things," *Bamberg Herald*, April 25, 1921, 5.

22. The Light, June 6, 1925, 2.

23. "Made Charge of Libel: Teacher at Allen University Before Magistrate Bowles," *The State*, Nov. 20, 1912, 12.

24. "C.G. Garrett Charged Libeling Preacher: First Case Under New Libel Law Heard at Coming Criminal Court," *The Columbia Record*, Jan. 4, 1913, 7.

25. Caldwell, *History*, 297–99 and 735–37.

26. "Made Charge," *The State*, Nov. 20, 1912, 12; *State v. CG Garrett*, case no. 5308, South Carolina Department of Archives and History, L 40059; "Wm. C. Swaffield Dies of Typhoid: Realty and Insurance Broker Passes Away," *The State*, July 24, 1915, 8.

27. *State v. CG Garrett*, case no. 5308, South Carolina Department of Archives and History.

28. Ibid.

7 — Martha's Trials

1. "Deserves Notice: Alleged Ingratitude of a Son to His Mother," *The State*, April 15, 1901, 5.

2. https://en.wikipedia.org/wiki/Leslie_Keeley.

3. "Prof. Garrett's Reply: What He Says of His Treatment to His Mother," *The State,* April 16, 1901, 2.

4. "Another Card," *The State,* April 16, 1901, 2.

5. "A Pitiful Case: The Mother of the Colored Professor Testifies Against Him," *The State,* April 17, 1901, 2.

6. Wright, *Centennial,* 94.

7. David T. Courtwright, "The Hidden Epidemic: Opiate Addiction and Cocaine Use in the South, 1860–1920." *Journal of Southern History* 49, no. 1 (Feb. 1983), 64.

8. Joseph M. Gabriel, "Opiate addiction and the history of pain and race in the US," https://theconversation.com/opiate-addiction-and-the-history-of pain-in-the-US.

9. Courtwright, 66, 64 (footnote 14), 57.

10. See Jim Downs, *Sick From Freedom: African-American Illness and Suffering during the Civil War and Reconstruction* (New York: Oxford, 2012).

11. Courtwright, 67.

8 — "For Editor of the A. M. E. Church Review"

1. "Allen University May Change Site: School May Be Moved to Lands Recently Acquired North of Columbia," *The State,* June 5, 1914, 3; "Negro Educator Dies in Columbia: Joseph W. Morris, Vice President of Allen University, Passed Away Last Night," *The State,* Sept. 14, 1913, 3; "Allen University, Thriving School: Has Had Nearly Seven Hundred Students During the Year Now Closing," *The State,* May 27, 1915, 5.

2. C. G. Garbet [*sic*], "South Carolina's Choice: For Secretary of the Sunday School Union," *Christian Recorder,* May 10, 1900, 1.

3. Wright, *Centennial,* 65.

4. "Meets May 4 at Norfolk, Va., General Conference of the A.M.E Church.

Great Meeting Anticipated. Large Delegation," *Nashville Globe,* March 13, 1908, 1.

5. "Dr. W.D. Johnson Goes to Pulpit: Dr. Chappelle Becomes President of Allen," *The State,* June 6, 1908, 3.

6. George A. Singleton, "Casper George Answers Final Call," source unknown. Photocopy of a typescript is in the possession of the author.

7. "Prof. C.G. Garrett, A.M., L.L.B., Vice President Allen University, Columbia, S.C., for Editor of the AME Review," *Christian Recorder,* March 16, 1916, 2; "Prof. C. G. Garrett for the Review," *Christian Recorder,* May 4, 1916, 5.

8. "The AME Church Holds Centennial," *New York Age,* May 11, 1916, n.p.n.; "Negro Methodists Balk at Bishop Rule: Insurgents at AME Conference Refuse to Confirm Committees," *Philadelphia Evening Ledger,* May 5, 1916, 9. See also: "A.M.E. General Conference: Celebrates Its 100th Anniversary in 'Mother' Bethel, the First Church Established by Richard Allen in Philadelphia, Pa.: Thousands of Delegates and Visitors in Attendance Many from Missouri and Kansas," *Kansas City Sun,* May 13, 1916, 1, which notes the formation of another layman's organization.

9. See, for example, Charles Spencer Smith, *A History of the African Methodist Episcopal Church* (Philadelphia: Book Concern of the AME Church, 1922), 290–306.

10. Larry Eugene Rivers and Canter Brown Jr., *Laborers in the Vineyard of the Lord: The Beginnings of the AME Church in Florida, 1865–1895* (Gainesville: University Press of Florida, 2001), 149.

11. Annetta L. Gomez-Jefferson, *The Sage of Tawawa: Reverdy Cassius Ransom, 1861–1959* (Kent, OH: Kent State University Press, 2002), 120.

12. "Saturday Morning Session, May 20, 1916," *Christian Recorder,* May 25, 1916, 2.

13. "To Our Erstwhile Competitor," *A.M.E. Church Review* (July 1916), 40–41.

14. Reverdy C. Ransom, *The Pilgrimage of Harriet Ransom's Son* (Nashville, TN: Sunday School Union, 1950), 76.

15. Reverdy C. Ransom, "The General Conference of 1920," *A.M.E. Church Review* (July 1920), 36–37, quoted in Gomez-Jefferson, 164.

16. Richard R. Wright Jr., *87 Years Behind the Black Curtain: An Autobiography* (Philadelphia: Rare Book Company, 1965), 218. Wright, 1878–1967, became the fifty-seventh bishop of the AME church in 1936.

17. "Things I saw in the General Conference and Around the AME Publishing House," *Christian Recorder*, Sept. 14, 1916, 2.

18. "Allen University Closes This Week: The Rev. W.W. Beckett, Now a Bishop, Retires as President of College for Negroes," *The State*, June 1, 1916, 6.

19. Wright, *Centennial*, 155.

20. ———, Matred to AMTG, March 24, 1937 (in the possession of the author). Probably Matred McKissick, an Aiken County Home Demonstration Agent who had attended South Carolina State University where she was a charter member of the Delta Sigma Theta sorority chapter. She was acquainted well enough with Mama to address her as "Mom Garrett."

21. "'Remarkable Session': Reflections Upon the Last General Conference.: Lack of Respect for the Episcopate More Apparent in Recent Years than Formerly.—The Episcopal Address.—Discusses the Church Politician," *Christian Recorder*, July 13, 1916, 1.

22. "Why discriminate against the laymen?" *The Christian Recorder*, July 27, 1916, 4. Papa had a point. Of the 117 churchmen serving on ten "connectional boards," only thirteen were laymen. ["Connectional Boards," *Christian Recorder*, July 20, 1916, 6.]

23. Myers, I. M. A., "Nine Thousand Dollars Raised for Allen University in Single Effort," *Christian Recorder*, Oct. 26, 1916, 2.

24. Simon, Bryant, "The Appeal of Cole Blease of South Carolina: Race, Class, and Sex in the New South," *Journal of Southern History* 61, no. 1, Feb. 1996, 57–86.

25. "Negroes Qualify Party Allegiance: To Vote Against Those Who Withhold Rights," *The State*, Feb. 5, 1919, 2.

26. Hudson, 190–191, and "Negro Students Hear C.L. Blease: Former Governor Speaks at Allen University," *The State*, Oct. 5, 1916, 5.

27. "The Palmetto Conference: Bishop William D. Chappelle, Presiding," *Christian Recorder*, Nov. 23, 1916, 1

28. "Negro Students," *The State*.

29. Wright, *Centennial*, 94.

30. "Allen University Closes Good Year: Sixty-five Diplomas and Certificates," *The State*, June 11, 1917, 2.

31. W. N. Hartshorn and George W. Penniman, eds, *An Era of Progress and Promise, 1863–1910: The Religious, Moral, and Educational Development of the American Negro Since his Emancipation* (Boston: Priscilla, 1910); Carolyn Wilson, "The Difficult Task: Fundraising for Small Southern Black Industrial Schools: The Case of Emma Jane Wilson and the Mayesville Educational and Industrial Institute," *American Educational History Journal* 30 (2003), 7–15; "'Saving Grace': Educating African American Children through Industrial Education in Mayesville," *Carologue* (Fall 2013), 20–24; "Emma J. Wilson," WPA Writers Project document (Columbia: Caroliniana Library, University of South Carolina Library); and *Twenty-Fifth Annual Report of the Commissioner of Labor 1910: Industrial Education*, (Washington, DC, Government Printing Office, 1911), 334, 652, 686, 762–763.

32. "Notice: School Opening Postponed," *The Light*, Jan. 17, 1918, 3.

9 — Change and the Great War

1. 1911–12 Allen Catalog, 86.

2. AMTG to MPGS [May 5–11, 1929].

3. Bethel Church Notes, *New York Age*, December 4, 1913, 2; "Allen Catalog," 1911–12, 82; "Allen Catalog," 1923–24, 60; "Columbia University in the City of New York, Catalogue 1914–1915," 572; *Columbia University Alumni Register*, 1754–1931, v.

4. Allen Catalog, 1923–24, 76.

5. David Levering Lewis, *When Harlem Was in Vogue* (New York: Knopf, 1981), 8.

6. Tap's registration card; "Teachers Elected for City School; Salary Increase: Three Additional Instructors Named—Many Re-elected—Four Did Not Apply—One Promotion," *Columbia Record*, May 19, 1917, 6.

7. "Boy Scouts Ready to Serve Country: Not Military Organization but Members are Trained to Useful Tasks," *The State*, April 7, 1917, 10; "Girls Would be Good Rifle Shots: Mrs. Murdaugh's Detachment Will Meet Each Wednesday for Practice in Marksmanship," *The State*, April 7, 1917, 10; "Darlington Ladies Make Pillow Cases: Unit of Red Cross Formed After Address by Miss Jane Evans," *The State*, April 7, 1917, 7.

8. "Close Ranks," *The Crisis* 16, no. 3 (July 1918), 111.

9. "Negroes Tender Their Services: Will Send Delegation to Gov. Manning," *The State*, April 5, 1917, 3.

10. "Negroes Pledge Loyalty of Race in War's Crisis: Committee Presents Resolutions to Governor Manning, Assuring Him of Willingness to Serve—Want Training," *Columbia Record*, April 7, 1917, 3.

11. "The Governor Elated over Negro Co-operation," *The Light*, Jan. 3, 1918, 1.

12. Lewis Broughton Porterfield [1879–1942], a 1902 graduate of the U.S. Naval Academy. He was from Alabama, so I doubt he wanted to see blacks serving with whites. ["Rear Admiral Porterfield Retires Here: Navy Veteran to Make Home in Berkeley After Distinguished Career as Naval Officer," *San Francisco Examiner*, July 9, 1937, 27; "Admiral L. B. Porterfield, Retired, Dies in Berkeley," *Oakland Tribune*, April 6, 1942, 11.]

13. "Wanted Only in Mess Branch of Navy," *New York Age*, April 26, 1917, 2.

14. CGG Jr. to Roy Nash, May 1, 1917, Library of Congress Manuscript Division, Box I:G196, folder 22.

15. "News of Greater New York," *New York Age*, Sept. 28, 1916, 7.

16. "Teachers Assigned for Work of Year," *The State*, Sept. 24, 1916, 2; "Teachers Elected for City School; Salary Increase: Three Additional Instructors Named—Many Re-elected—Four Did Not Apply—One Promotion." *Columbia Record*, May 19, 1917, 6.

17. "Increased Enrollment Shown in City Schools," *Columbia Record*, Nov. 26, 1916, 2.

18. "Negroes Will Take Officers Training," *Columbia Record*, May 29, 1917, 10.

19. "Negroes to Train as Officers Named: Forty-Three Selected to be Sent to Des Moines Training Camp from Palmetto State—Nine other Selections to be Made," *Columbia Record*, June 9, 1917, 10.

20. https://medium.com/iowa-history/first-black-officers-trained-for-world-war-i-at-fort-des-moines-100-years-ago-4f50ce8aaf04.

21. Emmett J. Scott, *Scott's Official History of The American Negro in the World War* (Chicago: Homewood Press, 1919), 63.

22. Scott, 84.

23. Scott, 90.

24. Scott, 471–81; W. Allison Sweeney, *History of the American Negro in the Great*

World War: His Splendid Record in the Battle Zones of Europe, [unk/unk] 1919, 119–30.

25. MPGS to AES, Feb. 24, 1918.

26. Ralston's Army record from digitized copies downloaded from familysearch.org and provided by New York State Archives; United States Army, "Pictorial History 367th Infantry, Army of the United States, 1942" (1942). *World War Regimental Histories*. Book 20, 8–11. [http://digicom.bpl.lib.me.us/ww_reg_his/20] *Battle Participation of Organizations of the American Expeditionary Forces in France, Belgium and Italy, 1917–1918*, (Washington, DC: Government Printing Office, 1920), x, 88, 95, 98.

27. Hudson, 12.

28. Her last name is given as Belling in the Philadelphia Orphans' Court Index, 1917–38.

29. "Conference of the A.M.E. Church," *Pensacola New Journal*, Dec. 12, 1912, 3; "Manhattan Personals," *New York Age*, Oct. 16, 1926, 10.

10 — Patriotism at Home

1. "Is Chap Pro-German Now?" *The Light*, Jan. 3, 1918, 2.

2. "Carroll Trying to Slobber Over Chappelle: Bishop and Recommendations of Applicants for the Officers' Training Camp," *The Light*, Jan. 17, 1918, 1.

3. The botts is a disease caused by larvae of the bott fly, which hatch in an animal's intestines or nose. "Carroll," 1.

4. "Allen Student Sues President and Bishop," *New York Age*, April 26, 1917, 7. The article was based on information from the *Allen Student*.

5. "Negro Newspaper Editors Arrested for Alleged Slander," *Greenville Daily News*, April 30, 1918, 11. The statements were made in the April 18, 1918, issue of *The Light*, which has not been found.

6. "Big Question of War: Negro Bishop Discusses Grave Situation," *The State*, Feb. 18, 1917, 11.

7. "Has No Position Now: President and Congress Have Spoken, Says Chappelle," *The State*, April 14, 1917, 4.

8. Theodore Hemingway, "Prelude to Change: Black Carolinians in the War Years, 1914–1920," *Journal of Negro History* 65, no. 3, 218.

9. "People are Taking to War Thrift Stamps," *Columbia Record*, Dec. 17, 1917, 3.

10. "Charleston News Gleaned in a Day," *The State*, Nov. 11, 1921, 8.

11. "Hit Him A Lick," *Columbia Record*, June 8, 1918, 4.

12. *The Light*, Jan. 3, 1918, 2.

13. See Hudson, 78–82.

14. "Negroes Assert Right to Serve: Committee Has Interview with Governor," *The State*, April 7, 1917, 3.

15. "Manning Voices Strong Protest: Opposed to Negroes Coming to Camp Jackson," *The State*, Aug. 19, 1917, 1; "Puerto Rican Men Won't Come Here: Island's Troops Will Not be at Camp Jackson," *The State*, Aug. 22, 1917, 1.

16. W. J. Megginson, "Black South Carolinians in World War I: The *Official Roster* as a Resource for Local History, Mobility, and African American History," *South Carolina Historical Magazine* 96, no. 2, April 1995, 153.

17. The name was changed to Christian Methodist Episcopal Church in 1954. "CME delegates vote to erase racial tag," *Baltimore Afro-American*, May 22, 1954, p. 21.

18. "Thousands See Negroes Parade: Overseas Soldiers March through Streets," *The State*, February 22, 1919, 10.

19. *The State*, March 25, 1919, 18.

20. In the author's possession.

21. Ann Douglas, *Terrible Honesty: Mongrel Manhattan in the 1920s*. (New York: Farrar, Straus and Giroux, 1995), 87.

22. Ball to Barnwell, Jan. 20, 1920, quoted in Hudson, 128.

23. "Army Uniform Cost Soldier His Life: 'Stay-at-Homes' Object to Presence of Khaki—Mob Acts," *The Chicago Defender*, April 5, 1919, 1.

24. Arkansas General Assembly SCR 6 Commemorating the 94th Anniversary of the US Supreme Court Ruling in *Moore v. Dempsey*.

25. "Red Summer," https://en.wikipedia.org/wiki/Red_Summer; "For Action on Race Riot Peril: Radical Propaganda Among Negroes Growing, and Increase of Mob Violence Set Out in Senate Brief For Federal Inquiry," *New York Times*, Oct. 5, 1919, 10; Cameron McWhirter, *Red Summer* (New York: St. Martin's Griffin, 2012 [paperback reprint]), 13.

11 — Mama Comes into Her Own

1. "High Hill AME Church," *Palmetto Leader*, Dec. 27, 1941, 6; and "Weston Chapel AME Church," *Palmetto Leader*, Oct. 16, 1943, 4.

2. L30237, Laurens County School Superintendent Ledgers, 1911–30, South Carolina Department of History and Archives.

3. Ledgers in the State Archives; AMTG to NMG [May 15, 1941].

4. AMTG to MPGS, Feb. 22, 1920.

5. AMTG to MPGS, April 17, 1922.

6. AMTG to MPGS, April 1, 1924.

7. "A Great Day at the Rock Hill Colored School," *Palmetto Leader*, Sept. 19, 1925, 2; "Rosenwald Schools, County: Richland," PDF from South Carolina Department of Archives and History website. https://scdah.sc.gov/sites/scdah/files/Documents/.

8. Danielle Dreilinger, in *The Secret History of Home Economics: How Trailblazing Women Harnessed the Power of Home and Changed the Way We Live* (New York:

Norton, 2021), discusses home economics at schools such as Tuskegee and Hampton and pioneers in the field such as Flemmie Kittrell, who earned a doctorate from Cornell University in 1938 and taught at Hampton Institute and Howard University.

9. Letter, AMTG to MPGS, March 6, 1922.

10. Theda Skocpol, Arian Lizzos, and Marshall Ganz, *What a Mighty Power We Can Be: African American Fraternal Groups and the Struggle for Racial Equality*" (Princeton, NJ: Princeton University Press, 2006), 56.

11. Skocpol et al., 13.

12. Skocpol et al., the Tents were incorporated in 1865, 24.

13. AMTG to MPGS, [Sept. 7, 1943]; Sydney, Dennis, "Women's group got start assisting runaway slaves," *Wilmington, Delaware Morning News*, July 8, 1982, p. 54; King, George F., "Founder of the Order of Tents: Remarkable Work of the Late Annetta Lane," *Baltimore Afro-American*, Sept. 7, 1912, 7; Anna M. Garrett, "Some Facts About the Grand United Order of Tents of the J.R.G. and J.U." [Leaflet in the possession of the author.] Mama was listed as "National Deputy and Pres. Ex. Board."

14. "A Partial Premium List of the Richland Co. Fair," *Palmetto Leader*, Nov. 28, 1925, p. 8

15. AMTG to MPGS, March 4, 1924.

16. AMTG to MPGS, n.d., but probably October 1923.

17. AMTG to MPGS, May 27, 1923.

18. AMTG to MPGS, Jan. 24, 1926.

19. AMTG to MPGS [1932].

20. AMTG to MPGS, May 31, 1926.

21. AMTG to MPGS, Aug. 1, 1927; AMTG to MPGS, Jan. 15, 1928.

22. CGG to AES, May 20, 1926.

23. AMTG to MPGS, May 31, 1926.

24. AMTG to NMG, Dec. 14, 1935.

25. Plaintiffs in these cases—numbers 15116, 17219, and 018077—were National Loan and Exchange and the Bank of Columbia. All are found in the South Carolina Department of Archives and History.

26. AMTG to MPGS, n.d., but probably around Christmas as she said she did not want any gifts.

27. AMTG to MPGS, September 2, 1929.

28. AMTG to MPGS, Nov. 13, 1923.

29. Ads from June 18 (p. 6), Sept. 24 (p. 6), and Dec. 7 (p. 5) issues of *The State*. Information about the model from https:// bringatrailer.com/listing/1923-ford-model -t-touring/ and https://www.oldcarsweekly .com/features/car-of-the-week-1923-ford -model-t-touring.

30. AMTG to MPGS, Nov. 13, 1923.

31. AMTG to MPGS, Nov. 26, 1923.

32. AMTG to MPGS, Sept. 4, 1925.

33. Salsi, 120; Zan Heyward, *Things I Remember* (Columbia: State-Record Company, 1964), 121, 123, quoted in Salsi; AMTG to MPGS, Jan. 24, 1926.

34. "Police Hold Negro: F.B. Shackelford Bruised in Auto Collision," *The State*, Oct. 24, 1923, 11; "Garrett Responsible for Shackleford Wreck," *Columbia Record*, Oct. 24, 1923, 5; "County Court Cases: Jurors Review Details of a Motor Car Collision," *The State*, Jan. 15, 1924, 9; AMTG to MPGS, Jan. 20, 1924.

35. AMTG to MPGS, June 1928.

36. AMTG to MPGS, March 4, 1924.

37. AMTG to MPGS, June 1928.

38. AMTG to MPGS, Oct. 1923.

39. AMTG to MPGS, Nov. 13, 1923; AMTG to MPGS, Nov. 26, 1923.

40. AMTG to MPGS, Oct. 1923.

41. AMTG to Ruth Eidier Garrett Valentine, Oct. 20, 1931.

42. AMTG to MPGS, June 26, 1937.

43. AMTG to MPGS, June 27, 1938.

44. AES Sr. to MPGS, Nov. 16, 1918.

45. AMTG to MPGS, April 17, 1922.

46. AMTG to MPGS, April 10, 1921.

47. AMTG to MPGS, April 17, 1922. Founded in 1880 as the Dixie Training School, the Berkeley Training High School was the first public school for Blacks in Moncks Corner, SC (https://www.hmdb .org/m.asp?m=41606). The commencement where Mama spoke must have been held in a new three-room school built in 1919–20 with aid from the Julius Rosenwald Foundation. The Foundation contributed more than $4.4 million in matching funds for the construction of Black schools, most of them in the South between 1917 and 1948. In one letter, Mama reports making arrangements for a visiting Rosenwald Field Agent.

48. Simon Gikandi, "Afro-Victorian Worlds," in *The Victorian World*, edited by Martin Hewitt Martin (New York: Routledge, 2012), 673.

49. AMTG to MPGS, May 22, 1922.

50. AMTG to MPGS, May 15, 1923.

51. Henig, 311.

52. Ibid.

53. AMTG to MPGS, March 23, 1920.

54. "Richland County School Board Minutes," April 26, July 27, 1917; June 7, 1920, 38.

55. "Richland County School Board Minutes," Aug. 24, 1924, 137; "Richland County Superintendent's Ledgers," 1925–26 enrollment figures.

56. AMTG to MPGS, Sept. 9, 1921.

57. AMTG to MPGS, April 25, 1925; letter n.d., but dated from reference to the death of a James Bailey; AMTG to MPGS, n.d.

12 — "We Are as Well as Common"

1. He appears as a freshman on p. 79 of the "*Catalogue of Lincoln University, Chester County, Penna., Sixty-Third Year, 1917–18*" (Philadelphia: Ferris & Leach, 1918).

2. Her last name is given as Duchett in the Philadelphia Orphans' Court Index, 1917–38.

3. *Student's Handbook Lincoln University*, 1914, 5; *Catalogue of Lincoln University, Chester County, Penna., Sixty-Third Year, 1917–18* (Philadelphia: Ferris & Leach, 1918), 36.

4. Marian Threewitts Garrett to MPGS, April 16, 1918.

5. *South Carolina State Agricultural and Mechanical College Catalog, 1918–1919*, 64.

6. AMTG to MPGS, Dec. 11, 1922.

7. 1920 census.

8. AMTG to MPGS, Feb. 22, 1920.

9. AMTG to MPGS, April 10, 1921.

10. AMTG to MPGS, April 17, 1922.

11. AMTG to MPGS, n.d., but likely after 1926.

12. Wright, *Centennial*, 95.

13. Program, Founder's Day Celebration Anna Boyd School, March 18, 1940 (in possession of the author).

14. AMTG to MPGS, March 26, 1923.

15. AMTG to AES, May 9, 1920.

16. AMTG to MPGS, March 7, 1926.

17. AMTG to MPGS, May 31, 1926.

18. AMTG to MPGS, Feb. 22, 1923.

19. AMTG to MPGS [1929?].

20. AMTG to MPGS, April 1, 1924.

21. AMTG to MPGS, Feb. 7, 1926.

22. AMTG to MPGS, April 17, Aug. 2, and Dec. 1, 1922. Seretha Cannon is listed as a domestic in the 1922 Columbia City Directory (p. 449), and as a teacher in 1927 (p. 568). Julia Saxon, the daughter of long-time Columbia teacher Celia Dial Saxon, married James Woodbury.

23. Letter from T. H. Wiseman to W. E. B. Du Bois, August 26, 1923. W. E. B. Du Bois Papers (MS 312). Special Collections and University Archives, University of Massachusetts Amherst Libraries; https://archive.org/details/.

24. AMTG to MPGS, March 11, 1924.

25. AMTG to MPGS, n.d. Mama gives only a first name, but this could have been Rosa Johnson who lived at 1616 Lady Street. She shot her husband on Oct. 22, 1929. ["Negro Shot by Wife Dies at Hospital," *Columbia Record*, Oct. 23, 1929, 8; "Widowed Herself, Negro Gets Bond: Rosa Johnson Admitted to $2,000 Bail," *The State*, Oct. 27, 1929, 2.]

26. AMTG to MPGS, June 8, 1938.

27. AMTG to NMG, Dec. 21, 1939.

28. Likely, Dora Dare Ricketts Baker. A milliner, she would have been forty-six at the time she encountered Mama. [Death certificate, no. 59008813; "Mrs. Baker, 74, of Columbia Dies," *The State*, June 30, 1959, 21.]

29. Mrs. F. A. Baker, "Re: Annie M. Garrett's Claim against City of Columbia;" letter from Austin T. Moore to John J. McMahan, Sept. 13, 1934; letter from Elise W. Goodwin of Good Samaritan Hospital, Sept. 13, 1934; Good Samaritan Hospital bill dated June 2, 1932. (All in the possession of the author.)

30. Phyllis Threewitts Simons Ferguson (PTSF) to RESN, July 30, 1943.

31. "Senior College Class of B.C. Entertained," *Palmetto Leader*, May 21, 1927, 7; "Correction," *Palmetto Leader*, May 28, 1927, 7.

32. AMTG to MPGS, Feb. 22, 1920.

33. AMTG to MPGS, April 4, 1920.

34. AMTG to MPGS, July 19, 1926.

35. AMTG to MPGS, Feb. 2, 1920.

36. AMTG to MPGS, Sept. 14, 1922.

37. AMTG to MPGS, May 27, 1923.

38. AMTG to MPGS, July 9, 1923.

39. "Negro Who for 55 Years Taught in City Schools Dies at Ripe Age of 77," *The State*, January 30, 1935, 12.

40. AMTG to MPGS, Aug. 14, 1923.

41. AMTG to MPGS, May 7, 1924.

42. AMTG to MPGS, Sept. 13, 1926.

43. AMTG to MPGS, June 10, 1929.

44. Theodora Blocker Thomas to David Nicholson, Aug. 29, 2012 (in possession of the author). Her father was Benjamin A. Blocker, the tailor who advertised in *The Light*.

45. NMG to MPGS, March 13, 1930.

46. Ibid.

47. "Aiken News," *Palmetto Leader*, Sept. 27, 1941, 8.

48. AMTG to NMG, Dec. 27, 1939.

49. AMTG to NMG, Jan. 1, 1943.

50. AMTG to MPGS, Sept. 28, 1919.

51. *Allen Catalog*, 1923–24, 11.

52. AMTG to MPGS, Oct. 7, 1919.

53. AMTG to MPGS, Aug. 5, 1925.

54. Certificate of Death, dated Sept. 2, 1925.

55. CGG Jr. to AMTG, April 1, 1935 (in possession of the author); "Police End Harlem Riot; Mayor Starts Inquiry; Dodge Sees a Red Plot," *New York Times*, March 21, 1935, 1; "Harlem Riot of 1935," https://en.wikipedia.org/wiki/Harlem_riot_of_1935.

56. Robin D. G. Kelley, "Introduction," in *Reflections in the Black: A History of Black Photographers 1840 to the Present*, edited by Debra Willis (New York: Norton, 2000), x.

57. Charity Adams Earley, *One Woman's Army: A Black Officer Remembers the WAC* (College Station, Texas: Texas A&M University Press, 1989), 6.

13 — The Editor and the Bishop, 1917–25

1. MPGS to AES [Feb. 1919].

2. Nathan Dial to William Ball, Aug. 9, 1922, Ball Papers, Duke University. I am indebted to Janet Hudson for providing a copy of the letter.

3. AES to MPGS, Jan. 23, 1919. Alfred didn't explain what a "two hand pole" was, but perhaps he meant one long and stout enough to require two hands.

4. "New Year Greetings," *The Light*, Jan. 3, 1918, 2.

5. "Editorial," *The Light*, Jan. 3, 1918, 2.

6. "Old Chap Will Sure Get Him," *The Light*, Jan. 3, 1918, 1.

7. See John R. Wilson, *A Brief Sketch of the Life and Career of the Right Rev. William David Chappelle, A.M., D.D., LL., Some of his Addresses and Sermons* (Columbia: The State Company, n.d.), 24–25.

8. "Editorial," 2.

9. "Carroll," 1.

10. "Rev. E.P. Ellis' Row: Still on At Greenwood—Forged Names?—He Woke Up the Wrong Man—Locked Out," *The Light*, Jan. 3, 1918, 1

11. *Catalogue of Allen University, Columbia, South Carolina, 1908–1910*, 84; "Rev. E. Philip Ellis, D.D.," *Palmetto Leader*, Feb. 18, 1928, 1; https://www.findagrave.com/memorial/156815096/e-philip-ellis."

12. "Country Negroes No More," *The Light*, Jan. 3, 1918, 2.

13. "Editor is Held for Newspaper Article," *Columbia Record*, May 3, 1918, 15.

14. *State v. CG Garrett*, case no. 6701, South Carolina Department of Archives and History, L 40559.

15. "Laymen Against Bishop Chappelle: Will Ask That Another Be Appointed in State," *The State*, April 24, 1920, 10.

16. Account of the attempt to remove Chappelle from the May 27, 1920, issue of *The Light*, 1–2, as well as a circular titled "The Way Bishop Chappelle Bulldozes People in South Carolina." A photocopy of the latter is in the author's possession.

17. "Judiciary Proceedings," 1920 General Conference Report, 215; "Resume of Judiciary Acts and AME Revisions: Charges Against Bishops Dismissed for Lack of Evidence—Vernon Wept at Being Sent to Africa," *New York Age*, May 29, 1920, 2. Mance's departure in 1924 was noted in "David H. Sims Made President:

Allen University Dean Succeeds R.W. Mance," *The State*, June 5, 1924, 9. The following year, the newspaper reported that Chappelle's successor, Reverdy C. Ransom, now a bishop, had appointed Mance to "one of the leading churches of his denomination" in Nashville.

18. "A Thief of the Cross," *The Light*, May 27, 1920, 2.

19. Ellis, E. Philip, "The Old Gray and the New Rider," *Palmetto Leader*, May 2, 1936.

20. *Catalogue of Allen University, Columbia, South Carolina 1923 and 1924*, 59.

21. Caldwell, *History*, 293.

22. "Bishop Chappelle Dead," *Christian Recorder*, June 18, 1925, 1.

23. "Bishop William David Chappelle Passes," *Palmetto Leader*, June 20, 1925, 1.

24. Hudson, 34–35.

25. Caldwell, *History*, 19.

26. "Thousands See," 10.

27. Chappelle Sounds Note of Warning: Calls on Negroes to Beware of Bolshevism," *The State*, July 31, 1919, 12.

28. "Heads of Colored State Fair Fight: Bad Blood Between Editor and Bishop Cause[s] Quarrel That Ends Meeting," *Watchman and Southron* (Sumter, SC), Nov. 8, 1922, 1.

29. "Bishop Chappelle Figures in Court: Claims C.G. Garrett Started Trouble at Meeting of Directors of Negro Fair," *The State*, Nov. 7, 1922, 8.

30. "Lectured Negroes," *The State*, Nov. 8, 1922, 5.

31. "Heads," 1.

32. "Dr. J.M. Carson In The City: Ministers Would like a Reconciliation With Bishop Chappelle in his Extremis," *The Light*, June 6, 1925, 1.

33. "Bishop William David Chappelle Passes at His Home in Columbia," *Palmetto Leader*, June 27, 1925, 1.

34. "Dr. J. M. Carson," 1.

35. The images are part of the Jackson Davis Collection of African American Educational Photographs at the University of Virginia Library Albert and Shirley Small Special Collections Library. Davis (1882–1947) spent fourteen years as a field agent for the General Education Board. An amateur photographer, he took thousands of photographs to show conditions at schools throughout the South (encyclopediavirginia.org).

36. "National Historic Landmark Nomination: Chappelle Administration Building."

37. Caldwell, A.B., ed., *History of the American Negro: Washington, D.C., Edition*, Atlanta, 1922, 202.

38. "Laymen Want Report; Full Time Professors," *The Light*, June 6, 1925, 2.

39. "Want Active Bishop for South Carolina," *The Light*, June 6, 1925, 1.

40. Richard R. Wright Jr., "Charges of Graft and Church Contributions," *Christian Recorder*, June 12, 1924, 1, 4.

41. Wright, *Centennial*, 258; Wright, *Encyclopaedia* (1947), 311–312.

42. Culp, 64.

43. Caldwell, *History*, 17–20.

44. Culp, 64.

45. Wright, *Centennial*, 355; Smith, *A History*, 323.

46. "Will of Bishop Filed for Probate," *Palmetto Leader*, June 27, 1925, 1.

14 — Beginnings and Departures

1. AMTG to MPGS, Aug. 13, 1921.

2. Ira B. Valentine (IBV) to MPGS, June 3, 1921.

3. Ibid.

4. AMTG to MPGS, Aug. 2, 1922.

5. AMTG to MPGS, Jan. 29, 1922.

6. AMTG to MPGS, n.d.

7. Ibid.

8. AMTG to MPGS, Aug. 14, 1923.

9. AMTG to MPGS [1923].

275 — Notes to Pages 156–165

10. Information from New York City directories, US census; Ralston's registration card; *New York Age*, Dec. 22, 1923, 10; "Building: The Marshall," https://streeteasy.com/building/the-marshall.

11. Ralston is listed as a porter in the 1930 and 1940 censuses. "Pullman Porters: From Servitude to Civil Rights," https://interactive.wttw.com/a/chicago-stories-pullman-porters.

12. A. B. Caldwell, *History of the American Negro: West Virginia Edition* (Atlanta: A. B. Caldwell Publishing Company, 1923), 47.

13. Caldwell, *History: South Carolina Edition*, 58, 376; also 490, 660, 720, 721.

14. Larry Tye, *Rising from the Rails: Pullman Porters and the Making of the Black Middle Class* (New York: Picador, 2005), xii, 46.

15. Ibid., 86, 87, 165; "Pullman Porters: From Servitude to Civil Rights," https://interactive.wttw.com/a/chicago-stories-pullman-porters; "Pullman porter," https://en.wikipedia.org/wiki/Pullman_porter.

16. Please see https://aprpullmanporter museum.org/searchnationalregistry/.

17. AMTG to NMG, Jan. 1, 1943.

18. New York City Municipal Archive; 1924 NYC Voter List, "The City Record," Supplement, 13, retrieved from ancestry.com.

19. AMTG to MPGS, Jan. 15, 1928.

20. AMTG to MPGS, Feb. 14, 1935.

21. AMTG to MPGS, Feb. 14, 1938.

22. Fleming Maceo Garrett (FMG) to CGG, April 11, 1939 (in possession of the author).

15 — Papa Returns to Allen

1. Ellis, E. Philip, "'The New Rider' Speaks now From the Trenches," *Palmetto Leader*, Oct. 19, 1935, 2.

2. AMTG to MPGS, Aug. 18, 1925.

3. AMTG to MPGS, Oct. 31, 1925.

4. AMTG to MPGS, Jan. 24, 1926.

5. Ibid.

6. *Palmetto Leader*, July 22, 1939, 5.

7. AMTG to MPGS [1940].

8. AMTG to MPGS [Sept. 7, 1943].

9. "Bishop Hurst Dies Tuesday: While at Home in Baltimore," *The State*, May 7, 1930, 5; AMTG to MPGS, May 6, 1930.

10. "Ransome [sic] Serves in Hurst's Place: Comes to South Carolina as Presiding Bishop, A.M.E. Church," *The State*, May 11, 1930, 6.

11. Gomez-Jefferson, 182. For a discussion of reform at the 1928 General Conference and Ransom's assignment to Louisiana, see Gomez-Jefferson, 182–85; and Singleton, *Romance*, 163–69.

12. AMTG to MPGS, undated, but likely May 1930. "Sims Renamed Allen's Head: Finals at University Come Today," *The State*, May 29, 1930, 20, lists Papa, as field agent, "among the new faculty members named today." Description of the job: "Allen Freshmen Get Early Start: Formal Opening Scheduled for September 17," *The State*, Sept. 7, 1930, 32.

13. "The Florence District S.S. and A.C.E. League Conv.," *Palmetto Leader*, Sept. 30, 1939, 5.

14. "Pleads for Allen: Garrett Addresses African Methodists," *The State*, May 20, 1937, 5.

15. Gomez-Jefferson, 191.

16. George A. Singleton, "Pointed Points," *Palmetto Leader*, May 31, 1930, 4.

17. Singleton, "Pointed Points," *Palmetto Leader*, June 14, 1930, 4.

18. Singleton, "Pointed Points," *Palmetto Leader*, July 26, 1930, 4.

19. Singleton, "Pointed Points," *Palmetto Leader*, June 11, 1932, 4.

20. E. Philip Ellis, "The Old Gray and the New Rider," *Palmetto Leader*, May 2,

1936, 2. Ellis's account appears under the subheading "Office of Custodian."

21. Ellis, *Palmetto Leader*, May 2, 1936, 2.

22. Philip Ellis, "Bishop Johnson Takes Up Work: Presides at Session of Allen Trustees," *The State*, May 27, 1936, 7. According to Ramon Jackson, whose doctoral dissertation concerns student activism at Allen and other HCBUs, Eugene had studied the issues the University faced and knew of Garrett's passion for the school and desire to help improve it.

23. Ellis, "Bishop Johnson"; AMTG to MPGS, undated letter.

24. E. Philip Ellis, "Negro Methodists Closing Sessions," *The State*, Nov. 28, 1936, 10; "Allen University to Have Library: Campaign for Funds to Begin in June," *The State*, Jan. 20, 1938, 2. Also, it's a four-decker headline, and I included only the first two. The third and fourth are "To Complete Gym; Executive Board Approves Building Plans, President McGill Says." E. Philip Ellis, "Presiding Elders AME Church Meet," *The State*, March 10, 1939, 11-B.

25. I am indebted to Ramon Jackson for providing his first and middle names. "Allen Students and Trustee Claim Dent Illegally Named: Not to Return to Classrooms Until Demands are Met," *The State*, March 21, 1939, 11-A; "Allen University Strike Settled; Classes Resumed: Dean O'Daniel Elected Acting President," *The State*, March 28, 1939, 14.

26. "Allen Students Strike; AME Churchman In Turmoil," *The Plaindealer* (Kansas City, KS), March 31, 1939, 2.

27. "Dr. Dent Still in Race No 100 Percent Orders Given by the Bishop," *Palmetto Leader*, June 17, 1939, 1.

28. An AME school founded in 1885 to train teachers and craftsmen. It closed in 1975; "Fired at Allen; Dent Named Kittrell Prexy," *Atlanta Daily World*, June 23, 1939, 1.

29. H. W. Baumgardner, "Dr. Casper G. Garrett Succumbs in South Carolina," *Christian Recorder*, Dec. 18, 1947, 7.

30. AMTG to NMG, June 6, 1940; AMTG to NMG, June 13, 1940; AMTG to NMG, undated letter.

31. "Bishops' Council Highlights," *Atlanta Daily World*, Feb. 15, 1940, 6; I. M. A. Myers, "Bishop Flipper is Honored by Church Leaders," *The State*, Feb. 25, 1941, 9; "AME Group Fetes Bishop And Mrs. Joseph Flipper," *Atlanta Daily World*, March 7, 1941, 2; "Corner Stone Laying Very Impressive At Allen University Last Wednesday," *Palmetto Leader*, Oct. 18, 1941, 3; "Corner Stone Laying Held At Allen University," *Pittsburgh Courier*, Oct. 25, 1941, 15. If Papa gave those dates, he was wrong. Allen was founded in 1870 and moved to Columbia a decade later.

16 — Tap's Almost Success

1. "New York, New York City Municipal Deaths, 1795–1949," FamilySearch database (https://www.familysearch.org /ark:/61903/1:1:2WZD-SNZ: 3 June 2020), Anna Louise Garrett, July 27, 1919; citing Death, Manhattan, New York City, New York, United States, New York Municipal Archives, New York; FHL microfilm 1,322,451.

2. Anna Josephine Simons Wade in conversation.

3. "'Goophered,' Negro Conjure Operette [sic] in Rehearsal for Harlem Presentation," NAACP news release dated April 30, 1926, NAACP III, Scrapbook 20, Library of Congress.

4. Ibid.

5. James De Jongh, *Vicious Modernism: Black Harlem and the Literary Imagination* (Cambridge, United Kingdom: Cambridge University Press, 1990), 10.

6. Cited by Ann Douglas, *Terrible Honesty: Mongrel Manhattan in the 1920s* (New York: Farrar, Straus and Giroux, 1996), 84.

7. Ibid., 80.

8. Eugene Thamon Simpson, *Hall Johnson: His Life, His Spirit, and His Music*, (Lanham, MD: Scarecrow Press, 2008), 2–3; "Hall Johnson," *New York Amsterdam News*, May 9, 1970, 42; Earl Calloway, "Tribute to Hall Johnson, Composer of Spirituals," *Chicago Daily Defender*, May 14, 1970, 20.

9. Arnold Rampersad, *The Life of Langston Hughes. Volume I: 1902–1941, I, Too, Sing America* (New York: Oxford, 1986), 186.

10. RESN found a letter from Tap to NAACP Secretary Roy Nash, dated May 1, 1917. Tap wrote asking for copies of the association's constitution and bylaws, as well as a membership card one member had not received. (Box G196 LOC MS Div.)

11. Stories appeared in the *New York Amsterdam News* (May 5, 1926), *Baltimore Afro-American* (May 8 and Sept. 4, 1926, and June 4, 1927), *Chicago Defender* (May 29, 1926), and *Pittsburgh Courier* (May 28 and June 9, 1927). And "Goophered" enjoyed sporadic mentions years afterward in the *New York Amsterdam News* (June 19, 1929), *New York Age* (June 22, 1929), and *Baltimore Afro-American* (March 10, 1934).

12. *Chicago Defender*, May 29, 1926, A1.

13. Josephine Tighe Williams, "Discovery of a New Writer of Poetry Among Workers at a Washington Hotel," *Sunday Star*, Dec. 13, 1925, magazine section, 4.

14. "Play of Rural Negro Life," *New York Times*, May 3, 1926, 27.

15. Gwendolyn Bennett, "The Ebony Flute," *Opportunity*, Aug. 1926, p. 261.

16. "Mother to Son" was first published in 1922. "Song for a Banjo Dance" appeared in Hughes's first book, *The Weary Blues*.

17. "New York's Show World Activities," Sept. 4, 1926, 3.

18. "Through the Lorgnette of Geraldyn Dismond," *Pittsburgh Courier*, May 28, 1927. Dismond did not name the songs for which

Hall won but, according to *Opportunity*'s July 1927 issue, he won for three compositions: "Sonata," "Fiyer," and "Banjo Dance." (p. 204). My guess is that the last two were from "Goophered."

19. The William E. Harmon Foundation Award for Distinguished Achievement Among Negroes was offered in 1926–31 for achievements in several categories, including art, literature, science, and business and industry.

20. Harman Foundation, Inc. Records, 1913–1967, Library of Congress Manuscript Division, Box 56, 1930.

21. "Johnson Show Deferred," *Baltimore Afro-American*, March 10, 1934, 6.

22. Johnson, Hall, "Fi-yer," unpublished manuscript. Hall Johnson Collection, Stuart A. Rose Manuscript, Archives, and Rare Book Library, Emory University.

23. Rampersad, 112, 113.

24. Rampersad, 159.

25. Rampersad, 166.

26. "Postal Employees," *Ebony*, November 1949, 15, Quoted in Philip F. Rubio, *There's Always Work at the Post Office: African American Postal Workers and the Fight for Jobs, Justice, and Equality* (Chapel Hill: University of North Carolina, 2010), 4.

27. CGG Jr. to RESN, Sept. 16, 1945.

28. Richland County records, L40095, 132, South Carolina Department of Archives and History.

29. "GARRETT, Colonel," [sic] Meharry Medical College Archives, accessed July 3, 2021, http://diglib.mmc.edu/omeka /items/show/4547; "Locals and Personals," *Palmetto Leader*, June 4, 1927, 7.

30. AMTG to MPGS, June 6, 1927.

31. "Dr. Garrett Passes Dental Board," *Palmetto Leader*, July 23, 1927, 7.

32. "Locals and Personalities," *Palmetto Leader*, Aug. 13, 1927, 7.

33. "*Leader* Representative Completes

State Tour," *Palmetto Leader*, Sept. 15, 1928, 3.

34. "Announcement," *Palmetto Leader*, Dec. 21, 1935, 3.

35. "Latta News," *Palmetto Leader*, Feb. 1, 1930, 3

36. "Dillon News," *Palmetto Leader*, Aug. 17, 1935, 3.

37. "Dillon News," *Palmetto Leader*, Aug. 30, 1930, 2.

38. "Dillon," *Palmetto Leader*, Jan. 18, 1930, 5.

39. "Dillon News," *Palmetto Leader*, Feb. 1, 1930, 3.

40. "Dillon News," *Palmetto Leader*, May 16, 1931, 5.

41. Advertisement, *Palmetto Leader*, Jan. 31, 1931; "Great Negro Tenor to Sing Here Soon: Much Demand for Seats to Hear Roland Hayes Next Month," *The State*, Jan. 21, 1931.

42. "New Colored School at Winnsboro Ready," *Columbia Record*, Nov. 22, 1925, 20.

43. AMTG to MPGS, Oct. 31, 1925.

44. AMTG to MPGS, May 17, 1926.

45. "Completes List School Teachers: City Board Fills Few Vacancies Existing," *The State*, July 28, 1929, 7.

46. "Under the Capitol Dome," *Palmetto Leader*, June 21, 1930, 7.

47. AMTG to MPGS, May 22, 1922.

48. AMTG to REV, Oct. 20, 1931.

49. AMTG to MPGS, Dec. 3, 1939.

50. AMTG to NMG, Jan. 26, 1940.

51. AMTG to NMG [Feb. 15, 1940].

52. Kershaw County adjoins Richland County to the northeast.

53. AMTG to MPGS [Nov. 26, 1942].

54. Dillon's population in 1930.

55. "Dillon News," *Palmetto Leader*, April 27, 1935, 6; "Dillon News," *Palmetto Leader*, May 11, 1935, 4; "Dillon News," *Palmetto Leader*, April 27, 1935, 6; "Dillon News," *Palmetto Leader*, July 24, 1935, 3;

"Dillon News," *Palmetto Leader*, Oct. 19, 1935, 8.

56. AMTG to NMG, Dec. 3, 1939.

57. AMTG to NMG [1940].

58. NMG to MPGS, April 16, 1944.

59. Evelyn Garrett (EG) to MPGS, Sept. 27, 1936 (in possession of the author).

60. AMTG to MPGS, February 1938.

61. AMTG to MPGS, May 14, 1943.

62. MTG to AMTG, Jan. 13, 1943 (in possession of the author).

63. MTG to MPGS, December 17, 1943.

64. MPGS to RESN, Jan. 8, 1958.

65. Interview with the author, June 21, 2022.

17 — Mills

1. Interview, NMG Jan. 1, 1984.

2. "Benedict Ends Work for Year: Lapsley Speaks to Graduates of College," *The State*, May 25, 1927, 2.

3. Mary S. Hoffschwelle, "Preserving Rosenwald Schools," National Trust for Historic Preservation, 2012 (p. 3).

4. NMG to MPGS, Oct. 5, 1927. Per the Rosenwald database at Fisk and a description in her letters, I believe it was the Bessemer City School, an eight-teacher school in Gaston County, NC. It was built at a cost of sixteen thousand dollars, which included a contribution of five hundred dollars from African-Americans and seventeen hundred dollars from the Rosenwald Fund. The website https://www.arcgis.com/apps/MapSeries/ says it was brick. "Directory of School Officials of North Carolina, 1929–1930," Educational Publication No. 143, Division of Publications No. 44, published by the State Superintendent of Public Instruction, Raleigh, lists (p. 39) an unnamed colored school in Bessemer city, whose principal was a D. H. Kearse.

5. Interview, NMG Jan. 1, 1984.

6. NMG to MPGS, Oct. 5, 1927.

7. Davie, 74.

8. Davie, 74.

9. NMG to MPGS Dec. 29, 1927, March 11, 1928.

10. NMG to MPGS Dec. 29, 1927.

11. Founded by the Rev. Alexander Bettis in 1882, the school focused on "the spiritual and industrial training of Negro youth, with emphasis on teacher education." It was accredited as a junior college in 1933 and closed in 1952 (http://memory .loc.gov/diglib/legacies/loc.afc.afc-legacies .200003514/).

12. NMG to MPGS, Jan. 23, 1936.

13. Davie, 74.

14. Félix Germain, "Mercer Cook and the Origins of Black French Studies," *French Politics, Culture & Society* 34 no. 1 (Spring 2016), 68.

15. Peyton Gray, "Kittrell in Comeback as Leading Church School: Survives Lean Years and Adverse Publicity," *Afro American*, Sept. 16, 1939, 16; "Negro College in Receivership: Kittrell College Asks Time to Meet Debts; Suit Was Pending," *News and Observer*, March 14, 1934, 4; "Negro College Owes Five Raleigh Firms: Kittrell College Lists Liabilities of $53,559 in Bankruptcy Schedule," *News and Observer*, April 13, 1934, 18; "Bishop Keeps Tabs on Kittrell's Progress," *Afro-American*, Sept. 16, 1939, 16.

16. NMG to MPGS, Jan. 24, 1938.

17. NMG to MPGS, Oct. 10, 1937.

18. NMG to MPGS, Jan. 24, 1938.

19. "Kittrell Head Dismissed by Trustee Board: Pres. Cochran 3 Faculty Members and Matron Are Ordered Out," *Chicago Defender*, June 17, 1939, 3; Gray, "Kittrell," 16.

20. AMTG to NMG, April 18, 1941.

21. NMG to AMTG, Jan. 22, 1939.

22. Davie, 75.

23. NMG to MPGS, Oct. 29, 1941.

24. Davie, 75.

25. Elmer A. Henderson (EAH) to NMG, Aug. 11, 1942 (in possession of the author).

26. "Dr. Elmer A. Henderson (1887–1951)," *Journal of Negro History* 36, no. 4 (October 1951), 481–483; "Elmer Henderson Dies in Baltimore," *Baltimore Afro-American*, July 14, 1951, 1.

27. AMTG to NMG, Sept. 24, 1942.

28. NMG to MPGS, November 4, 1946.

29. "Teachers' Salaries," Letter to the Editor, *Baltimore Sun*, Nov. 8, 1943. Maryland passed legislation to pay Black and white teachers equal salaries in 1941. Salaries of Black teachers in Washington were equal to those paid to whites because all were federal employees.

30. AMTG to NMG, Sept. 24, 1942.

31. Probably the Rev. Thomas J. Miles, who lived at 1230 Pine Street, near the intersection with Lady Street. NMG to AJSW, Aug. 7, 1942.

32. AMTG to NMG, Dec. 3, 1942.

33. AMTG to NMG, Nov. 25, 1942.

34. AMTG to NMG, Dec. 17, 1942.

35. "Board Won't Release Tutor," *Afro-American*, Jan. 30, 1943, 10. This appears to have been true: "More than 450 Baltimore teachers, or 12.5 percent . . . have quit their jobs since Sept. 1, 1942," the *Baltimore Sun* reported (Oct. 7, 1943, 28).

36. NMG to MPGS, Jan. 17, 1943.

37. "Elmer Henderson Dies in Baltimore," 1.

38. NMG to MPGS, Nov. 16, 1943.

39. AMTG to NMG [Jan. 1, 1943].

40. AMTG to NMG [Jan. 7, 1943].

41. "Board Won't Release Tutor," 10; NMG to AMTG, Jan. 17, 1943.

42. "Columbia [sic] Wins Teaching Fellowship to Haiti," *Palmetto Leader*, Feb. 6, 1943, 1.

43. "Benedict College Club Honors Miss Naomi M. Garrett," *Palmetto Leader*, March 6, 1943, 7.

44. AMTG to NMG [Jan. 7, 1943].

45. NMG to MPGS, Feb. 10, 1943.

46. AMTG to MPGS, n.d.

47. "Seven Teachers Arrive in Haiti," *Atlanta Daily World*, March 27, 1943, 5.

48. "James Forsythe Dies; Taught at Sidwell School," *Washington Post*, Jan. 6, 1982, B6.

49. "D.C. Youth to Aid Haiti Set Up English Courses," *Evening Star*, March 20, 1943, A15; "Six Howard Students Given Travel Awards," *Chicago Defender*, May 6, 1939, 11.

50. "Some members of Virginia Union's War Time Faculty: John Matthew Moore," *Virginia Union University Bulletin*, January 1946, 10; "Scholarships," *Opportunity* 10, no. 2 (Feb. 1932), 60.

51. "Forrest O. Wiggins papers," https://archives.lib.umn.edu/repositories /14/resources/1692; "Opening Smith University on September 19: Start Co-Educational Work at Institution here—Additions are Made to Faculty," *Charlotte News*, Sept. 11, 1932, 7; "Haiti," *News and Observer* (Raleigh, NC), March 21, 1943, 1.

52. "Rites Held for DeWitt Peters, Founder of Haitian Art Center," *Journal News* (White Plains, NY), July 26, 1966, 2.

53. Henry Charles Schwartz, registration card dated Oct. 16, 1940, retrieved from familysearch.org.

54. NMG to AJSW, Feb. 14, 1943.

55. NMG to AMTG, March 4, 1943.

18 — Fiftieth Anniversary and Nearing the End

1. AMTG to MPGS [n.d., probably spring 1938].

2. AMTG to NMG, June 1, 1940, July 18, 1940, Sept. 12, 1940, Nov. 1 and 7, 1940.

3. AMTG to NMG, Oct. 10, 1940.

4. AMTG to NMG [Sept. 5 and 12], 1940.

5. AMTG to NMG, Sept. 5, 1940.

6. AMTG to NMG, Dec. 6, 1940.

7. There's that name again.

8. AMTG to NMG [May 8, 15, and 22, 1941] The bill allowed teachers to retire at age sixty-five, but retirement was not mandatory. A total of six thousand dollars was appropriated. ["Nine Richland Acts Approved by Legislature: Supply Measure, Bond Issue Plan Most Important of Local Bills," *Columbia Record*, May 28, 1941, 16.].

9. "Minutes of the Richland County Retirement Board, 1941–1964," South Carolina Department of Archives and History, L40118.

10. "Two-Year[-]Old Fort Jackson is a Complete City: Size of Fort Tripled Since World War I," *The State*, Aug. 15, 1942, 2-B; "Fort Jackson," *The State*, April 14, 2002, 60.

11. "Sixty Deaths Listed at Fort in 14 Months," *The State*, Oct. 14, 1941, 14.

12. Salsi, 136.

13. AMTG to NMG, Feb. 8, 1940.

14. AMTG to MPGS, Sept. 29, 1941.

15. Salsi, 135, 137, 138; comparison of grocery store ads, *The State*, Jan. 12, 1940, and Jan. 12, 1945.

16. AMTG to MPGS, July 13, 1942.

17. "More Police Held Need of Section: For Officers says Expansion of Forces Essential to Curb Rise in Vice," *Columbia Record*, Jan. 9, 1941, 1, 2.

18. NMG to AJSW, Aug. 7, 1942.

19. Ibid.

20. "Fort Jackson News: Service Club For Negro Soldiers at Fort Jackson," *Palmetto Leader*, July 19, 1941, 3.

21. "New Service Club For Negro Soldiers at Fort Jackson," Nov. 1, 1941, *Palmetto Leader*, 7.

22. AMTG to MPGS, Dec. 24, 1942.

23. AMTG to MPGS, Jan. 1, 1943.

24. AMTG to NMG, Dec. 17, 1942. Gaylord is mentioned several times in Mama's letters, once with his wife, Lillian.

Occupation from the 1920 and 1942 censuses.

25. AMTG to MPGS, March 6, 1942.
26. AMTG to MPGS, Nov. 26, 1942.
27. AMTG to MPGS, Sept. 10, 1942.
28. AMTG to MPGS, Nov. 3, 1942.
29. AMTG to MPGS, March 1943.
30. Ibid.
31. NMG to RESN, March 25, 1943.
32. AES to MPGS, April 4, 1943.
33. AES to MPGS, March 21, 1943.
34. "Personal Mention," *Palmetto Leader*, May 1, 1943, 7.
35. CGG Jr., to AMTG, May 2, 1943 (in possession of the author).
36. AMTG to MPGS [March 1943].
37. AMTG to MPGS, Oct. 22, 1943.
38. AMTG to MPGS, April 17, 1943.
39. AMTG to MPGS [n.d., but probably June or July 1943].
40. AMTG to MPGS, July 8, 1943.
41. Arnold Rampersad, ed., *The Collected Poems of Langston Hughes* (New York: Vintage Classics, 1994), 368.
42. AMTG to MPGS, July 8, 1943.
43. "Fleming Maceo Garrett Passes," *Palmetto Leader*, July 10, 1943, 2.
44. AMTG to MPGS, Nov. 30, 1943.

19 — Mills in Haiti

1. Naomi M. Garrett, "St.-Marc, Haiti," *Opportunity* XXV, Winter issue (Jan.–March 1947), 9, 35.
2. Sténio Joseph Vincent, 1874–1959, president of Haiti 1930–41.
3. NMG to MPGS, May 15, 1944.
4. NMG to AMTG, March 4, 1943.
5. NMG to AMTG, March 4, 1943.
6. Ibid.
7. NMG to AJSW, June 5, 1943.
8. NMG to MPGS, April 18, 1943.
9. NMG to AJSW, March 16, 1943.
10. NMG to MPGS, April 18, 1943.
11. NMG to MPGS, May 5, 1943.
12. Zora Neale Hurston, *Tell My Horse* (Berkeley, CA: Turtle Island, 1981), 166.
13. NMG to MPGS, May 5, 1943.
14. NMG to MPGS, May 9, 1943.
15. NMG to RESN, Oct. 17, 1943.
16. NMG to MPGS, April 16, 1944.
17. NMG to RESN, Oct. 17, 1943.
18. Wiggins wanted to stay but had attracted the attention of the FBI. According to Jesse Leo Kass, an informer reported Wiggins as "an active anti-White and anti-British propagandist." He was interviewed by an agent when he returned to the United States. Though no action was taken, Wiggins's politics—he was "a self-professed socialist"—would cause him much trouble. He was fired from posts at the University of Minnesota and Allen University. He and Mills were reunited in 1968, when he came to West Virginia State College (now West Virginia State University), where Mills headed the Department of Romance Languages. https://blindmanwithmathdegree.blogspot.com/2020/12/. NMG to [AJSW], Aug. 24, 1943.
19. Ibid.
20. Ibid.
21. NMG to MPGS, Sept. 16, 1943
22. NMG to AJSW, June 5, 1943.
23. NMG to AJSW, Oct. 28, 1945.
24. NMG to MPGS, June 14, 1944.
25. NMG to MPGS, June 19, 1944.
26. Ibid.
27. Ibid.
28. NMG to [AJSW], Aug. 6, 1943.
29. NMG to MPGS, Sept. 16, 1943.
30. NMG to MPGS, June 19, 1944.
31. NMG to AJSW, Jan. 22, 1945.
32. She called him "'Ezekiel Hezekiah' Tindel" in one letter.
33. Charlesina Garrett (CG) to NMG [May 8, 1940] (in possession of the author).
34. NMG to AJSW, May 12, 1943.
35. NMG to AJSW, June 5, 1943.

36. Ibid.

37. See "Office of the Coordinator of Inter-American Affairs," https://en.wikipedia.org/wiki/.

38. NMG to MPGS, Jan. 4, 1944.

39. NMG to MPGS, Nov. 16, 1943.

40. NMG to MPGS, Oct. 31, 1943.

41. Gérmain, 67.

42. NMG to MPGS, Dec. 15 [1943].

43. NMG to MPGS, Oct. 5, 1927.

44. NMG to AJSW, March 16, 1943.

45. NMG to MPGS, Dec. 27, 1943.

46. NMG to MPGS, May 21, 1944.

47. NMG to MPGS, April 27, 1944.

48. "Rosenwald Fellowships to 22; Seniors Get Grants," *Baltimore Afro-American*, May 20, 1944, 1.

49. NMG to MPGS, March 8, 1944.

50. NMG to MPGS, February 29, 1944, and April 16, 1944.

51. AMTG to MPGS, June 26, 1937.

52. NMG to AJSW, May 9, 1944.

53. Ibid.

54. Ibid.

55. NMG to MPGS, May 7, 1945.

56. NMG to MPGS, July 29, 1943.

57. NMG to MPGS, Dec. 8, 1943.

58. NMG to MPGS, June 14, 1944.

59. The term comes from the 1958 novel *The Ugly American* by William Lederer and Eugene Burdick.

60. Port-au-Prince.

61. NMG to AJSW, March 16, 1943. In her letter of June 19, 1944, Mills wrote that she had learned that Carter was dead.

62. "An Influential Collector of Modern Haitian Art," *New York Times*, June 7, 1993, C13; "Haitian Art in New Orleans," *Post-Signal* (Crowley, LA), Oct. 9, 1979, 10; "Haitian Art Auction Set for May 22," *Journal News* (White Plains, NY), May 14, 1969, 55; "Rites Held For DeWitt Peters, Founder of Haitian Art Center," *Journal News* (White Plains, NY), July 26, 1966, 2.

63. NMG to AJSW, Jan. 25, 1944.

64. NMG to MPGS, April 1, 1944.

65. NMG to MPGS, April 16, 1944.

66. "High School Teacher Leaves Friday, Takes Position in Haiti," *La Grande Observer*, Feb. 3, 1944, 3.

67. NMG to MPGS, Jan. 24, 1944.

68. NMG to MPGS, July 29, 1943.

69. Davie earned a master's degree from Columbia and led the Department of Foreign Languages at West Virginia State College, 1974–84.

70. NMG to AJSW, March 25, 1945. Piquion, 1906–2001, was dean of the College of Arts and Sciences at the University of Port-au-Prince.

20 — Mills Returns to America

1. Davie, 86.

2. NMG to AJSW, March 25, 1945.

3. Garrett file, Rosenwald Papers, 1945, 1, quoted in Linda M. Perkins, "The History of Black Women Graduate Students, 1921–1948," in *The Sage Handbook of African American Education*, edited by Linda C. Tillman, (Thousand Oaks, CA: SAGE Publications, 2009), 62–63.

4. NMG to AJSW, March 24, 1946.

5. NMG to MPGS, May 7, 1945.

6. NMG to RESN, Oct. 21, 1945.

7. NMG to AJSW, March 24, 1946.

8. Train, interview AJSW; NMG to AJSW, March 24, 1946.

9. AMTG to AJSW, March 8, 1945.

10. NMG to AJSW, March 1, 1945.

11. NMG to MPGS, March 19, 1945.

12. NMG to AJSW, July 2, 1945.

13. NMG to AJSW, May 26, 1946.

14. Ibid.

15. NMG to AJSW, Feb. 20, 1946.

16. NMG to AJSW, Oct. 28, 1945.

17. NMG to AJSW, Feb. 20, 1946.

18. NMG to MPGS, Aug. 6, 1946.

19. Please see "Columbia College Today," https://www.college.columbia.edu/cct_archive/sep05/cover.html.

20. NMG to MPGS, March 19 and April 14, 1947.

21. NMG to AJSW, May 26, 1946.

22. "Skinner to Head Anthropology; First Black Named Chairman," *Columbia Spectator*, April 11, 1972, 1. Immediately above the story about the appointment of Elliott P. Skinner, there's another about Columbia's president "personally" submitting the University's affirmative-action plan to the Department of Health, Education and Welfare's Office of Civil Rights. ("President Submits Final HEW Plan: Agency's Action on Anti-Bias Proposal Is not Expected for Several Weeks," *Columbia Spectator*, April 11, 1972, 1.) The cynic in me suspects that Skinner's appointment was no coincidence.

23. "Noted Black Historian Named to Tenured Faculty Position," May 6, 1970, 1.

21 — Death and Funerals

1. *Palmetto Leader*, Sept. 4, 1943, reported Mama's return from the Tents meeting in Atlantic City. Two weeks later, *The Leader* reported that Mama had been among the women attending a Tents meeting in Charleston.

2. Ruth Edier Garrett Butcher (REGB) to AMTG, Dec. 7, 1943 (in possession of the author).

3. NMG to MPGS, Jan. 24, 1944.

4. AMTG to MPGS, Aug 5 [1943], Aug. 14, 1943, Oct. 22, 1943.

5. Owner of Pearson and Champion Funeral Home, which was incorporated in 1929. Henry (1900–1954) was also a postman for thirty-five years.

6. "Mrs. A.M. Garrett Passes," *Palmetto Leader*, Feb. 19, 1944, (p. 1); "President Hinton Writes Teachers: Asks for Contributions to Carry on New Cases," *Palmetto Leader*, Feb. 19, 1944 (p. 1); Felder, 26–33.

7. NMG to MPGS, Oct. 9, 1946.

8. NMG to MPGS, March 19 and April 14, 1947.

9. NMG to MPGS, Sept.r 1, 1946.

10. NMG to MPGS, April 14, 1947.

11. NMG to MPGS, Aug. 24, 1947.

12. NMG to MPGS, Oct. 11, 1947.

13. Baumgardner, "Dr. Casper G. Garrett."

14. Christopher Threewitts Garrett (CTG) to MPGS [Dec. 11, 1947].

22 — And Their Children after Them

1. AMTG to NMG, Dec. 3, 1939.

2. NMG to MPGS, Jan. 24, 1944.

3. Colon Hunter Garrett (CHG) to CGG, Feb. 13, 1944 (in possession of the author).

4. CHG to CGG, March 6, 1945 (in possession of the author).

5. AMTG to NMG, Dec. 17, 1942.

6. NMG to MPGS, Jan. 24, 1944.

7. REGB to AMTG, Dec. 7, 1943 (in possession of the author).

8. NMG to MPGS, Oct. 22, 1947.

9. "Ruth 'Aunt Ruth' Butcher," *Philadelphia Daily News*, April 26, 1996, 44.

10. NMG to MPGS, March 2, 1955.

11. NMG to MPGS, Sept. 14 and Oct. 15, 1957.

12. "Jaworski opens Honors Week: special prosecutor joined by others," *The Denisonian*, April 11, 1979, 1.

13. "Integration: Negro College's Newest Challenge: Problems and Prejudices Mar Relationships on Campuses," *Ebony*, March 1966, 36. Mill's picture appears on p. 46.

14. "Not Just for Blacks, but for Everybody": West Virginia State College Celebrates 100 Years," *Charleston Gazette-Mail*, March 17, 1991, 1B.

23 — They, Too, Sang America

1. "Leevy, Isaac Samuel," https://www.scencyclopedia.org/sce/entries/leevy-isaac-samuel/; Hudson, 23–24; "City Mortician

I.S. Leevy Dies After Illness," *The State*, Dec. 10, 1968, 1.

2. Caldwell, *History,* "Preface," n.p.n.

3. CGG, Jr. to Ruth Esther Simons (RES), Sept. 16, 1942 (in possession of the author).

4. REGB to AMTG, April 1, 1935; CHG to AMTG, April 2, 1935 (in possession of the author).

5. AMTG to MPGS, March 23, 1920.

6. AMTG to MPGS, Dec. 11, 1922.

7. AMTG to MPGS, May 5–11, 1929.

8. AMTG to MPGS, Nov. 8, 1933.

9. *The State vs. William D. Chappelle, Jr.*, Richland County Court of General Sessions, Indictments 5940 (1915), South Carolina Department of Archives and History; "Carroll is Cleared: Son of Negro Leader is Acquitted of Arson," *The State*, May 10, 1917, p. 3.

10. AMTG to MPGS, May 5–11, 1929.

11. Douglas, p. 90. She's quoting philosopher Alain Locke and writer Arna Bontemps respectively.

12. De Jongh, p. 6.

13. De Jongh, p. 1.

14. AMTG to MPGS, January 20, 1924.

15. Wright, *Centennial*, p. 27.

16. AMTG to NMG, Sept. 5, 1940.

17. AMTG to MPGS, May 17, 1926.

18. AMTG to MPGS, Sept. 13, 1926.

Afterword

1. University of South Carolina Press, Columbia, 1973, p. 3.

2. *Random House Webster's College Dictionary*, Random House, New York, 1997, p. 266.

3. Newby, p. 15.

4. "Resources Associated with Segregation in Columbia, S.C., 1880–1960," National Register of Historic Places Multiple Property Documentation Form; Kennedy, Stetson, *Jim Crow Guide to the U.S.A.: The Laws, Customs and Etiquette Governing the Conduct of Nonwhites and Other Minorities as Second-Class Citizens,* University of Alabama Press, Tuscaloosa, 1990 [reprint and also on www.stetson kennedy.com]; "New Negro Theater Opens Tomorrow; Named for Carver," *Columbia Record*, April 30, 1942, p. 14

5. "Lectured Negroes," *The State*, Nov. 8, 1922, p. 5.

6. Hudson, p. 34.

7. AMTG to NMG, June 6, 1941.

8. NMG to AJSW, Aug. 7, 1942.

9. Guy Vanderhaeghe, *The Englishman's Boy* [paperback reprint] (New York: Picador, 1998), 148.

Cast of Characters

1. Bobby J. Donaldson, "Carroll, Richard," in *101 African Americans Who Shaped South Carolina*, ed. Bernard E. Powers Jr. (Columbia: University of South Carolina Press, 2020), 67.

2. "Church Figures, Laymen Crowd Bishop's Funeral," *Baltimore Afro-American*, February 21, 1953, p. 1.

BIBLIOGRAPHY

Some sources—including the Columbia and New York City censuses; Columbia, New York, and other city directories; draft registration cards and other military records; newspaper articles; and death certificates—are not included here, though they may appear in the footnotes. Letters—including those from Anna Maria Garrett to her daughters, Mattie, Ruth, and Mills, as well as letters from Mills to her mother, sister, and nieces, and letters from Phyllis Simons to her sister, Ruth—are among the family letters in the Library of Congress. They, and other letters in the author's collection, appear in the footnotes.

The word Negro was often left lowercase in older documents. I have silently capitalized it, except when it appears in Dublin Hunter's manumission papers. In addition, I have often corrected spelling and grammatical errors when quoting from letters and other documents. When a letter's date appears in brackets, the original is undated and the date is inferred from internal evidence or taken from the envelope postmark. Letters that cannot be dated are referred to as "n.d."

Interviews

Naomi Mills Garrett, January 1, 1984, interviewed by David Nicholson (DN), notes and transcript in the possession of the author.

———, interviewed by Beryl Dakers, n.d. transcript in possession of the author.

Sue-Lynn Garrett, June 21, 2022, interviewed by DN, notes in possession of the author.

Josephine Wade, January 6, 2010, interviewed by DN, notes and transcript in the possession of the author.

———, January 22, 2010, interviewed by DN, notes and transcript in the possession of the author.

———, March 2, interviewed by DN, notes and transcript in the possession of the author.

———, July 22, 2010, interviewed by DN, notes and transcript in the possession of the author.

———, September 17, 2011, interviewed by DN, notes and transcript in the possession of the author.

———, February 16, 2012, interviewed by DN, notes and transcript in the possession of the author.

Books

Angell, Stephen Ward. *Bishop Henry McNeal Turner and African American Religion in the South*. Knoxville: University of Tennessee Press, 1992.

Battle Participation of Organizations of the American Expeditionary Forces in France, Belgium and Italy, 1917–1918. Washington, DC: Government Printing Office, 1920.

Beadles Dime Dialogues No. 27. New York: Beadle and Adams, 1880.

Brown Jr., Canter. *Florida Black Public Officials, 1867–1924*. Tuscaloosa: University of Alabama Press, 1998.

Caldwell, A. B. (Arthur Bunyan), ed. *History of the American Negro: South Carolina Edition.* Atlanta: A. B. Caldwell Publishing Company, 1919.

———, ed. *History of the American Negro: Washington, D.C., Edition.* Atlanta: A. B. Caldwell Publishing Company, 1922.

———, ed. *History of the American Negro: West Virginia Edition.* Atlanta: A. B. Caldwell Publishing Company, 1923.

Catalogue of Columbia University, 1914–1915 (New York: Columbia University).

Catalogue of Allen University, 1890 and 1891 (Columbia, SC: The Bryan Printing Company, 1891).

Catalogue of Allen University, 1908–1910 (Columbia, SC: The R.L. Bryan Company, 1910).

Catalogue of Allen University 1911 and 1912 (Columbia, SC: The R.L. Bryan Company, Book Builders, 1912).

Catalogue of Allen University, 1923 and 1924 (Columbia, SC: Allen University Print).

Catalogue of Lincoln University, Chester County, Penna., Sixty-Third Year, 1917–18 (Philadelphia: Ferris & Leach, 1918).

Columbia University Alumni Register, 1754–1931 (New York: Columbia University Press, 1932). Available from https://library.columbia.edu/libraries/cuarchives/resources/alumni.html.

Culp, D. W., ed. *Twentieth Century Negro Literature or a Cyclopedia on the Vital Topics Relating to the American Negro by 100 of America's Greatest Negroes.* Atlanta: J. L. Nichols & Company, 1902.

Davie, Ethel O. "Naomi M. Garrett, 1906–." In *Missing Chapters II: West Virginia Women in History*, edited by Frances S. Hensley, 73–84. Charleston: West Virginia Women's Commission, 1986.

De Jongh, James. *Vicious Modernism: Black Harlem and the Literary Imagination.* Cambridge, United Kingdom: Cambridge University Press, 1990.

Donaldson, Bobby J. "Standing on a Volcano: The Leadership of William Jefferson White." In *Paternalism in a Southern City: Race, Religion, and Gender in Augusta, Georgia*, edited by Edward J. Cashin and Glenn T. Eskew, 135–76. Athens: University of Georgia Press, 2012.

Douglas, Ann. *Terrible Honesty: Mongrel Manhattan in the 1920s.* New York: Farrar, Straus and Giroux, 1995.

Douglass, Frederick. *My Bondage and My Freedom.* New York: Miller, Orton & Mulligan, 1855.

Downs, Jim. *Sick from Freedom: African American Illness and Suffering during the Civil War and Reconstruction.* New York: Oxford, 2012.

Dreilinger, Danielle. *The Secret History of Home Economics: How Trailblazing Women Harnessed the Power of Home and Changed the Way We Live.* New York: Norton, 2021.

Earley, Charity Adams. *One Woman's Army: A Black Officer Remembers the WAC.* College Station: Texas A&M University Press, 1989.

Felder, James L. *Civil Rights in South Carolina: From Peaceful Protests to Groundbreaking Rulings.* Charleston, SC: The History Press, 2012.

Finnegan, Terence. *A Deed So Accursed: Lynching in Mississippi and South Carolina, 1881–1940.* Charlottesville: University of Virginia Press, 2013.

Friend, Craig Thompson, "From Southern Manhood to Southern Masculinity: An Introduction." In *Southern Masculinity: Perspectives on Manhood in the South Since Reconstruction*, edited by Craig Thompson Friend Athens: University of Georgia, 2009.

Gikandi, Simon. "Afro-Victorian Worlds." In *The Victorian World*, edited Martin Hewitt. by New York: Routledge, 2012.

Gomez-Jefferson, Annetta, L. *The Sage of Tawawa: Reverdy Cassius Ransom, 1861–1959*. Kent, Ohio: Kent State University Press, 2002.

Goodspeed's History of Tennessee. Nashville, TN: Goodspeed Publishing Company, 1886–87. Available at www.tngenweb.org /records/shelby/history/goodspeed /history7.html.

Harris, William J. *Deep Souths: Delta, Piedmont, and Sea Island Society in the Age of Segregation*. Baltimore: Johns Hopkins University Press, 2001.

Hartshorn, W. N., and Penniman, George W., eds. *An Era of Progress and Promise, 1863–1910: The Religious, Moral, and Educational Development of the American Negro Since His Emancipation*. Boston: Priscilla, 1910.

Haskins, Jim, and Kathleen Benson, *African American Religious Leaders*. San Francisco: Jossey-Bass, 2008.

Hennig, Helen Kohn, ed. *Columbia: Capital City of South Carolina, 1786–1936*. Columbia, SC: Columbia Sesqui-centennial Commission, 1936.

History of Wages in the United States from Colonial Times to 1928, Bulletin of the United States Bureau of Labor Statistics No. 604. Washington, DC: Government Printing Office, 1934.

Howe, George. *History of the Presbyterian Church in South Carolina, Vol. II*. Columbia, SC: W. J. Duffie, 1883.

Hudson, Janet G. *Entangled by White Supremacy: Reform in World War I-era South Carolina*. Lexington: University Press of Kentucky, 2009.

Hurston, Zora Neale. *Tell My Horse*. Berkeley, CA: Turtle Island, 1981.

Johnson, Alonzo, and Paul T. Jersild, eds. *Ain't Going to Lay My 'Ligion Down: African American Religion in the South*. Columbia: University of South Carolina Press, 1996.

Johnson, Michael P., and Roark, James L. *Black Masters: A Free Family of Color in the Old South*. New York: Norton, 1984.

Journal of the Twenty-first Quadrennial Session of the General Conference of the African M.E. Church, Held in the Auditorium, Columbus, Ohio, May 7th to May 25, 1900, Philadelphia: AME Book Concern.

Journal of the Twenty-Sixth Quadrennial Session of the General Conference of the African Methodist Episcopal Church, Held in St. Louis, Missouri, May 3rd to 18th, 1920. Nashville, TN: A.M.E. Sunday School Union, 1922.

Kelley, Robin D. G. "Introduction." In *Reflections in the Black: A History of Black Photographers 1840 to the Present*, edited by Debra Willis, p. x. New York: Norton, 2000.

Kennedy, Stetson. *Jim Crow Guide to the U.S.A.: The Laws, Customs and Etiquette Governing the Conduct of Nonwhites and Other Minorities as Second-Class Citizens*. Tuscaloosa: University of Alabama Press, 1990.

LaBorde, M [Maximillian]. *History of the South Carolina College from the Incorporation December 19, 1801, to December 19, 1865, Including Sketches of its Presidents and Professors, With an Appendix*. Charleston, SC: Walker, Evans & Cogswell, 1874.

Lewis, David Levering. *When Harlem Was in Vogue*. New York: Knopf, 1981.

McCord, David J., ed. *The Statutes at Large of South Carolina, Vol. 7: Containing the Acts Relating to Charleston, Courts, Slaves, and Rivers*. Columbia, SC: A. S. Johnston, 1840.

McWhirter, Cameron. *Red Summer*. New York: St. Martin's Griffin, 2012.

Moore, John Hammond. *South Carolina Newspapers*. Columbia: University of South Carolina Press, 1988.

Motes, Margaret Peckham. *Blacks Found in the Deeds of Laurens & Newberry Counties, S.C.: 1785–1827, Listed in Deeds of Gifts, Deeds of Sale, Mortgages, Born Free and Freed, Abstracted from Laurens County, SC Deed Books A-L and Newberry County, SC Deed Books A-G*. Baltimore, MD: Clearfield, 2002.

Nash, Gary B. *Forging Freedom: The Formation of Philadelphia's Black Community, 1720–1840*. Cambridge, MA: Harvard University Press, 1988.

Neuffer, Claude Henry, ed. *Names in South Carolina*. Spartanburg, SC: The Reprint Company, 1983.

Perkins, Linda M. "The History of Black Women Graduate Students, 1921–1948." In *The Sage Handbook of African American Education*, edited by Linda C. Tillman, 62–63. Thousand Oaks, CA: SAGE Publications, 2009.

Rampersad, Arnold. *The Life of Langston Hughes: Volume I: 1902–1941, I, Too, Sing America*. New York: Oxford, 1986.

Random House Webster's College Dictionary. New York: Random House, 1997.

Ransom, Reverdy C. *The Pilgrimage of Harriet Ransom's Son*. Nashville, TN: Sunday School Union, 1950.

Richardson, Joe M. *Christian Reconstruction: The American Missionary Association and Southern Blacks, 1861–1890*. Athens: University of Georgia Press, 1986.

Rivers, Larry Eugene, and Canter Brown, Jr. *Laborers in the Vineyard of the Lord: The Beginnings of the AME Church in Florida, 1865–1895*. Gainesville: University Press of Florida, 2001.

Rubio, Philip F. *There's Always Work at the Post Office: African American Postal Workers and the Fight for Jobs, Justice, and Equality*. Chapel Hill: University of North Carolina, 2010.

Salsi, Lynn Sims. *Columbia: History of a Southern Capital*. Charleston, SC: Arcadia, 2003.

Schweninger, Loren, and Howell, Marguerite Ross, eds. *Race, Slavery, and Free Blacks: Series II, Petitions to Southern County Courts, 1775–1867: Part D: North Carolina (1775–1867) and South Carolina (1784–1867)*. Bethesda, MD: LexisNexis, 2005.

Scott, Emmett J. *Scott's Official History of The American Negro in the World War*. Chicago: Homewood Press, 1919.

Simpson, Eugene Thamon. *Hall Johnson: His Life, His Spirit, and His Music*. Lanham, MD: Scarecrow Press, 2008.

Skocpol, Theda, Arian Lizzos, and Marshall Ganz. *What a Mighty Power We Can Be: African American Fraternal Groups and the Struggle for Racial Equality*. Princeton, NJ: Princeton University Press, 2006.

Smith, Charles Spencer. *A History of the African Methodist Episcopal Church*. Philadelphia: Book Concern of the AME Church, 1922.

South Carolina State Agricultural and Mechanical College Catalog, 1918–1919.

Stroup, Rodger E. *Meet Me at the Rocket: A History of the South Carolina State Fair*. Columbia, University of South Carolina Press, 2019.

Student's Handbook. Lincoln University, PA, 1914.

Sweeney, W. Allison. *History of the American Negro in the Great World War: His Splendid Record in the Battle Zones of Europe. Including a Resume of His Past Services to his Country in the Wars of The Revolution, of 1812, the War of the Rebellion, the Indian Wars on the Frontier, the Spanish-American War, and the Late Imbroglio with Mexico*. G.G. Sapp, 1919.

Tindall, George Brown. *South Carolina Negroes, 1877–1900*. Columbia, University of South Carolina Press, 1952.

Twenty-Fifth Annual Report of the Commissioner of Labor 1910: Industrial Education. Washington, DC: Government Printing Office, 1911.

Tye, Larry. *Rising from the Rails: Pullman Porters and the Making of the Black Middle Class.* New York: Picador, 2005.

Underwood, James Lowell, and W. Lewis Burke Jr., eds. *At Freedom's Door.* Columbia: University of South Carolina Press, 2000.

Vanderhaeghe, Guy. *The Englishman's Boy.* New York: Picador USA, 1998.

Wilson, John R. *A Brief Sketch of the Life and Career of the Right Rev. William David Chappelle, A.M., D.D., LL., Some of His Addresses and Sermons.* Columbia, SC: The State Company, n.d.

Wright, Richard R. Jr. *87 Years Behind the Black Curtain: An Autobiography.* Philadelphia: Rare Book Company, 1965.

———, ed. *Centennial Encyclopedia of the African Methodist Episcopal Church.* Philadelphia: Book Concern of the AME Church, 1916.

———, ed. *Encyclopaedia of the African Methodist Episcopal Church.* Second Ed. Philadelphia: AME Church, 1947.

Articles

Brown, Canter, Jr., and Larry E. Rivers. "The Pioneer African American Jurist Who Almost Became a Bishop: Florida's Judge James Dean, 1858–1914," *Florida Historical Quarterly* 87, no. 1 (Summer 2008): 16–49.

"Close Ranks," *The Crisis* 16, no. 3 (July 1918): 111–14.

Courtwright, David T. "The Hidden Epidemic: Opiate Addiction and Cocaine Use in the South, 1860–1920." *Journal of Southern History* 49, no. 1 (February 1983): 57–72.

Datiri, Dorothy Hines. "'Saving Grace':

Educating African American Children through Industrial Education in Mayesville." *Carologue* 29, no. 2 (Fall 2013): 20–24. Available at https://dokumen .tips/documents/.

"Dr. Elmer A. Henderson (1887–1951)." *Journal of Negro History* 36, no. 4 (October 1951): 481–83.

Ford, Lacy. "Reconfiguring the Old South: 'Solving' the Problem of Slavery, 1787–1838." *Journal of American History* 95, no. 1 (June 2008): 95–122.

Garrett, Naomi M. "St.-Marc, Haiti." *Opportunity* XXV, no. 1 (January–March 1947): 9–11, 35–36.

Germain, Félix. "Mercer Cook and the Origins of Black French Studies." *French Politics, Culture & Society* 34, no. 1 (Spring 2016): 66–85.

Hemingway, Theodore. "Prelude to Change: Black Carolinians in the War Years, 1914–1920." *Journal of Negro History* 65, no. 3 (Summer 1980): 212–27.

Jackson, David H. Jr. "Booker T. Washington in South Carolina, March 1909." *South Carolina Historical Magazine* 113, no. 3 (July 2012): 192–220.

Leach, Frank Willing. "Old Philadelphia Families." *North American,* July 7, 1912. http://archiver.rootsweb.ancestry.com/th /read/philly-roots/200308/1061232877.

Marszalek, John F. "The Black Leader in 1919—South Carolina as a Case Study." *Phylon* 36, no. 3 (Third quarter, 1975): 249–59.

Matthews, John M. "Black Newspapermen and the Black Community in Georgia, 1890–1930." *Georgia Historical Quarterly* 68, no. 3 (Fall 1984): 356–81.

Megginson, W. J. "Black South Carolinians in World War I: The Official Roster as a Resource For Local History, Mobility, and African American History." *South Carolina Historical Magazine* 96, no. 2 (April 1995): 153–73.

"Scholarships." *Opportunity* X, no. 2, (February 1932): 60.

"Some members of Virginia Union's War Time Faculty: John Matthew Moore." *Virginia Union Bulletin* 46, no. 2 (January 1946): 10–13.

Simon, Bryant, "The Appeal of Cole Blease of South Carolina: Race, Class, and Sex in the New South." *Journal of Southern History* 61, no. 1 (February 1996): 57–86.

Wilson, Carolyn. "The Difficult Task: Fundraising for Small Southern Black Industrial Schools: The Case of Emma Jane Wilson and the Mayesville Educational and Industrial Institute." *American Educational History Journal* 30 (2003): 7–15.

Zug, James. "The Color of Our Skin: Quakerism and Integration at Sidwell Friends School." *Quaker History* 98, no. 1 (Spring 2009): 35–47.

Other Documents

"Annual Report of the School Commissioner of Laurens County S.C. of Claims Approved by him during the year 1885." L30158, South Carolina Department of Archives and History.

Arkansas General Assembly SCR 6 Commemorating the 94th Anniversary of the US Supreme Court Ruling in *Moore V. Dempsey.*

Army of the United States. "Pictorial History 367th Infantry, Army of the United States, 1942," World War Regimental Histories, Book 20.

"Emma J. Wilson." WPA Writers Project document. Columbia: Caroliniana Library, University of South Carolina Library.

Gabriel, Joseph M. "Opiate addiction and the history of pain and race in the US." *The Conversation*, June 19, 2018. https://theconversation.com/.

Garrett, Anna M., "Some Facts About the Grand United Order of Tents of the J.R.G.

and J.U." [leaflet in the author's possession].

"'Goophered,' Negro Conjure Operette in Rehearsal for Harlem Presentation," NAACP news release, April 30, 1926, NAACP III, Scrapbook 20. Washington, DC, Library of Congress.

Hoffschwelle, Mary S. "Preserving Rosenwald Schools." [PDF.] Washington, DC, National Trust for Historic Preservation, 2012.

Laurens County School Superintendent Ledgers, 1911–1930, L 30237, South Carolina Department of Archives and History.

Laurens District, Deed Books L, 66.

"Life and Works of Henry McNeil [*sic*] Turner: The Bishop's Four Wives," typescript, "Moorland-Spingarn Research Center, Howard University, Box 1, folder 14.

"Lynching in America: Confronting the Legacy of Racial Terror," 2nd ed. Montgomery, AL, Equal Justice Initiative, 2015.

Minutes of the Richland County Retirement Board, 1941–1964, L40118, South Carolina Department of Archives and History.

"National Historic Landmark Nomination: Chappelle Administration Building."

"National Register of Historic Places Multiple Property Documentation Form," Resources Associated with Segregation in Columbia, S.C., 1880–1960. http://www.nationalregister.sc.gov/MPS/MPS048.pdf.

Richland County School Board Minutes, April 26, 1917, July 27, 1917, June 7, 1920, and August 24, 1924, South Carolina Department of Archives and History.

Richland County Records, L40095, South Carolina Department of Archives and History.

"Rosenwald Schools, County: Richland" [PDF], South Carolina Department of Archives and History.

"Sale Bill of the Estate of Charles Simmons deceased" (photocopy in the author's possession).

Singleton, George A. "Casper Geo Answers Final Call" (photocopy in the author's possession).

State v. C. G. Garrett, case no. 5308, L 40059, South Carolina Department of Archives and History.

State v. C. G. Garrett, case no. 6701, L 40559, South Carolina Department of Archives and History.

State v. William D. Chappelle Jr., Richland County Court of General Sessions, Indictments 5940 (1915), South Carolina Department of Archives and History.

"The Way Bishop Chappelle Bulldozes People in South Carolina" (leaflet, photocopy in the author's possession).

Twenty-First Annual Report of the Board of Managers of the Massachusetts Colonization Society. Presented at the Annual Meeting, May 28, 1862, Boston; .

"Twenty-Sixth Annual Report of the State Superintendent of Education of the State of South Carolina." In *Reports and Resolutions of the General Assembly of the State of South Carolina at the Regular Session Commencing November 27th, 1894,* Vol. 2 (Charles A Calvo, Jr., State Printer). Columbia, SC, 1894.

Ward, Virginia B., ed. "The History of South Carolina Schools." Study commissioned by the Center for Educator Recruitment, Retention, and Advancement (CERRA–SC), MS.

Zimmerman, David, Laura Zimmerman, and Anne Sheppard. "Our History." www.firstpreslaurens.org/our_history (last revised April 2007).

Websites

"College Columbia Today," https://www.college.columbia.edu/cct_archive/sep05/cover.html.

"Building: The Marshall," Streeteasy.com. https://streeteasy.com/building/the-marshall.

"Car of the Week: 1923 Ford Model T Touring." https://www.oldcarsweekly.com/features/car-of-the-week-1923-ford-model-t-touring.

"First Black Officers Trained for World War I at Fort Des Moines 100 Years Ago," Iowa History," Iowa Culture. https://medium.com/iowa-history/first-black-officers-trained-for-world-war-i-at-fort-des-moines-100-years-ago-4f50ce8aafo4.

"Harlem Riot of 1935," Wikipedia. https://en.wikipedia.org/wiki/Harlem_riot_of_1935.

"Jackson Davis Collection of African American Photographs," University of Virginia Library. https://v4.lib.virginia.edu/sources/images/items/uva-lib:330516.

"Leslie Keeley," Wikipedia. https://en.wikipedia.org/wiki/Leslie_Keeley.

National A. Philip Randolph Pullman Porter Museum. https://aprpullmanportermuseum.org/searchnationalregistry/.

"No Reserve: 1923 Ford Model T Touring." https://bringatrailer.com/listing/1923-ford-model-t-touring/.

"Office of the Coordinator of Inter-American Affairs," Wikipedia. https://en.wikipedia.org/wiki/Office_of_the_Coordinator_of_Inter-American_Affairs.

"Pullman Porter," Wikipedia. https://en.wikipedia.org/wiki/Pullman_porter.

"Pullman Porters: From Servitude to Civil Rights." https://interactive.wttw.com/a/chicago-stories-pullman-porters.

"Red Summer," Wikipedia. https://en.wikipedia.org/wiki/Red_Summer.

INDEX

Page numbers in italics refer to illustrations.